D1761123

OXFORD BROOKES UNIVERSITY
Harcourt Hill
A fine will be levied if this item becomes
overdue. ~~To renew please ring 01865 483133~~
(reserved items cannot be renewed).
Harcourt Hill enquiries 01865 488222
www.brookes.ac.uk/services/library

The Nature of Philosophical Problems

The Nature of Philosophical Problems

Their Causes and Implications

John Kekes

OXFORD
UNIVERSITY PRESS

Great Clarendon Street, Oxford, OX2 6DP,
United Kingdom

Oxford University Press is a department of the University of Oxford.
It furthers the University's objective of excellence in research, scholarship,
and education by publishing worldwide. Oxford is a registered trade mark of
Oxford University Press in the UK and in certain other countries

Published in the United States of America by Oxford University Press
198 Madison Avenue, New York, NY 10016, United States of America

British Library Cataloguing in Publication Data

Data available

Library of Congress Control Number: 2014932278

ISBN 978–0–19–871275–6

Printed and bound by
CPI Group (UK) Ltd, Croydon, CR0 4YY

Links to third party websites are provided by Oxford in good faith and
for information only. Oxford disclaims any responsibility for the materials
contained in any third party website referenced in this work.

For J.Y.K.

Preface

> What is the use of studying philosophy if all it does for you is to enable you to talk with some plausibility about some abstruse questions of logic, etc., & if it does not improve your thinking about the important questions of everyday life.
>
> Ludwig Wittgenstein[1]

Many years ago I wrote a youthful essay about the nature of philosophical problems, sent it to an eminent philosopher I deeply respected, and asked for his comments. He responded kindly and advised me to choose some specific problem to work on rather than worry about the nature of problems in general. His advice reflected the prevailing view, but I did not accept it. I became a philosopher because I was interested in philosophical problems about how it is reasonable to live: problems like What makes lives good? Is there a providential order? Can there be an ideal political state? Can we control how we live? What can we reasonably hope? Are there absolute moral values? I thought then, and continue to think still, that following his advice would not have helped me think better about these problems, because if we do not understand their nature, we cannot know what work we should do on them. In this book I am still thinking about their nature, but I have come to realize along the way that being perennial is part of their nature and that is why they are exceptionally difficult and why many centuries of hard work by excellent minds has not resulted in a generally accepted solution of any of them.

The approach I have adopted is contrary to the prevailing view that good philosophical work should divide whatever basic problem it begins with into manageable smaller problems, concentrate on one of them, take account of the increasingly technical literature on it, clarify it by finer distinctions and more perspicuous analyses, show how the resulting view can accommodate difficult cases, and why contrary views cannot handle ever more ingenious counterexamples. Many excellent books and articles have been and are being written in this way. However, their connection with the basic problem that prompted all the highly skillful work gets lost in the accumulation of increasingly complex detail whose significance only a handful of specialists working on that small segment of the basic problem can understand.

My approach, for better or worse, is to propose an explanation of why the basic problems are philosophical. I do not think that this would turn philosophical problems into ordinary ones. If the explanation is right, no approach can do that. What can be done is to explain why philosophical problems are perennial, why they are formidably difficult, and why excellent philosophers have advanced throughout the ages so many conflicting solutions of them. My proposed approach does not to add to the already vast body of technical work yet another plea for the superiority of a method, nor finer-grained analyses than those already available, nor more searching historical scholarship. If readers look for any of these, they will not find it. My aim, I repeat, is to explain why basic philosophical problems are and will remain perennial and to say a little about how we might nevertheless cope with them reasonably. I do not say that it is little out of false modesty.

I know that I need good reasons for deviating from the prevailing expectations about how philosophical work should be done. My reasons are cultural and philosophical. The cultural one is that philosophy has changed. It no longer occupies the centrally important role it used to have in forming the Western world-view. In the past, philosophers have aimed to construct a general outlook about the nature of reality and humanity's place in it, an outlook in terms of which their contemporaries and perhaps even their successors could make sense of their lives. Philosophers used to think that this was their calling, which is what it then was. Now, philosophers, at least in the English-speaking world, proceed very differently. Philosophy has become an academic specialty, research in it is a skill, and philosophers are more likely to belong to a union than to the secular equivalent of a priesthood.

There is little point in debating whether this change is good or bad. It is probably a mixture of both, as most changes are, but, in any case, I doubt that it is reversible. It does have a consequence, however, that seems to me very bad indeed. Philosophy has become remote from everyday life. The cultural niche philosophers used to occupy is now filled with perfervid ideologues, fundamentalist preachers, sensation-seeking journalists, charlatans selling salvation, and cynics bent on unmasking all values. The airwaves, cyberspace, the media, and talk shows are filled with psychobabble, propaganda, imported oriental cults, absurd conspiracy theories, and abysmally ignorant dogmatic claims about science, history, religion, politics, and economics. The sleep of reason breeds monsters, and they haunt the niche vacated by philosophers. I think that we, as philosophers, should make a greater effort than we are doing to help our contemporaries distinguish between reasonable and unreasonable approaches to basic problems about how to live in our complex and dangerous world. I do not think that this can be done merely by practicing our skill well enough to meet the prevailing professional expectations. In this book, I take a tentative and much too small a step in another direction.

My philosophical reasons are, first, that the countless journal articles and specialist books written in conformity to the prevailing expectations have not resulted in a generally accepted solution to any of the philosophical problems. Second, many of the great works in the history of philosophy, works that still fundamentally influence our thinking about how we should live, would not now be judged good enough to meet the prevailing professional expectations. Painful satires could be written of the rejection notices that would be sent, say, to Plato's *Republic*, Machiavelli's *Prince*, Montaigne's *Essays*, Hume's *Dialogues*, Nietzsche's *Genealogy*, or Wittgenstein's *Investigations*. It is perhaps more reasonable to conclude that these works cast more doubt on the prevailing expectations than the unmet expectations do on the works. And third, I believe that the general approach I propose leads to a better understanding of philosophical problems and of why they are perennial than the specialist approach favored by prevailing expectations. The first two reasons seem to me very strong, whether the third is strong enough depends on the argument of this book.

Acknowledgements

I am grateful to David Wootton, Leo Zaibert, and to two readers for Oxford University Press for their enormously helpful comments, criticisms, and suggestions that have made the final version much better. None of them should be taken to endorse any of the constructive or critical views I express.

Peter Momtchiloff, my editor, has once again been unfailingly helpful in various ways in guiding the making of this book. I acknowledge his help with pleasure and gratitude.

The book is dedicated to my wife who has made it possible.

Ithaca
Charlton
New York

Acknowledgements

Contents

Part II. Problematic Approaches

Part III. Toward a Pluralist Approach

Introduction

On the one hand, philosophers, more than any other type of investigator, per-
sistently work at what appear to be the same unchanging problems. On the
other hand, although these problems appear not only to be unchanging but
to admit of rational or even necessary solutions, yet the history of philosophy
presents them as the centres of unending conflicts and debates, punctuated
briefly from time to time by claims that a revolution has taken place and that
philosophical problems will now be speedily wound up—after which things
go on very much as before.

W.B. Gallie[1]

Time passes, circumstances change, our knowledge and experience grow, yet we
continue to face the same problems about how we should live. Here they are once
again: What makes lives good? Is there a providential order? What would be an
ideal political state? Can we control how we live? What can we reasonably hope?
Are there moral absolutes? The solutions, if only we had them, would help to make
our lives better, but the many that have been proposed conflict and exclude one
another. There are good reasons for some of the conflicting solutions, and so they
continue to endure, but there are no less good reasons against them. And thus their
conflicts have persisted in changing forms throughout the centuries, the present
one included.

The difficulty is not that we lack the relevant facts. They have long been available and known. The difficulty is rather that the answers are based on conflicting
evaluations of the significance of familiar facts. Defenders of the evaluations agree
that finding the right ones is the key to improving our lives, but they disagree about
which ones are right. It would be simple if we could dismiss all but one solution
as unreasonable, but we cannot. Longstanding persistent disputes have not led to
a generally accepted approach to a reasonable solution of the conflicts between
incompatible evaluations and reasons. That is why the problems are perennial.

Perennial problems are philosophical, but not all philosophical problems are perennial. Philosophical problems arise when we try to form an overall understanding of the world and our situation in it. We have pursued this aim in two directions: toward an impersonal, godlike understanding of the world and everything in it, and toward an anthropocentric understanding of our situation in the world and of how we could make our lives better. The first aims at understanding regardless of how it might affect us; the second is centrally concerned with it. Their aims differ, but their approaches overlap. The first treats the conditions of our lives as one set of facts among countless others, understanding the conditions, however, helps us to improve our lives. The second concentrates on improving our lives, yet the conditions in which we can do so are what they are regardless of whether they aid or hinder our efforts. Still, the two aims are different and give rise to different problems. The philosophical problems I am concerned with (from now on I omit the qualification that there are also other kinds of philosophical problems) arise in the context of seeking the second kind of understanding, which is anthropocentric and evaluative.

A basic aim of this second kind of understanding is to explain why philosophical problems are so very difficult and why the proposed approaches to coping with them are controversial. This is my main concern. The particular difficulty in the way of finding the explanation we need is that there are several different modes of understanding—historical, moral, political, religious, scientific, and personal, among others—and they lead to conflicting evaluations of the significance of the facts on which the improvement of our lives depends. The explanation I propose will eventually suggest an approach to how we should go about finding the most reasonable evaluations of the relevant facts and cope with philosophical problems, but much has to be said to prepare the ground for it.

The right explanation, however, will not be one that once found needs only to be remembered. It will require continued efforts that take different forms in different contexts, as do balancing conflicting political interests, living prudently in changing conditions, or acquiring broader and deeper knowledge. That is why I stress throughout that dealing with philosophical problems is a matter of coping with them, rather than solving them once and for all. If we find the right ways of coping in one context, it will not obviate the need to keep finding it in forever changing contexts. The key to the right explanation, however, is to reject the widely shared assumption that the evaluations that follow from one of the modes of understanding should always override the conflicting ones that follow from the other modes. Finding the right evaluations and ways of coping with philosophical problems requires particular and context-dependent explanations and approaches.

"Modes of understanding" is an expression some of whose cognates are "scale of forms," "modes of experience," "modes of thought," "symbolic forms," "linguistic frameworks," "language games," "ways of worldmaking," "cultural forms," and "conceptual schemes."[2] "Categories," "universes of discourse," and other near-synonyms could no doubt be found. The general idea implicit in all of them is that by following different modes of understanding, we ascribe to facts various more or less different significance.

It is a matter of much controversy in the history of this idea what exactly is or is not a mode of understanding; how many of them there are; whether they can be arranged in a hierarchy, and, if so, in what order; whether they are merely different and parallel or at least sometimes conflicting; whether they rest on a common ground; whether there are standards external to all of them by which they can be compared, justified, or criticized; whether they are merely interpretations of our experiences or descriptions of genuine properties or qualities that exist regardless of how we interpret them; and so on.

These controversies continue to exist, but instead of entering into them, I will proceed instead by making clear how I understand modes of understanding. A fuller account of them will emerge only gradually. My view is, then, that modes of understanding are plural and irreducible; do not form a hierarchy; routinely conflict; aim to interpret and evaluate the significance of familiar facts of everyday life from the point of view of making our lives better; they are reasonably or otherwise committed to claims that can be true or false and justified or criticized on reasonable grounds; each is often challenged by defenders of conflicting modes of understanding; and each is essentially evaluative and action-guiding.

In the discussion that follows it will be helpful to have a general term for the mentality or sensibility of a society at a particular time that is informed by a combination of the available modes of understanding; their characteristic conflicts; the shifting flux of the prevailing and changing conditions; and the more or less conscious assumptions, prevalent beliefs, strongly felt emotions, and widely shared motives. I will use, not without hesitation, "world-view" as a shorthand expression to refer to all this. I might have opted instead for "form of life," "culture," "the spirit of an age," "climates of opinion," or borrowed *Weltanschauung* from German, but, for better or worse, I settled on world-view, because it has the generality I intend and is perhaps the least encumbered with connotations I do not intend.

The particular forms in which philosophical problems occur and the arguments about the relative merits of the conflicting ways of coping with them are characteristic features of the world-view of a society at a particular time. If we are reflective about how we should live, such problems and arguments seem particularly important and difficult, because they are obstacles to forming a reasonable view of what makes our lives good, what we should think about a providential order, what would be better political arrangements than the existing ones, what we could do to take greater control of our lives, what we can reasonably hope for the future, and what force moral values have.

These problems have recurred in historically changing forms from ancient times to our own. This is but another way of saying that they are perennial. If we reflect on them, we will find ourselves in a predicament. We will know that reason should guide our efforts to choose the best among the conflicting ways of coping with them, but we will also know that it would be arbitrary simply to claim that one of the historical, moral, political, religious, scientific, or personal modes of understanding is overriding, and subordinate the others to it. We will, then, look for an approach that avoids arbitrariness and enables us to find the most reasonable way of coping with the philosophical problems that stand in the way of improving our lives. We might turn to philosophy for help, but we will not get it.

Hume's damning observation is correct:

Principles taken upon trust, consequences lamely deduced from them, want of coherence in the parts, and of evidence in the whole, these are every where to be met with in the systems of the most eminent philosophers, and seem to have drawn disgrace upon philosophy itself.... Even the rabble without doors may judge from the noise and clamour, which they hear, that all goes not well within. There is nothing which is not subject to debate, and in which men of learning are not of contrary opinions. The most trivial question escapes not our controversy, and in the most momentous we are not able to give any certain decision.[3]

Hume is not alone in holding this view. According to Descartes:

regarding philosophy, I shall say only this: seeing that it has been cultivated for many centuries by the most excellent minds and yet there is still no point in it which is not disputed and hence doubtful.... And, considering how many diverse opinions learned men may maintain on a single question—even though it is impossible for more than one to be true—I held as well-nigh false everything that was merely probable.[4]

Kant concurs:

it seems almost ridiculous, while every other science is continually advancing, that in this, which pretends to be wisdom incarnate, for whose oracle everyone inquires, we should constantly move round the same spot, without gaining a single step.... In this domain there is actually as yet no standard weight and measure to distinguish sound knowledge from shallow talk.[5]

Mill agrees:

from the dawn of philosophy, the question concerning the *summum bonum*, or ... the foundation of morality, has been accounted the main problem of speculative thought.... And after more than two thousand years the same discussions continue, philosophers are still ranged under the same contending banners, and neither thinkers nor mankind at large seem nearer to being unanimous on the subject than when the young Socrates listened to the old Protagoras.[6]

Russell says:

there are many questions—and among them those that are of the profoundest interest to our spiritual life—which, so far as we can see, must remain insoluble to the human intellect, unless its powers become of a quite different order from what they are now.[7]

It is an irony—or a disgrace—of philosophy that these devastating observations about the subject were made by philosophers as preliminaries to their own proposals to put right what has gone wrong before them. They could all have said at first what Wittgenstein said with a young man's amazing confidence in his infallibility that "the *truth* of the thoughts that are here communicated seems to me unassailable and definitive. I therefore believe myself to have found, on all essential points, the final solution of the problems."[8] But their proposals, like Wittgenstein's, fared no better than those of their predecessors. If these philosophers had been as self-critical as Wittgenstein later became, they would have reached the same conclusion as he arrived at after he had reflected on the criticisms of his "unassailable and definitive" truths: "I have been forced to recognize the grave mistakes in what I wrote in that first book."[9] The history of philosophy is replete with grave mistakes, as the search for the right way of coping with philosophical problems throughout many centuries by excellent minds so amply shows.

Familiarity with these endless disputes may lead, depending on one's temperament, to impatience, a sense of futility, distrust of reasons, arbitrary preference for one proposal over the others, or to ignoring the whole mess and turning one's attention to other matters. If philosophical problems were merely arcane theoretical puzzles, they could be left to those who happened to be interested in them. But finding the right ways of coping with them is important, I repeat, because the problems are obstacles to making our lives better. Yet, as their persistence seems to suggest, we cannot reasonably judge the relative merits of the conflicting proposals for coping with them.

This is the background of my modest proposal. I emphasize its modesty. It is an approach, not yet another hubristic attempt to formulate unassailable and definitive truths. I call the approach pluralist, and argue that it is more reasonable than the absolutist and relativist alternatives to it. The pluralist approach stresses the particularity and the relatively short life-expectancy of reasonable ways of coping with philosophical problems in particular contexts at particular times. There are strong reasons, I believe, that can be given in favor of particular ways of coping and against conflicting ones. But the reasons do not carry over to other contexts and times. This approach is not relativist, because it rests on reasons and the balance of reasons can be judged without claiming that one of the historical, moral, political, religious, scientific, or personal modes of understanding should always override the others. Nevertheless, the balance of reasons in favor of any particular way of coping holds only temporarily, so the approach I favor is not absolutist either. Contexts change as a result of the unavoidable contingencies of life, the improvements of modes of understanding, the correction of faulty judgments, and the constant flux of conditions in which we must do as well as we can. Certainty and finality will always elude us. Still, we can reasonably judge which of the proposed ways of coping are more reasonable than the others. This is the context in which we must cope with philosophical problems. Our efforts are not hopeless because we can reasonably rely on the available modes of understanding to suggest the most reasonable ways of coping. Or so I will argue.

Cynics may conclude that the persistence of philosophical problems is yet a further symptom of our feeble reasons, rampant emotions, and futile efforts to find a way out of the swamp we have created. But the cynics are wrong. Philosophical problems are symptoms of health, not of maladies. The conflicts between modes of understanding indicate that our historical, moral, political, religious, scientific, and personal understandings are growing in breadth and depth. If they stagnated, the problems that result from their conflicts would not be perennial. They would be as deservedly forgotten as those of alchemy, astrology, and phrenology. Our modes of understanding are alive and well, not stagnant, and provide multiple strategies for reducing our ignorance of the vastness and complexity of the world and for coping with contingent and ever-changing conditions on which the improvement of our lives depend. We should be encouraged by the multiple strategies at our disposal, rather than discouraged by their conflicts. Philosophical problems are difficult, but that is part of the burden of having many modes of understanding.

Part One is about modes of understanding, their conflicts, and the resulting philosophical problems. Part Two is a critical examination of problematic proposals for coping with philosophical problems. Part Three is an account of the pluralist approach.

Each chapter is headed by an epigraph intended to express the central point of the discussion that follows. Readers wanting to form a preliminary idea of the conclusions I have reached, although without the reasons I give for them, may consider reading the epigraphs one after the other.

From Modes of Understanding to Philosophical Problems

PART I

From Modes of Understanding
to Philosophical Systems

1

Modes of Understanding: A General Account

Philosophical questions have a certain desperateness about them, are accompanied by a degree of emotional pressure, a craving for an answer whose nature is not clear, a sense at once of urgency and insolubility which indicates not a quest for facts...but rather that there is a conflict...a head-on crash, a confusion and interreaction of entire conceptual systems, of whole methods of looking at the world and describing it, which leads to the so-called "perennial" problems such as free will versus determinism, theism and atheism, materialism and immaterialism, liberty and order, authority and equality, happiness and justice, self-sacrifice and the pursuit of happiness.

Isaiah Berlin[1]

Practical and Reflective Approaches

Each mode of understanding provides a point of view from which facts may be described and evaluated. Each has a set of conventions and methods, notable achievements, strengths and weaknesses, standards by which contributions can be judged, criteria for distinguishing between relevant and irrelevant considerations, especially prized values, and ideals to be approximated. Each may be approached in two ways. One is by those who use the resources of a particular mode to cope with some problematic aspect of a particular segment of their world-view. This is the approach of historians, moral agents, politicians, religious believers, scientists, or individuals concentrating on their personal concerns. Theirs is the practical approach. The other is the approach of those who stand back from the activities appropriate to a mode of understanding, reflect on the larger significance of the descriptions and evaluations that follow from it, compare and contrast their own favored mode with other less favored ones, and give reasons for it and against the others. This is the reflective approach.

The practical approach proceeds by using the resources of a particular mode to understand present conditions by understanding the historical influences that have formed it, or to make reasonable moral or political decisions, or to apply the teachings of a religion to how believers should live and act, or to provide scientific explanations that make it possible to understand better and cope with natural adversities, or to pursue personal interests and preferences. Those who follow the practical approach of a mode of understanding need not combine it with the reflective approach, but there are strong reasons, both internal and external to modes of understanding, why they should.

The internal reason is that the appropriate conventions, methods, standards, criteria, values, and ideals of a mode of understanding are often controversial, as is the explanation of what makes its significant achievements possible. It may be the invention of a new method, synthesis of the apparently unrelated contributions of others, the depth or acuity of a particular thinker, and so forth. Those who seek understanding in a particular mode often disagree about whether current practices should be followed, reformed, or abandoned; which new developments are worth exploring; where the important issues lie; which assumptions should be questioned; what the relative importance of agreed upon values is; and so forth. These and other internal controversies make it natural for them to stand back and reflect on their practices, try to justify them, and criticize those of others.

The external reason for the reflective approach is that virtually no one is committed to only one mode of understanding. Scientists are moral agents, historians hold political views, religious believers have personal interests and preferences, and so on. Most of us have many different commitments to different modes of understanding, which have many different conventions, methods, standards, criteria, and values, and these commitments routinely guide us to act in incompatible ways. We need to reflect in order to decide which of our commitments are more and which less important than the others.

The problems that stand in the way of improving our lives make it reasonable to turn to modes of understanding for help. Controversies within them prompt us to reflect on our practices. And reflection leads us to realize that our various commitments often conflict. Thus we find that step by reasonable step we are brought to the realization that the modes of understanding to which we believe ourselves to be reasonably committed conflict. We, then, come up against philosophical problems caused by conflicting commitments that follow from different modes of understanding. It adds to the difficulty that these commitments are often not merely those of reflective people in the public sphere who share a world-view, but our own when we take both sides in arguments we are having with ourselves.[2]

Our need to cope with basic problems about how we should live and act makes us realize that we have incompatible commitments to conflicting modes of understanding. Such conflicts prompt us to reflect, and reflection may lead us to understand that we are divided about how we should resolve conflicts between our moral values and personal interests, between the scientific and the religious aspects of our world-view, between traditional ideals we hold and political reforms we regard as important, and so forth. This is part of the reason why conflicting modes of understanding lead to philosophical problems that are not only epistemological, but also psychological. They engage us because our beliefs about how we should live and act conflict. These beliefs, however, are not impersonal abstractions. We have strong feelings about the evaluative commitments they involve and we have made. Philosophical problems are difficult partly because they reveal our ambivalence about our commitments.

Generality

Generality is a distinguishing characteristic of modes of understanding. Those who are committed to a particular mode aim to describe and evaluate the significance of facts from its point of view. Historians explain present facts by tracing the past influences that have formed them; scientists fit them into a nomological network; religious believers locate them in the providential order; moral agents, politicians, and individuals evaluate how they affect the welfare of human beings, or of a society, or of their own. The generality of modes of understanding requires that they should have the resources, at least in principle, to distinguish between facts whose significance they should accommodate, facts that are unimportant from their point of view, and facts that present problems for them.

Historians have problems with explaining apparently senseless, irrational decisions; moral agents with assigning responsibility for the character of individuals formed by influences beyond their control; politicians with setting limits to permissible interference with individual freedom; religious believers with distinguishing between real and apparent miracles and religious experiences; scientists with coincidences and anomalies; and individuals with the frequency of self-deception. The usual strategy for dealing with such problems is to claim that they are minor, or that the resources for coping with them are available but insufficiently developed, or that the problems of other modes of understanding are far more serious.

These attempts to deal with problems often look suspiciously ad hoc, but even ad hoc attempts may be justified. The salient point is that problems are normal for all modes of understanding. They become threatening only if they are numerous and the attempts to cope with them repeatedly fail. This may happen, of course, and then the affected mode of understanding ought to go the way astrology, magic, and numerology have, or should have, gone.

I stress this point to make clear that I am not assuming that our modes of understanding are justified. Justified or not, they are part of our world-view. Critics may or may not be reasonable in regarding history as naïve science, morality as a sham, politics as unavoidably corrupted by indefensible ideologies, religion as a snare and a delusion, science as incapable of accommodating the values that make life worth living, or individuality as the self-indulgence of selfish, decadent aesthetes. For present purposes, what matters is to understand why philosophical problems occur, not whether the modes of understanding whose conflicts cause them are justified.

There are also facts that are unimportant from the point of view of a mode of understanding. There is no reason why historians should be concerned with lullabies, moral agents with quarks, politicians with puns, religious believers with inflation, scientists with abstract expressionism, or individuals with the Fibonacci sequence. Those who seek a particular mode of understanding may be reasonably indifferent to many facts that have no significance from their points of view. But they cannot be reasonably indifferent to facts that present problems for their modes of understanding. If they ignore some facts or if critics claim that some facts they ignore ought not to be ignored, then both defenders and critics of a mode must explain what reasons there are for regarding the contested facts as irrelevant or relevant. I do not think that it is possible to have a more precise way of distinguishing between what is and what is not relevant than this case-by-case method. Modes of understanding are general and it is impossible to say in advance what consideration may become relevant to historical or scientific explanations, or to moral, political, religious, or personal evaluations.

The generality of modes of understanding, therefore, does not mean that they are comprehensive accounts of all the facts—only of relevant ones. Still, the facts relevant to history, morality, politics, religion, science, and individuality are far more numerous and come from far more varied contexts than the facts that are relevant, say, to agriculture, commerce, poetry, or sports. This makes it possible to distinguish between modes of understanding and less general approaches to the significance of facts, but the distinction should not be drawn sharply. Economics, jurisprudence, linguistics, and medicine are borderline cases, because a wide variety of facts drawn from a wide variety of contexts may acquire significance for them. Virtually all distinctions must allow for grey areas, borderline cases, and disputed instances. In all of them there will be clear cases that fall on one or the other side. And the modes of understanding I am concerned with are, I think, clear cases of the most general approaches our world-view presently has. I readily acknowledge that there may be other no less clear cases, but that does not make the ones I concentrate on less clear. My aim is not to draw up a complete list of all modes of understanding, but to understand how conflicts between some of them lead to philosophical problems that we must cope with since the improvement of our lives partly depends on it.

What has so far emerged, then, is that modes of understanding combine practical and reflective approaches; aim to understand the significance of relevant facts; are general but not comprehensive; and may or may not be justified. The reason for concentrating on them is that their conflicts lead to philosophical problems.

Implications

If modes of understanding are the most general ways of describing and evaluating the significance of facts, then it should be possible to derive from history, morality, politics, religion, science, and personal concerns an account of the significance of the fact that the other modes of understanding account for the significance of facts differently. It may seem at first sight that this is not hard to do. Historians can provide an account of the past influences that have formed the present state of the other modes of understanding. Moral agents can evaluate them on the basis of their moral values or principles. Politicians can do the same from the point of view of the welfare of their society. Religious believers can criticize or justify them by forming a view of whether they conform to or violate the providential order. Scientists can give an account of the causes that have led them to be what they are. And individuals can similarly judge the significance of facts as they seem to those who pursue other modes of understanding by asking how they affect the pursuers' personal interests and preferences. Each mode of understanding, therefore, seems to have the capacity to account for the significance of the facts as they appear from the point of view of other modes. If a mode of understanding lacks this capacity, it is a strong reason for regarding it as deficient.

Contrary to first appearances, however, all modes of understanding are deficient in this respect. It is true that defenders of each mode can explain, at least in principle, from their own point of view why the other modes account for the significance of the facts as they do. But they must think that the other modes' accounts of significance misjudge the significance of relevant facts. The trouble they find with accounts other than their own is not that they are false. Their description of the facts may be true, but their evaluations go wrong by emphasizing what is shallow and miss the deeper significance of the facts that they may have accurately described.

Historians and scientists must see the significance of moral, political, religious, or personal evaluations as the products of past influences or causal conditions that have formed them, and they must see them as resting on contingent historical assumptions or causal conditions that change with time. The salient point for historians and scientists is not whether the evaluations that follow from other modes of understanding are reasonable or true, but what historical or causal conditions have led those who are committed to them to regard them as reasonable or true. They think that moral, political, religious, or personal evaluations are not really of the significance of the facts, but of what their significance is believed to be by moral agents, politicians, religious believers, or individuals. The real significance of the facts emerges from understanding the historical or causal conditions that led to whatever happen to be the prevailing moral, political, religious, or personal evaluations.

Similarly, moral agents are primarily concerned with the evaluation of historical, political, religious, scientific, or personal considerations on the basis of the relevant moral values or principles. They are not concerned with the past influences or the causal conditions that have formed these considerations, nor with their evaluation on the basis of political, religious, or personal values or principles. They will say that non-moral explanations and evaluations are shallow unless they are favorably evaluated by moral values or principles, and that the improvement of our lives depends on moral evaluations, not merely on what historians, politicians, religious believers, scientists, or individuals happen to favor. According to them, moral evaluations take precedence over non-moral ones, because the true significance of the facts depends on the moral evaluation of them.

Politicians, religious believers, and individuals are likewise concerned with how historical, scientific, or moral considerations ought to be evaluated from the point of view of the welfare of their society, or the providential order, or their personal interests and preferences, not on how they are in fact evaluated from the point of view of other modes of understanding. They will say that the improvement of our lives ultimately depends on the welfare of the society in which we live, or on conforming to the providential order, or on pursuing our own interests and preferences. Historical and scientific explanations of moral evaluations are acceptable only insofar as they serve this purpose.

Defenders of each mode of understanding, therefore, must regard the accounts of significance that follow from other modes as misguided. This, of course, is not how defenders of the supposedly misguided modes regard them. They are all committed to thinking that defenders of the others modes attribute the wrong significance to their own evaluations. Thus they all lack the capacity to account for the significance of the relevant facts as they appear from the point of view of the other modes. And since the generality of modes of understanding requires those who are committed to them to account for the significance of all relevant facts, they all fail to meet this requirement, because they are unavoidably committed to denying that those who are committed to the other modes have understood the real significance of the facts. It seems, therefore, that all modes of understanding are deficient, because they account for the significance of the facts from their own point of view that excludes the significance of facts that follow from the point of view of other modes.

It may be thought that such accounts are simply arbitrary because they question-beggingly take for granted their own account of significance in order to cast doubt on the accounts of significance that follow from other modes of understanding. But they need not be arbitrary, provided those who give them explain what error has led to the misguided accounts of significance that followed from other modes. Reflective historians and scientists will say that the error is that they miss the crucial significance of the fact that moral, political, religious, or personal evaluations are what they are because of the historical influences or causal conditions that have formed them. Reflective moral agents, politicians, religious believers, and individuals will say that the error is that participants in modes other than their own fail to evaluate the significance of relevant facts on the basis of the values or principles on which the improvement of our lives depends. Reflective defenders of each mode of understanding, therefore, can provide reasons for their rejection of the accounts of significance that follow from other modes.

Nevertheless, these reasons will not be strong enough to save them from the charge of arbitrariness. For defenders of the criticized mode will level exactly the same charge against their critics. Each will say that the mode of understanding on which critics base their criticisms arbitrarily assumes that the true significance of facts emerges from the mode they favor. Defenders of a mode will ask why they should accept that the historical, moral, political, religious, scientific, or personal significance of facts is more important than the significance they attribute to them. None of them needs to deny that the descriptions and evaluations of the other modes are relevant, but they will all continue to think that those that follow from their own mode of understanding are more important than the others. And so the argument among them will take the form of stressing the importance of one mode of understanding at the expense of the others.

Defenders of each mode owe an explanation of why their own mode is more important than the others. Each will provide an explanation, but it will consist in the elaboration of the assumption with which they start, namely, that the true significance of relevant facts is historical, or moral, or political, or religious, or scientific, or personal. The elaborated explanation will aim to show how the significance of relevant facts, including the points of view that follow from the other modes of understanding, should be understood when described and evaluated from the point of view of the mode of understanding they favor. Such arguments will go on and on because the defenders of each mode will provide ever more perspicuous elaborations of their own mode and ever more sophisticated criticisms of the others.

The obvious question that needs to be asked at this point is why defenders of a mode of understanding could not simply accept that understanding the true significance of the relevant facts depends on the combination of all or most of the accounts of significance that follows from different modes of understanding? The answer is that they could not accept it because, as we have seen, different modes of understanding do not merely provide different accounts of the significance of the relevant facts, but conflicting accounts of them. That is what causes philosophical problems.[3] And philosophical problems imply that the world-view of which the conflicting modes of understanding are incompatible parts is incoherent.

Reflection on a Case

The discussion has so far been general and abstract. In order to make it less so, consider a concrete case to illustrate how conflicts among modes of understanding may impinge on everyday life. There can be no reasonable doubt that AIDS is a serious problem in whatever society it occurs. Many have died and more are slowly dying from it worldwide; sexual relations are altered by it; and considerable resources, much-needed elsewhere, are spent on its prevention and treatment. Whatever anyone thinks of the sexual revolution brought about by the pill and other effective methods of contraception, the decriminalization of homosexuality, the normalization of extramarital sex, increasingly larger number of women entering the workforce, and the resulting changes in traditional family life, AIDS has basically influenced how the sexual revolution affects everyday life. We cannot just ignore it, and we must face the question of what to do about it. A reasonable answer depends on understanding AIDS, but the historical, moral, political, religious, scientific, and personal modes of understanding it are very different and lead to very different proposals for coping with it.

We may try to understand AIDS historically by identifying the larger social influences that have led to it. We may concentrate on the sort of considerations I have just mentioned. But history has become a discipline that goes far beyond the sort of obvious, albeit anecdotal, observations I offer above. Historians may proceed statistically by quantifying the changes that have occurred, or by focusing on the forces that have led to changes in the laws and in their enforcement in the direction of greater sexual permissiveness, or by comparing the history of epidemics and attempted ways of coping with them at very different times and places, or by contrasting and comparing changes from past to present sensibility as reflected in the press or in literature, and so on. Historians who proceed in one of these ways, of course, disagree with others who proceed differently, not so much about the description of the facts, but about their evaluation, and the relative significance they attribute to acknowledged facts, as well as about the best method of pursuing historical understanding.

We may think about AIDS from a moral point of view and ask how far we ought to hold responsible those who contracted it, what we owe to our stricken fellow citizens, how we ought to weigh the many different moral demands on our scarce resources, how far our moral responsibility extends beyond the borders of our country, what are the morally permissible limits of the various measures we might take to prevent the spread of the disease, what group, institution, or policy, if any, can be reasonably blamed for the epidemic we face, and so on. Serious moral thought will appeal to principles and values, but there are many of them, and they often lead to incompatible moral judgments. There will be moral disagreements about what we ought to do about AIDS, as there are moral disagreements about many of the important decisions we have to make to cope with the various problems we face.

We may also try to understand AIDS from a political point of view. Politicians, holders of the relevant offices, and public health authorities must consider what to do about it. They must judge how far public policies can legitimately interfere with the private sexual conduct of consenting mature adults, how threatening the spread of the disease really is, what policies would be acceptable to a large population with very different views about where to draw the line between permissible and impermissible sexual practices, whether citizens already burdened by taxation would accept higher taxes if they could be convinced that there is an emergency, and so on. Of course, those who have to make such policy decisions will themselves be divided among each other and within themselves about how these questions should be answered.

Since religion is a potent force even in increasingly secularized societies, it matters what the religious understanding of AIDS should be. Should believers regard AIDS as divine punishment for sin, should they respond with charity and compassion to those who have contracted it, is it a consequence of more and more people seeking sensual pleasures and turning away from spiritual life, how can widespread doubts about sin be convincingly countered in a society where temptations are ubiquitous, how literally should biblical prohibitions of promiscuity and homosexuality be interpreted, and what are the obligations of various religious organizations toward those who suffer from AIDS? These are difficult questions, but they are made more difficult still, because there is no authoritative religious understanding that transcends those that follow from particular religions. There are substantial differences between the understandings that follow from different religions, and within each religion there will be deep disagreements between the orthodox who follow traditional teachings and the heterodox who want to reform them in order to respond to the changing concerns of believers in changing times.

There will also be a scientific approach to AIDS. Epidemiologists, hematologists, immunologists, microbiologists, pharmacologists, and others, in their different ways, are doing both basic research into the causes of the disease, its treatment and prevention, and effective immunization against it. Their theories and methods take them in many different directions, and they often have serious disagreements about the lines of research they regard as more and as less promising. Their disagreements are not simply the usual professional wrangles, but involve the far more complicated matter of deciding how scarce resources should be allocated among the competing directions in which future research might go.

We may also consider AIDS in personal terms. We will then ask how it should affect our own behavior, how far it should or should not change the sexual education of our children, can we trust that our sexual partner(s) will be sufficiently prudent in their own sexual contacts, what are the chances that we or those we love may contract AIDS, not only by direct sexual contacts, but indirectly by exposure to contaminated blood, how effective we think the various public safety measures are that have been taken to prevent its spread, how should we respond to friends or acquaintances who have contracted it, how trustworthy is the information we have about AIDS, is it perhaps just a scare generated by the media, self-declared experts, and ambitious politicians, or is it a serious threat? We will give many, often conflicting, but, in any case, different answers to these very natural questions, and often we will be uncertain.

AIDS is a serious problem. Reflection on it makes us realize, however, that it is a symptom of the even more serious problem that we are vulnerable to the contingencies of life over which we have, at best, only limited control. It shows us that the different approaches that follow from the modes of understanding we have developed to cope with our problems are not merely different ways of pursuing the same aim, but different ways of pursuing different aims. The different evaluations and the resulting accounts of the significance of facts that follow from different modes of understanding reflect deep differences among them on account of their assumptions about explanation, evaluation, anthropocentrism, impersonality, and prudence.

Historical and scientific modes of understanding are alike in aiming at explanations, but scientific explanations aim to fit facts into a nomological network, while historical explanations are typically of unique events, trends, or decisions that reflect changing circumstances and fallible, often irrational, human beings, not laws. Scientific explanations are not anthropocentric, whereas historical explanations focus on human concerns. Moral, political, religious, and personal modes of understanding have a central evaluative dimension, but political and religious evaluations are impersonal, in contrast with moral and personal ones that are at least partly personal. Moral and religious evaluations typically override conflicting prudential considerations, but political and personal ones are essentially connected with them. Political and religious modes of understanding have an important explanatory aspect, whereas the moral and personal modes are intended to be action-guiding, not explanatory. Moral, political, religious, and personal evaluations concentrate on making human lives better, whereas historical and scientific explanations aim at the truth, regardless of how it might affect us.

One implication of these and other differences among modes of understanding is that the conflicts among them cannot be resolved by comparing their relative success in achieving a shared aim. Scientists hold moral, political, personal, and perhaps also religious values, but science itself aims to be neutral toward such values; religion is not bad science; politics is not morality writ large; history is no longer a search for causal laws that govern human affairs; personal understanding is not just a matter of internalizing moral, political, and religious evaluations. The resulting philosophical problems are obstacles to coping with the pressing problems we face. They are serious obstacles because the conflicting practical and reflective approaches of different modes of understanding lead us to pursue different aims in different ways, and because it is typically a matter of sharp controversy which ways, aims, and understandings are more reasonable than the others.

If this account of philosophical problems as the results of conflicts among modes of understanding is correct, then it follows that these problems are not generated by philosophers benighted by complications they have invented, but central aspects of the world-view of a society at a particular time. A world-view, then, is not characterized merely by the modes of understanding that partly form it, but also by the conflicts among them, and by the philosophical problems their conflicts cause.

It is part of our world-view here and now that we know that history has influenced how we think and feel, but we disagree whether we can partly or wholly free ourselves from those influences. We know that science is amazingly successful and makes our lives immeasurably better, but we disagree about how far we should limit scientific research by our moral, political, religious, or personal values. We know that our moral and non-moral values often conflict, but we disagree about how their conflicts could be reasonably resolved. We know that we cannot live without politics, but we disagree about how far it should control our lives and actions. We know that secularization and vast social changes have led to the diminishing influence of religion, but many look to it for consolation, hope, and the meaning and value of life. We know the importance of pursuing our interests and preferences, but we sharply disagree about how far we should subordinate them to impersonal considerations. Philosophical problems are behind such disagreements. So long as conflicting modes of understanding are parts of our world-view, philosophical problems matter and are here to stay. We cannot make them go away, and we must cope with them. The question for us is how we should do that.

Problematic Approaches

I will briefly consider three approaches to coping with philosophical problems. I will keep returning to them in subsequent chapters, but it is important to see at this stage of the argument, even if only in an introductory way, that none of them provides an obvious way of coping with philosophical problems.

The absolutist approach is that the various modes of understanding should be arranged in a hierarchical order.[4] When modes of understanding conflict, the one that stands higher in the hierarchy should take precedence over and override those that stand lower. There is one mode of understanding, however, that stands highest in the hierarchy, because it provides the supreme action-guiding principle, or the authoritative method, not just for coping with, but for resolving philosophical problems once and for all. At one time or another, each one of the historical, moral, political, religious, scientific, and personal modes has been claimed to be overriding. Hegelians claimed it for history and its dialectic; Kant for morality and the unconditional requirement of the categorical imperative; Hobbes for politics as a precondition of civilized life; Augustine and Aquinas for religious faith as the key to salvation; positivists and logical empiricists for science as the standard of truth and rationality; and classical liberals and existentialists for individuality as involving a basic commitment to whatever manner of living seems best to us.

The problem with the absolutist approach is that, regardless of what mode of understanding is thought to be overriding, it is question-begging. This becomes evident if we ask what the force is of the "should" in the assertion that the supposedly highest mode of understanding should override the supposedly lower ones. If this assertion is not just an arbitrary preference for one mode of understanding over the others, it must be supported by reasons that explain why the supposedly overriding mode should actually be overriding. If the reasons are derived from the overriding mode itself, they simply assume what is in question, namely, that the overriding mode should override the others if they conflict. Of course there are moral reasons why moral reasons should override conflicting political reasons. But there are also political reasons why political reasons should override conflicting moral reasons. And the same is true regardless of what the conflicting modes of understanding are.

If the reasons for regarding one mode of understanding as overriding go beyond arbitrary preferences, then they must be neutral between all the conflicting modes of understanding. There are such reasons: logical consistency, explanation of relevant facts, responsiveness to criticism, and the like. But defenders of all the modes of understanding I am considering can adduce such neutral reasons in favor of their own mode. The problem is that the neutral reasons are not strong enough to decide between the conflicting modes of understanding that conform to them. Reflective defenders of modes of understanding are usually highly intelligent, analytically sophisticated thinkers who are unlikely to make elementary mistakes in logic, explanation, and responding to criticisms. What is in question is the relative weight that should be ascribed to conflicting non-neutral reasons, and that question defenders of each mode of understanding answer in their own favor. That is part of the reason why the approaches for resolving the conflicts between modes of understanding lead to the philosophical problems that concern us. I conclude for the moment, until further discussion, that defenders of the absolutist approach have no obvious way of meeting this difficulty.

The second approach for coping with philosophical problems is relativist. Its defenders acknowledge the plurality of conflicting modes of understanding, but claim that in a society during a particular age, the consensus is to regard one of the modes of understanding as overriding. Doing so has been during that period part of the shared world-view of those who live together in a society. They show their acceptance of one mode as overriding by relying on its practical and reflective approaches to cope with the problems of everyday life they encounter.[5] Reflective people in that society may acknowledge that others in other societies or at other times may reasonably proceed differently, but, they will claim in support of their own way of proceeding, that what others do elsewhere does not cast doubt on the reasons they have then and there in their society for regarding one mode of understanding as overriding.

What, then, are the reasons relativists give in their own context for regarding a mode of understanding as overriding? The reasons cannot just be that it is their custom to do this, because that is as question-begging as the absolutist approach. The question is, what reasons are there for the custom they follow? And that needs a better answer than that it is what they do. Of course they may be accustomed to doing it, but if that exhausts their reasons, then they have run out of reasons for doing it. This is a dangerous pass to come to since their customs may be cruel, destructive, unjust, impoverished, stupid, or contrary to human well-being in other ways.

Why is it still not reason enough for relativists to add that when they proceed in their customary ways, then they manage to cope with their problems? Because each of the modes of understanding reflects a genuinely important aspect of human life. If one of them overrides the others, then the others must be subordinated to it, and that means that genuinely important aspects of human life are stifled in the course of regarding one as overriding. It is painfully familiar from our past and present what miseries people suffer in societies that are ruled by authorities who claim that historical, moral, political, religious, scientific, or personal considerations must override whatever other considerations conflict with them. Such decisions lead to tyranny or chaos, and often to one after the other. If our age can lay claim to having become at least in some respects a little more civilized than its predecessors, it must be based on our recognition that tyranny or chaos in any form is incompatible with the improvement of our lives. There is much, therefore, that seems, at least initially, to tell against the relativist approach.

The third approach is skeptical. Skepticism has many versions, but perhaps the strongest one is Pyrrhonian, and that is the one I will now briefly consider. Skeptics agree that the preceding two approaches are arbitrary. Their own approach is to avoid philosophical problems, rather than embark on what skeptics regard as a futile search for ways of coping with them. Their point expressed in terms of my discussion is that since philosophical problems occur because modes of understanding conflict, the way to avoid them is to make no commitment to any mode of understanding. Making that commitment would lead to futile arguments about the relative merits of unreasonable efforts to go beyond the obvious and readily available resources of everyday life.[6] Skeptics acknowledge that everyday life is beset by problems, but they deny that we must rely on modes of understanding to cope with them. And even if we must rely on them, skeptics deny that having them would help, and they can adduce the resulting philosophical problems as confirmations of their view. They conclude that it is far more reasonable and conducive to our peace of mind to try to cope with our problems by relying on the resources of everyday life than on modes of understanding that lead to irresolvable philosophical problems.

There is much to be said in favor of the skeptical approach, but it remains problematic for modes of understanding are not gratuitous abstractions that serve no reasonable purpose. They provide far better practical approaches than everyday life does to coping with our problems. The tangible benefits of the practical approaches that follow from history, morality, politics, religion, science, and individuality have made our lives immeasurably better. Historical understanding aims to help us to evaluate our institutions and practices on the basis of how well they serve their objectives. Morality aims to make it possible to explain and give reasons for judgments about what is good or bad. Political understanding aims to show why it is important to limit the power of each branch of the government, to hold politicians accountable, and to demand conformity to the law. Religion aims to reconcile us to the adversities of life that lie beyond our control, to console us for our miseries, and to give us hope for a better future. Science aims to enable us to acquire greater control over natural conditions and helps us to improve the quality of our lives. And personal understanding clarifies how we want to live and what reasons we have for it. Their aims are important and the extent to which they approximate them is one of the great benefits of civilized life. No reasonable person can fail to appreciate how much better some of the modes of understanding have made our lives, even if they deny that some one or another of the others is defensible. The skeptical approach fails to take account of the genuine benefits we derive from at least some of the modes of understanding.

Skeptics nevertheless have an important point, and the distinction I drew earlier between the practical and reflective approaches helps to make clearer what it is. The practical approach of a mode of understanding may help to cope with problems and secure the sort of benefits I have just mentioned. The reflective approach, however, is also needed because, as we have seen, modes of understanding are continually handicapped by internal and external conflicts. The need to resolve their conflicts forces defenders of a particular mode of understanding to claim that it should override the conflicting ones. But defenders of each mode of understanding make that claim, and all their claims are questionable. I interpret the importance of the skeptics' point as the recommendation to avoid the reflective approach on the ground that it leads to intractable philosophical problems.

According to this interpretation, skeptics have no objection to following the available practical approaches of modes of understanding to coping with problems. Nor do skeptics deny the obvious benefits that such efforts may yield. What they recommend against is turning to the reflective approach in order to resolve conflicts among practical approaches. And the reason they may give for this recommendation is that the reflective approaches unavoidably lead to philosophical problems that can be resolved only by making an arbitrary decision to regard one mode of understanding as overriding. The skeptical approach to coping with philosophical problems, then, is the recommendation to avoid generating them by refusing to go beyond practical approaches.

My reason for thinking that the skeptical approach is also problematic is that the reflective approach is unavoidable. We are driven to it because the problems of everyday life compel us to seek a practical approach to coping with them, and we are compelled to do so by relying on the available modes of understanding. But there are several modes available, and we have to decide which one we should follow. If our decision is reasonable, it must involve deciding which mode of understanding is more likely than the others to enable us to cope with our problems. We can make that decision only by deciding which mode is more important. And that leads to the reflective approach that skeptics recommend avoiding. If we follow their recommendation, we will not know how to cope with our problems, nor how to resolve conflicts among practical approaches to coping with them. Their recommendation, therefore, has unacceptable consequences. If we do as they recommend and avoid the reflective approach, we end up with arbitrary and conflicting claims that one mode of understanding should override the others. And that, in turn, produces the philosophical problems we seem not to be able either to avoid or to cope with in a reasonable way.

The upshot is that we face a dilemma that appears unavoidable regardless of whether we opt for the absolutist, relativist, or the skeptical approach. If we arbitrarily regard one mode of understanding as overriding, then we ultimately we have no good reason for relying on it to cope with our problems. If we try to decide reasonably which mode of understanding is overriding, then we unavoidably end up with the philosophical problems that prevent us from making a reasonable decision. This is the predicament that makes it reasonable to look with favor on the pluralist approach to coping with philosophical problems that is different from these three.

The Pattern

There is a pattern that emerges from the preceding discussion. I think it is one that characterizes all philosophical problems of the kind I am considering. The background is the quotidian everyday life as it is at a certain time and place. It is the shared context in which virtually all of us in a society live. Everyday life is disrupted in various ways by various problems. We can cope with some of them by relying on the resources of everyday life, but others are far more serious and threatening. These latter problems force us to seek a practical approach to coping with them beyond the resources of everyday life. We, then, turn to the available modes of understanding and derive from them a practical approach based on historical understanding, or moral and political values or principles, or religious teachings, or scientific explanation, or personal interests and preferences. But these practical approaches conflict and suggest incompatible ways of coping with the problems that have led us to seek practical approaches in the first place. We need to cope with their conflicts, and for this we need a reflective approach. Different modes of understanding, however, provide different reflective approaches, and they conflict as much as the practical approaches do. We need to cope with their conflicts as well. We can do so by trying to make a reasonable decision to rely on one of the conflicting modes of understanding and use its reflective approach to cope with conflicts among the available practical approaches. Our predicament is that the only reasons we seem to have for deciding which reflective approach we should follow derive from the available modes of understanding. And, naturally enough, those reasons will favor the reflective approach of the mode from which we derive them. We, then, have to decide which of these reasons is the best. But, once again, we can make that decision only by relying on the available modes of understanding, and each will prompt us to regard its reasons as the best. We are thus led to philosophical problems because we seem to have no reasonable way of deciding about the relative merits of the modes of understanding that provide the conflicting practical and reflective approaches. We thus cannot cope with the serious problems that stand in the way of improving our lives.

This is merely a general outline of the pattern. In subsequent chapters I will make it less general by filling in the gaps. In Chapter 2 I aim to explain why if we are reflective and familiar with the various modes of understanding available in our world-view, we may actually commit ourselves to one of them in preference to the others.

2

Modes of Understanding: Particular Accounts

There often arise quarrels between...lines of thought, which are...irreconcilable with one another. A thinker who adopts one of them often seems to be logically committed to rejecting the other, despite the fact that the inquiries from which the theories issued had, from the beginning widely different goals. In disputes of this kind, we often find one and the same thinker—very likely oneself—strongly inclined to champion both sides....He is both satisfied with the logical credentials of each of the points of view, and sure that one of them must be totally wrong if the other is even largely right.

Gilbert Ryle[1]

Historical, moral, political, religious, scientific, and personal modes of understanding are important components of our world-view. Each combines a practical approach to coping with problems that stand in the way of improving our lives and a reflective approach to understanding the significance of relevant facts. Reflective defenders of each mode contrast and compare their own approaches with those that follow from the others, and give reasons why their own should override the others when they conflict. The aim of this chapter is to understand their reasons. In Chapters 5–8 I will argue that their reasons are inadequate. In order to avoid cluttering the text with long quotations, I often, but not always, proceed by reconstructing their reasons in my own words. Supporting documentation can be found in the Notes.

The Historical Mode

Our world-view, containing modes of understanding and their assumptions, beliefs, values, and practices, forms a whole whose parts are connected with one another in countless ways. When we find them conflicting, have anomalous experiences, encounter new problems, or find new ways of dealing with old problems, we have to revise parts of our world-view. In this way, we continually change parts of it, but we do so by relying on the other parts that have remained temporarily unaffected. As a result of such adjustments, the world-view is at once continuing and changing. As time goes on, the changes may become more and more numerous, so much so that the old world-view with which we began is gradually transformed into one that resembles the old in some ways and differs from it in others. It is futile to try to identify a point at which a world-view is replaced by a new one. Who could tell at what point was the ancient world-view replaced by the medieval one, or when the Renaissance replaced it? Who could say exactly when modernity started? And who could take literally Virginia Woolf's witticism that human nature changed on or about December 1910?

This fluidity has a crucial implication for how historical understanding proceeds. It is committed to understanding the significance of facts—be they ideas, values, decisions, actions, events, or processes—by understanding their context. And the context is a world-view, the prevailing conditions, and the state of its modes of understanding. But conditions and modes of understanding continually change, and the significance of facts changes with them. Descriptions of facts typically change much less than their evaluations, but changes of some kind are unavoidable, and so are changes of significance. There is, therefore, no such thing as the one true significance of any fact. Good reasons can be given for accounts of significance, and one account can be more or less reasonable than another. But what counts as a reason and how heavily it counts changes with changing world-views. There are also reasons that can be given for or against world-views themselves. The reasons, however, are not theoretical but practical. They have to do with how helpful the world-view is in coping with the prevailing problems. Conspicuous successes or repeated failures in coping with serious problems are reasons for or against a world-view. And over time the balance of reasons shifts and the world-view is thereby strengthened or weakened.[2]

By way of illustration, here are three synecdoches each of which stands for the complex world-view it represents. The first is of 5th-century BC Athens reflected in Pericles' funeral oration:

Taking everything together then, I declare that our city is an education of Greece, and I declare that in my opinion each single one of our citizens, in all the manifold aspects of life, is able to show himself the rightful lord and owner of his own person, and do this, moreover, with exceptional grace and exceptional versatility. And to show that this is no empty boasting for the present occasion, but real tangible fact, you have only to consider the power which our city possesses and which has been won by those very qualities which I have mentioned.... Future ages will wonder at us, as the present age wonders at us now.... Our adventurous spirit has forced an entry into every sea and into every land; and everywhere we have left behind us everlasting memorials of good done to our friends or suffering inflicted on our enemies.[3]

The second is the medieval world-view of 13th-century Christian Europe:

In this climate of opinion it was an unquestioned fact that the world and man in it had been created in six days by God the Father, an omniscient and benevolent intelligence, for an ultimate if inscrutable purpose.... Man had through disobedience fallen from grace into sin and error, thereby incurring the penalty of eternal damnation. Yet happily a way of atonement and salvation had been provided through the propitiatory sacrifice of God's only begotten son. Helpless in themselves to avert the just wrath of God, men were permitted, through his mercy, and by humility and obedience to his will, to obtain pardon for sin and error. Life on earth was but a means to this desired end, a temporary probation for the testing of God's children. In God's appointed time, the Earthly City would come to an end... good and evil men would be finally separated. For the recalcitrant there was reserved a place of everlasting punishment; but the faithful would be gathered with God in the Heavenly City, there in perfection and felicity to dwell forever.[4]

The third world-view is philosophical, held at the beginning of the 20th century by many educated English speakers:

Man is the product of causes which had no prevision of the end they were achieving; that his origin, his growth, his hopes and fears, his loves and his beliefs, are but the outcome of accidental collocations of atoms; that no fire, no heroism, no intensity of thought and feeling, can preserve an individual life beyond the grave; that all the labours of the ages, all the devotion, all the inspiration, all the noonday brightness of human genius, are destined to extinction in the vast death of the solar system, and that the whole temple of Man's achievement must inevitably be buried beneath the debris of a universe in ruins— all these things, if not quite beyond dispute, are yet so nearly certain, that no philosophy which rejects them can hope to stand. Only within the scaffolding of these truths, only on the firm foundation of unyielding despair, can the soul's habitation henceforth be safely built.[5]

Now consider the evaluations that emerge from these world-views of history, morality, politics, religion, science, and individuality; the relative importance attributed to various modes of understanding; and of the very different meanings of concepts central to the human condition, such as of nature, good and bad, happiness, hope, the meaning of life, and so forth. Historians aim to reconstruct these evaluations, standards of relevance, and meanings in a particular period, and reflective historians will compare and contrast their own with those that follow from different periods and world-views. If they are asked for their reasons for assigning priority to the historical mode of understanding over the other modes, they will say that the others, typically unbeknownst to their defenders, presuppose the historically conditioned assumptions, beliefs, and values of the world-view that happens to be prevalent in their context, and that is as true of past as of present modes of understanding.

Reflective historians will say that defenders of the other, non-historical modes are right to stress that they are forces for moral progress, political order, religious consolation and hope, scientific understanding and coping with natural adversities, and for the creation of conditions in which individuals can pursue their personal preferences. Their indisputable achievements, however, count as such only within the world-view that they all, in their different ways, take for granted. The special excellence of historical understanding, its defenders will say, is that it alone can lead to the deeper understanding of the forever-changing world-views that make possible and form the basis of what are within them recognizable achievements. They will acknowledge that non-historical modes of understanding have standards of relevance, truth, reason, and goodness by which the significance of facts can be judged. But they will point out that the standards rest on historically conditioned, forever changing presuppositions. This is the deeper understanding of the significance of the facts and the special excellence, they will say, that the historical mode has and other modes lack. And that is the reason why it has and should be recognized as overriding the other modes if they come into conflict.

The Moral Mode

It is difficult to give a neutral account of the moral mode of understanding. The available accounts typically proceed from the point of view of particular moral theories, and are thus not neutral. Consequentialists, contractarians, deontologists, eudaimonists, and natural law theorists each give an account of morality biased in their own favor. The account I propose is intended to avoid bias. I have defended it elsewhere and will make use of its basic approach here, but for a purpose quite different from the previous one. I call it a three-dimensional view of morality.[6] What follows is no more than the barest outline, but it is sufficient for the present purpose, which is to indicate the reasons reflective moral agents have for regarding the moral mode as overriding, without assuming the correctness of any particular moral theory.

Morality is three-dimensional both literally and metaphorically. It has three dimensions and it is capacious enough to accommodate a wide variety of different moral theories. Its aim is to describe various moral concerns, their differences and similarities, and the reasons that may be given for the significance and importance of these moral concerns. The moralities of the different world-views are different, but if a morality is reasonable, it must aim to secure some of the conditions of individual well-being. These conditions are universal, social, and personal. The dimensions of morality correspond to these conditions: its universal dimension is concerned with conditions that are the same for all human beings; its social dimension includes conditions that hold in a particular society and may or may not hold in others; and its personal dimension focuses on conditions that hold for particular individuals but not for others.

In each dimension, securing the conditions counts as good and violating them as bad. Since they are secured or violated primarily by actions, there are universally, socially, and personally right and wrong actions. Each dimension has possibilities and limits. The possibilities are various conditions of well-being, and the limits are the prohibitions against violating these conditions. In order to pursue the possibilities and prohibit the violation of limits each dimension has conventions establishing what actions are right or wrong. The justification or criticism of the morality of a society, then, depends on how well or badly its conventions secure the conditions of well-being in each of the three dimensions.

The universal dimension is concerned with the satisfaction of basic needs that are the same for all human beings at all times and places and under all conditions. The most obvious ones are physiological needs for nutrition, oxygen, protection from the elements, rest and motion, consumption and elimination, and so forth. To these may be added basic psychological needs for companionship, appreciation, the absence of terror and self-loathing, and the like. There are also basic social needs for a civilized form of life in which there is order and security, division of labor, protection against crime and illness, coordination of individual activities, adjudication of conflicts, education of children, and life beyond mere subsistence.

The satisfaction of these basic physiological, psychological, and social needs is a condition of all reasonable conceptions of well-being. For the prolonged frustration of these needs seriously damages everyone in all circumstances. The specific satisfactions of specific basic needs are universal goods. Since all reasonable moralities aim to secure these elementary conditions of well-being, each must have conventions specifying what the universal values are and providing protection against being deprived of them. These conventions are morally required because well-being is impossible without them. The aim of the universal dimension is thus to secure universal values. Required conventions are means to securing them. They are universal because the basic needs they aim to satisfy are the same for all human beings, and they are impersonal because they apply to all human beings equally. From this follows the standard of evaluation by which, in the universal dimension of morality, actions and conventions are evaluated. Their rightness or wrongness is proportional to their success or failure in satisfying the basic needs of people in a particular context.

The social dimension is concerned with securing the social values recognized by people living in a society. In all societies there are conventions that aim to secure them and prohibit their violation. These conventions vary with societies and ages, but when they hold, they apply to everyone in that society. They are, therefore, general, although not universal. Some variable conventions are impersonal because they are supposed to secure social values for everyone equally, like police protection or the use of public roads. Others secure social values selectively, since they are competitive, scarce, or attached to specific positions, roles, or relationships. Social values and variable conventions constitute a large part of a particular society's system of values. Part of the upbringing and socialization of children consists in acquainting them with the prevailing system of values, from which they eventually derive both their moral identity and the standard by which they justify or criticize actions and variable conventions in the social dimension of morality.

Social values are of two types. One is formed of the particular ways in which the universal values are interpreted in a particular context, such as the satisfaction of basic needs for food, companionship, and the adjudication of conflicts. The need for food must be met, otherwise we die. But there are great differences in how it is met. All societies have conventions guiding what is eaten, when, with whom, what should be raw and what cooked, who prepares the food, what is served to guests, and so forth. In all societies there are shared ways of interpreting universal values and shared conventions aiming to secure the values thus interpreted, but the interpretations and conventions vary with societies and times.

Another type of social value includes aspects of life whose connection with universal values is more remote, such as ethnicity, religious affiliation, ways of making a living, education, high and popular culture, hobbies, and so forth. It includes also the countless customs, rituals, and ceremonies of everyday life that mark significant occasions, like birth, marriage, and death; conventions about flirtation, competition, clothing, and housing; and the appropriate ways of expressing gratitude, regret, contempt, resentment, admiration, and the like.

People living in a society are familiar with both types of social values. Their familiarity creates expectations and leaves their mark on those who have lived in that society for a sufficiently long time. The values are part of the system of values by which they live. Their expectations, characters, and ways of life jointly form a significant part of their moral identity.

As the satisfaction of basic needs is a condition of well-being and the standard of evaluation in the universal dimension of morality, so moral identity is a condition of well-being and the standard of evaluation in the social dimension of morality. Reasonable moralities, therefore, must protect social values and variable conventions. The protection, however, is of the system of social values and variable conventions, not of the changing components of it. It is having a moral identity that is a condition of well-being, not the particular social values and variable conventions that are temporarily parts of it. Reasonable moralities must combine the recognition of the importance of protecting moral identity with a great deal of flexibility that allows for changes in its parts. The conditions of well-being in the universal dimension, therefore, will be largely the same in different societies, whereas the conditions of well-being in the social dimension will be the same only as far as the protection of moral identity is concerned, but they will differ in respect to the changing social values and variable conventions that constitute moral identity in different societies or in different ages.

The personal dimension is concerned with individuals pursuing their well-being. The values of this dimension may differ from person to person. They are usually derived from the available social values and adapted to reflect preferences that vary with individuals. The possibilities and limits of this dimension vary with societies and individuals, so that they are not universal, general, or impersonal. The protection of these personal possibilities and staying within their limits largely takes the form of adapting social values to fit individual characters, preferences, and circumstances.

The advantages of the three-dimensional view of morality are that its universal dimension leaves room for the concerns of universalist moral theories without commitment to any of them. Its social dimension can accommodate relativist moral theories, without denying that human beings have permanent interests even as conditions change. And its personal dimension can accept individualist moral theories that emphasize that what matters most from the moral point of view is the well-being of individuals.

Another advantage of the three-dimensional view is that it can recognize and suggest ways of coping with moral conflicts. Conflicts within each dimension of morality can be resolved by appealing to its standard of evaluation: to the joint satisfaction of all the various basic needs; to the protection of the moral identity; and to the well-being of individuals. There will also be conflicts between evaluations that follow from different dimensions. These conflicts can be resolved by appealing to the need to protect the whole system (formed of universal, social, and personal values) as it exists in a particular society at a particular time. The resolution of both kinds of conflict is likely to be often disputed. If the disputants are reasonable, they will accept the standards and dispute only about how they should be applied in particular cases. The disputants, of course, are often not reasonable, but that reflects on them, not on the standards of the three-dimensional view. And what makes it reasonable to accept the proposed standards of each dimension and the overall standard is that the well-being of those who live in a society at a certain time depends on it.

This account of three-dimensional morality makes obvious the reason reflective moral agents have for claiming that the moral mode of understanding is overriding. The reason is that all modes of understanding depend on the existence of conditions in which they can be pursued. The moral mode of understanding is concerned with creating and maintaining those conditions. All the other modes, therefore, presuppose it, and that is the reason for assigning priority to it.

The Political Mode

Most of the existing accounts of political understanding lean toward one of the main contending contemporary political theories: conservative, liberal, or socialist. It complicates matters further that each has different versions, and they often combine elements of the different theories. This makes it hard to say whether they are conservative, liberal, or socialist. I will try to give a neutral account by distinguishing between the universal and conventional approaches; either may be conservative, liberal, or socialist.

Defenders of the universal approach focus on one political value, and aim to transform societies so that its institutions and policies approximate more closely this highest political value. Each one of equality, justice, liberty, and rights has been claimed to be the highest.[7] This approach is universal in the sense that it claims that the highest value should govern the institutions and policies of all societies regardless of historical, cultural, economic, and other differences among them. Defenders of different universal approaches, then, disagree about which political value is the highest, how it should be interpreted, and what the best policies are in different circumstances for approximating it.

Defenders of the conventional approach deny that there is a highest political value. There are many political values, they are connected in various ways, sometimes conflict, at other times support and strengthen one another. In contemporary Western societies there is a fairly short list of generally accepted political values, including, in addition to the ones above, democracy, order, peace, private property, prosperity, rule of law, security, stability, and toleration. In other societies, at other times, in other circumstances, the political values are likely to be more or less different. The aim of politics, according to this approach, is to cope with the particular political problems a society faces at a particular time in particular circumstances as guided by the system of values. This requires policies that temporarily favor one of these values over others. But as times change, policies need to change with them.[8]

The two approaches need not always conflict. It may happen that in the circumstances of a society the highest political value favored by the universal approach and the particular value temporarily favored by the conventional approach actually coincide. When this happens, defenders of the two approaches will still disagree, not necessarily about the policies they favor, but about the reasons they give for the value they believe should guide their policies.

The reason defenders of the universal approach give for the assumption that politics must be guided by a highest value is that in all circumstances what is recognized as a problem and as a solution of it presupposes that there is some value whose approximation is hindered by the problem and aided by the solution. Their claim is that without commitment to some such value, no one could know what policies would be reasonable to follow. And the highest value should be one whose pursuit is more important than the others for the improvement of the conditions of people in a society.[9]

Defenders of the conventional approach are guided by a very different reason. They think that the political problems a society faces at a particular time are those that stand in the way of living and acting according to the prevailing conventions that have stood the test of time, commanded the allegiance of a large number of people in that society, and to which they voluntarily adhered even when, and especially when, they had an opportunity to do otherwise. The solution to such problems is a policy that copes with the problem by allowing conventional life to go on with as little interruption as possible. They key is not to follow a plan for approximating whatever the highest value is thought to be, but to protect the institutions and pursue the policies that enable people in a society to live in the conventional ways in which they are accustomed to pursue the betterment of their lives.[10]

In our society at the present time, defenders of the conventional approach tend to be conservative and defenders of the universal approach tend to be liberal or socialist. These, however, are only contingent associations depending on how their defenders evaluate the existing conventions. If liberals or socialists were to judge the political arrangements on the whole satisfactory, they may well adopt the conventional approach to political problems and their solutions. If defenders of the conventional approach found the existing conventions largely unsatisfactory, as they may do, they would not be conservative.

Another contingent association is between defenders of the universal approach and the universal dimension of morality, on the one hand, and between defenders of the conventional approach and the social dimension of morality, on the other hand. These associations are contingent because defenders of both approaches often distinguish between morality and politics. They may well acknowledge that morality has three dimensions, and insist that political institutions and policies should leave room for them. Or they may regard as reasonable only those institutions and policies that conform to the standard of one or more of the dimensions of morality. I do not think that there is anything in the nature of morality and politics that requires that they be identified or that they be distinguished. Politics may or may not be thought of as applied morality, and morality may or may not be thought of as politics pursued by other means.

Reflective defenders of these two approaches may disagree in the ways I have described, and no doubt in other ways as well. But they will agree on the point crucial for present purposes that the political mode of understanding, however it is interpreted, should override other modes of understanding if they conflict. For politics is concerned with creating and maintaining the conditions without which the pursuit of historical, moral, religious, scientific, or personal understanding is impossible. None of these modes of understanding can be pursued outside of a political framework that makes civilized life possible. The political institutions and policies of a society, of course, may be influenced by considerations that follow from non-political modes of understanding, but they can be influenced by them only if the necessary prior political conditions have been secured. In a primitive state of nature or in barbaric political regimes these conditions do not exist, whereas in civilized circumstances they do. That is one reason why defenders of the political mode of understanding think that it should override any other mode of understanding that may conflict with it.

The Religious Mode

I must preface the discussion that follows with a warning: I have no religious beliefs and my account of the religious mode understanding is that of an outsider. I acknowledge the social, moral, personal, and aesthetic importance religious understanding has for many people, even though I do not accept the ontological assumptions that go with them.

Central to the religious mode of understanding is the belief in a providential order that permeates the scheme of things. The order is providential in that it is divinely ordained. Defenders of different religions conceive of the order differently, but they agree that it exists. I will ignore their differences and focus on what they agree about. Their agreement includes that the order, in its totality, is good. And it includes further that human affairs go well if they conform to this good order and go badly if they deviate from it. They interpret the order, the nature of its goodness, and its accessibility to human understanding differently, but their differences are about its interpretation, not about its existence and goodness.[11]

This central belief of the religious mode of understanding is a complex amalgam of cognitive, emotive, and action-guiding components. The cognitive component includes the belief that the providential order exists and that there are reasons for or against competing interpretations of its nature. This is largely the province of theologians. Most religious people take the cognitive element for granted, accept it on faith or on the authority of a text or of theologians. They are far more concerned with the emotive component of their religion, which is its greatest source of power and the attraction. It gives hope in the face of adversity; consoles for grief, injustice, failure, and man's inhumanity to man; inspires by its vision of goodness; and makes life meaningful by portraying its contingencies and vicissitudes, not as senseless episodes in an indifferent universe, but as the insufficiently comprehended manifestations of a deeper and far more basic providential order.[12]

The attraction of religious belief, however, is not only that it enriches the inner lives of believers, but also that it creates a community whose members share, and thereby strengthen, the emotive appeal of their belief. This sense of belongingness is reinforced in some religions by rituals and ceremonies, and in others by simple, unadorned religious services in which the faithful come together to express their allegiance to whatever happens to be their interpretation of the providential order. If believers were to lose their sense of the meaningfulness of life and the warmth that comes from their membership in their community, it would be traumatic indeed. Even if they have doubts about the cognitive component of their religion, they also have very strong motives for not dwelling on it. And if their doubts grow, so does their sense of the loss they would suffer if they allowed their doubts to grow so strong as to threaten both the meaning of their lives and their membership in a community to which they have long belonged.

There is yet more. It comes from the action-guiding component of religion that motivates the faithful to live and act in ways that conform to the providential order and thereby become, in a small way, a force for good. The practical guidance of religion improves the character and dispositions of the faithful, leads them to treat others well, defines their general obligations and particular responsibilities, and thereby makes them better human beings, as that is understood by their religion. This is the ideal they aim at, even if they often fall short of it. Nevertheless, the action-guiding component of their religious belief gives them, what so many people without religious belief lack, an ideal to aim at, a standard by which they can evaluate their own conduct, and it forms a considerable part of what makes their lives meaningful.[13]

Responding to the religious mode of understanding, reflective historians may point at the great variability and changes in religious beliefs, ideals, and practices; moral thinkers may stress the importance of cognitive considerations and the plurality of conceptions of well-being; politicians may emphasize the necessity of protecting the conditions of civilized life in the face of the often violent conflicts between faiths; scientists may deny that any evidence supports religious belief; and individualists may insist that individual conceptions of well-being should be formulated, as it were, from the inside out rather than from the outside in. To all of them, reflective defenders of religious belief will respond by saying that to do these fine things and to participate in all these non-religious modes of understanding depends on having a meaningful life that motivates us to engage in the activities we value, hope for the future, and have the faith that all is not vain as we face the adversities that unavoidably beset us. These are the reasons defenders of religion have for insisting that their mode of understanding overrides all the other modes if they come into conflict. They claim that it is a deeper, more fundamental condition of making lives better than those that may be derived from any of the other modes of understanding. And they claim that the religious mode of understanding has the special excellence of recognizing and responding to the emotional needs that few human beings lack, the need to feel that there is more to life than the daily grind of routine activities and the small pleasures of mundane existence.

They will add that it is not a coincidence and that it needs an explanation why some historically conditioned world-views are more conducive to making lives better than others, why some moral theories, political institutions and policies, scientific theories, and personal conceptions of well-being are better than others. Reflective defenders of the religious mode will say that the explanation is that some world-views, moral theories, political arrangements, scientific theories, and personal conceptions are better than others because they approximate more closely the providential order. And that is another reason why religious belief in the providential order and in the evaluation of the facts relevant to how it is reasonable to live and act overrides other modes of understanding.

The Scientific Mode

Reflection on the scientific mode of understanding and its amazing success leads its defenders to claim that it overrides other modes of understanding if they come into conflict. The reasons for their claim are the many achievements of science that have immeasurably increased our knowledge, its predictive capacity that is unique among modes of understanding, and the countless ways in which science has improved our lives. The key to these achievements is thought to be the scientific method.

The method is to explain an event by forming a hypothesis that proposes an explanation of the event as the effect that will predictably occur if precisely specified causes and conditions are present. The method requires testing the hypothesis to determine whether the predicted event indeed occurs if the hypothesized causes and conditions are present. If it does occur, the hypothesis is confirmed; if it does not, the hypothesis is disconfirmed. The testing relies on direct observation by the unaided senses, or indirect observation by reading and interpreting instruments. The ultimate test of the original hypothesis, therefore, is some form of observation. If the hypothesis is repeatedly confirmed and if attempts to disconfirm it are unsuccessful, it becomes acceptable as establishing a nomological connection between the specified causes and effects, provided the specified conditions are present.[14]

This is the method working scientists apply to whatever events they intend to explain. Its application has resulted in the unprecedented growth of knowledge, roughly since the 17th century in Europe when science gradually started to become a systematic inquiry pursued by a community of scientists. It has greatly increased our understanding of cosmology, physics, chemistry, and biology, and, much more recently, it is being applied in the various social sciences. But the claim reflective defenders of the scientific mode of understanding make for the method is much wider than this. They think that it is not merely a reasonable method, but that it is *the* rational method that must actually be followed by whoever, in whatever area of life, is seeking understanding by rational means.[15]

Science is one of the very few human activities—perhaps the only one—in which errors are systematically criticized and fairly often, in time, corrected. This is why we can say that, in science, we often learn from our mistakes, and why we can speak clearly and sensibly about making progress there. In most other fields of human endeavour there is change, but rarely progress ... for almost every gain is balanced, or more than balanced, by some loss. And in most fields we do not even know how to evaluate change.[16]

Those who identify the rational method with the scientific one acknowledge that not all questions are answerable by the application of the method. But they claim that if the questions are rational, then the method will be applicable to them. As the early Wittgenstein put it, before he changed his mind, "we feel that even when all *possible* scientific questions have been answered, the problems of life remain completely untouched." And he continued by adding that "of course there is then no question left, and this itself is the answer. The solution of the problem of life is seen in the vanishing of the problem."[17] If a question has a rational answer, then the method can be applied to finding it. If a question is unanswerable by the application of the method, it is not a genuine question. Those who realize this and are rational will cease to think of the question as deserving of an answer.

The dismissal of questions to which the method does not apply is not arbitrary. Consider, for instance, having moral, political, religious, or personal values. Holding them is either rational or not. If it is rational, it is because whatever purpose they intend to serve can be achieved by their means. But whether their purpose is actually achieved must be ascertained, and the only way in which that can be done is by observing the effects that follow when the cause is an action prompted by the value in question. If the action leads to its intended purpose, it is a reason for holding the value that guides the action; if the action repeatedly fails to lead to the intended purpose, it is a reason against holding the value. If it makes no observable difference what consequences an action prompted by a value has, then the value is idle. It then serves no purposes and holding it, once again, is not rational.

Reflective defenders of the scientific mode of understanding readily acknowledge that human beings are often motivated by non-rational and even irrational values, and that such values may motivate scientists as much as other people. But the testing of reasonable hypotheses does not depend on the rationality of holding the values that led to their formulation. It depends on the confirmation or disconfirmation of the hypothesis by the method. Furthermore, the non-rational or irrational values by which scientists or others may be motivated are themselves the effects of causes, and, consequently, it can be explained why anyone is motivated by them even though acting on the values has no observable consequences. Providing such explanations is the task of the social sciences, which, it should also be acknowledged, are in their infancy and cannot yet actually provide the explanations. In principle, however, nothing stands in their way of finding such explanations in the future.[18]

A similar argument holds if the historical mode of understanding is correct and the rationality of holding values cannot be tested piecemeal, but only by testing the whole world-view of which they are parts. The rationality of a world-view ultimately depends on ascertaining whether or not it contributes to or hinders the improvement of the lives of those who hold it. The result is likely to be the equivocal one that in some respects it does one and in other respects the other. But the result can be made much less equivocal if the testing is made more precise. This can be done by comparing world-views and their specific contributions to the improvement of their adherents' lives in specific respects, and by observing how well they protect their security, nutrition, liberty, health, and so forth. The rationality of the historical mode of understanding, therefore, is as much dependent on the scientific mode and its method as is the rationality of the moral, political, religious, and personal modes.

It is for these reasons that defenders claim that the scientific mode of understanding the significance of relevant facts and the scientific method for testing the evaluations involved in this kind of understanding should override the conflicting understandings and evaluations of other modes of understanding. And they claim also that the scientific mode has the special excellence of yielding more reliable predictions that contribute greatly to bettering human lives than whatever may follow from other modes of understanding.

The Personal Mode

The aim of the personal mode is to understand the significance of facts from our individual point of view. It is not personal in the different sense that the understanding we manage to have is made reasonable by the mere fact that we have it. Our supposed understanding may be misunderstanding: our beliefs may be false, emotional reactions inappropriate, motives misguided, commitments unreasonable, and actions misdirected. Nor does the personal understanding mean that its aim is bound to be self-centered or self-interested. Its aim may be to love well, be loyal or dutiful, live a creative life, or be faithful to moral, political, religious, or other commitments. But, for better or worse, the understanding is our own, and our descriptions and evaluations of the relevant facts direct—or misdirect—how we live and act.

The personal mode of understanding has a long history. One of its earliest inspirations was the admonition inscribed on the temple at Delphi: Know thyself (in Greek, *Gnothi sauton*).

It was taken up by Augustine, and became an important step in the love of God, as Christians understand it. Later it was memorably transformed into a way of life by Montaigne. Inspired by his *Essays*, which owed much to Augustine's *Confessions*, the genre of autobiography was created and became a familiar part of literature. Psychoanalysis added a dimension to it, and so did romanticism, Proust, stream of consciousness novels, and the countless memoirs, diaries, and biographies published during the past centuries. It is also a crucial component of contemporary moral and political thought in which the Kantian notion of autonomy has pivotal importance.

The Whigish spirit is a notable feature of the personal mode. At the conclusion of a scholarly study of the history of autobiography, we find the characteristically optimistic paean:

In the ideal of individuality Western man obtained matters of very high value. When understood in the best terms, a view of life resting on loving admiration for the diversity and manifold richness of life is a magnificent one. It embodies the deepest respect for the formative powers of man. Even if we know nothing about ultimate human purpose and the end objectives of this mysterious process of life, we can derive gratification and hope from a conception of cosmic order where creative individuality adds forever to the growing richness of the world.[19]

We find the same ideal in a study of the history of autonomy in moral thought:

most moral philosophy now starts by assuming...that the people we live with are capable of understanding and acknowledging in practice the reasons for moral constraints we all mutually expect ourselves and others to respect. We assume, in short, that people are equally competent as moral agents unless shown otherwise.

This is, the author writes, "the conception of morality as self-governance" and it is "a distinctly modern way of understanding ourselves as moral agents."[20]

One basic reason for commitment to the personal mode of understanding is that it enables us to achieve clarity about our preferences and live according to them. Preferences are typically for the realization of possibilities available in our context. In civilized societies such possibilities are many, and they are often provided by other modes of understanding. They may be enduring historical traditions and practices, or moral, political, or religious values and ideals, or scientific research and technological innovation that result from it. We may discover that some few of these possibilities enable us to articulate and then pursue our preferences. In this discovery social and personal considerations are inextricably mixed. The possibilities are social, the preferences personal. But we see the possibilities as psychologically suitable for ourselves, not just as abstract logical possibilities. We feel some affinity for some of them, but such feelings are vague, inarticulate velleities unless we articulate them and connect them to some object, which are typically possibilities available in our social context.[21]

It is, therefore, a mistake to think of the personal mode of understanding as a form of inwardness. Inwardness is part of it, but it is only a part, because its aim is the discovery of what outward orientation fits our preferences. In civilized societies, most of us know of many more possibilities that might fit our preferences than we can reasonably pursue, given limitations of time, energy, talents, resources, and opportunity. If we are reasonable, we endeavor to impose order on our preferred possibilities, distinguish between more and less important ones, judge our own talents and opportunities, and try to make a prudent decision about how we should live. Making such decisions is another central part of the personal mode of understanding.[22]

Another mistake is to suppose that the personal mode commits us to retreat from public life and devote ourselves to the fine-tuning of our soul. What it commits us to is to try to clarify, articulate, and impose reasonable order on our preferences, but that leaves room for many very different kinds of preferences and different orderings of them. Understanding our preferences may lead us to become moral reformers, political activists, religious advocates, or join a community of historians or scientists. From the point of view of the personal mode of understanding, the important consideration is that whatever our preferences happen to be, we should have arrived at them and decided to pursue them as guided by our judgment, and not by external pressure or authority other than our own.

A fine expression of what motivates commitment to the personal mode is that:

I wish my life and decisions to depend on myself, not on external forces. . . . I wish to be the instrument of my own, not of other men's, acts of will. I wish to be a subject, not an object; to be moved by reasons, by conscious purposes, which are my own, not by causes which affect me, as it were, from outside. I wish to be...conceiving goals and policies of my own and realizing them. This is at least part of what I mean when I say that I am rational....I wish, above all, to be conscious of myself as a thinking, active being, bearing responsibility for my choices and able to explain them by references to my own ideas and purposes.[23]

Understanding the significance of relevant facts, evaluating the possibilities available in our context, and articulating our preferences, taken jointly, is, according to defenders of the personal mode, a necessary condition of the reasonable pursuit of any other mode of understanding. And it is also a necessary condition of living and acting reasonably in accordance with whatever conception of well-being we have. It is not a necessary condition of well-being itself, for the conception may be faulty and its pursuit may be led astray by our weaknesses, mistakes, imprudence, and the contingencies and vicissitudes of life. Nevertheless, the reasonable pursuit of well-being is impossible without it. This is one reason that leads defenders of the personal mode to claim that it overrides whatever conflicting evaluations of the significance of relevant facts follows from the other modes. Another reason is the special excellence that the personal mode of understanding alone among the modes has. By stressing the importance of self-understanding it enables us to identify ourselves with the possibilities we are trying to realize and thereby rightly feel that we have some control over how we live.

The Pattern

In this chapter I have tried to present as sympathetically as possible the reasons that lead well-informed and reflective people to commit themselves to evaluating the significance of relevant facts from the point of view of a particular mode of understanding in preference to the others. They are not ignorant of the other modes, acknowledge their achievements, nevertheless have two reasons for claiming that their preferred mode has priority over the others. One is that it is a necessary condition of the reasonable pursuit of other modes of understanding. The other is that their mode has a special excellence that the others lack. These reasons explain their motivation, but do not justify their claims. The problem is not that the reasons are faulty. They are good reasons. The problem is defenders of all the modes could and, as we have seen, do make the same reasonable claims for the overriding importance of the mode they favor. Yet their claims conflict, and unless their conflicts are resolved in some reasonable way, their defenders have not justified their claim that the mode they favor should have priority over the modes they do not favor. It is true that defenders of each mode can lay claim to an excellence that the other modes lack. But defenders of each mode claim a special excellence for their own mode, but none of these claims convince defenders of conflicting claims.

The required justification cannot be derived from one of the modes of understanding, because it is the claim that any one of them should always override the others that needs to be justified. Appealing to epistemological standards that all reasonable modes must meet—logical consistency, explanation of the relevant facts, openness to criticism, and so forth—will not yield the required justification, because all the modes I have discussed meet such elementary standards. If the justification cannot be derived from any of the modes, and if there is no strong enough neutral standard specified that could be appealed to for resolving the conflicting claims about which mode is overriding, do we then have to conclude that all these claims are arbitrary?

One reason for thinking that this is the case is that no reasonable way has been found in the course of centuries of search for avoiding philosophical problems caused by the conflicts between modes of understanding. But we should not leave it at this. The philosophical problems stand in the way of making our lives better. Reason requires that we find some way of dealing with them, even if past search for it has been frustrated by the pattern of conflicts I am engaged in describing.

The pattern is that everyday life is disrupted by problems, and the usual ways of coping with them are inadequate. We turn then to history, morality, politics, religion, science, or personal concerns in the hope of deriving from them an approach to coping with the problem. But from each mode of understanding several practical approaches follow, and their conflicts are multiplied manifold by the conflicting practical approaches that follow from other modes of understanding. We need some reasonable way of deciding which of these many practical approaches is the best. This leads to seeking a reflective approach to resolving the conflicts between practical approaches.

We find as we reflect that defenders of different modes of understanding propose different and no less conflicting reflective approaches to resolving conflicts between practical approaches. And these latter conflicts can be resolved only by showing that the reflective approach of one mode is more basic, deeper, or more fundamental than the reflective approaches of the other modes. But, since defenders of each mode claim this for the mode they favor, we do not know how to resolve the conflicts that prevent us from finding a reasonable way of coping with the problems that stand in the way of improving our lives. The sources of philosophical problems are these conflicts, and their endless recurrence is a consequence of our need for and lack of a reasonable solution. In Chapter 3, I will examine some of the philosophical problems that occur when modes of understanding conflict.

3

Conflicts and Problems

Neither in the social order, nor in the experience of an individual, is a state of conflict the sign of vice, or defect, or a malfunctioning. It is not a deviation from the normal state of a city or of a nation, and it is not a deviation from the normal course of a person's experience. To follow through the ethical implications of these propositions about the normality of conflicts, these Heracleitean truths, a kind of moral conversion is needed.

Stuart Hampshire[1]

In the previous chapters I proposed an account of the modes of understanding whose conflicts lead to philosophical problems. But reflective defenders of modes of understanding do not accept that the philosophical problems are perennial. They think that they have good reasons for claiming that their mode of understanding should override other modes if they conflict. If this were generally recognized, they claim, the philosophical problems would be solved and arguments about them would come to an end. As I have endeavored to show, however, reflective defenders of each of the modes of understanding believe themselves to have such reasons for claiming that their own mode of understanding is overriding, the arguments do not come to an end, and the problems are, do not just seem, perennial. The aim of this chapter is to show how specific conflicts between modes of understanding lead to perennial philosophical problems.

These problems and the arguments about their proposed solutions are complicated enough. To avoid making them still more complicated, I treat the conflicts that lead to philosophical problems as between two modes of understanding. In fact, however, philosophical problems may be caused by conflicts between more than two modes of understanding, but I do not discuss this possibility. I defend the claim that none of the proposed solutions of philosophical problems is acceptable. This is not because they are unreasonable. All of them are based on reasons derived from various modes of understanding. They are unacceptable because they conflict and there are reasons both for and against each of the conflicting proposals.

Accepting any one of them is ultimately based on an arbitrary preference for the mode of understanding from which the favored approach follows. Defenders of the conflicting modes of understanding work hard to strengthen the reasons for the mode they favor and against the ones they reject, but their efforts consist in the refinement of the mode of understanding with which they began. They offer more subtle distinctions, perspicuous clarifications, ingenious examples that favor their mode of understanding, and counterexamples that defenders of the rejected modes find difficult to accommodate. The ensuing arguments—each with a history running back many centuries—concern more and more minute points whose relevance and significance only a handful of experts can appreciate.

The result is that the problems that stand in the way of improving our lives recede into a barely remembered background. And when people are troubled by the original problems that still await a solution after endless increasingly more minute and technical arguments, reflective defenders of the conflicting modes explain to them how naïve they are. This is an unsatisfactory state of affairs, and improving our lives depends on making it less so. In order to avoid a possible misunderstanding, I stress that my concern here is not to make a case for any of the conflicting modes of understanding, but to understand the reasons for and against them and the nature of their conflicts. My aim, I repeat, is to understand, not to justify or criticize.

The conflicts I discuss are likely to be familiar to readers of this book. I decided not to clutter the pages with pedantic references to classic proposals and to their more recent reformulations, and to keep the discussion no more detailed than necessary for showing that the philosophical problems follow the same pattern. This pattern leads to the endless, recurrent arguments from which no decisive solutions follow and to our inability to cope with the problems that stand in the way of improving our lives.

What Makes Lives Good?

A widely shared simple view is that a life is good if it is morally responsible and personally satisfying. We might say, then, that a good life has a moral and a personal component. The moral component is to live and act in a way that conforms to the requirements of morality as they are understood in a particular world-view. The personal component is to live and act in ways we find satisfying. Both components are necessary. We cannot reasonably call our lives good if we derive our satisfaction from activities that harm innocent people, or if we scrupulously meet moral requirements, but are miserable most of the time. A good life must be on the whole both personally satisfying and morally responsible. Episodes of irresponsibility and dissatisfaction, of course, need not make a life bad, only less than perfectly good.

This view of good lives is too simple. It takes no account of frequently occurring complications. One of them is that what are taken to be moral requirements may not be, because they involve false beliefs about the possibilities and limits of health, law, patriotism, politics, religion, sex, wealth, and so forth. Or the supposed requirements may be inconsistent, dogmatic, too demanding, or not demanding enough. It cannot be part of good lives to live and act according to mistaken moral requirements. Another complication is that we may be mistaken in what we believe is personally satisfying. We may believe that a way of living or acting would be satisfying, but it turns out not to be. Or we may actually find it satisfying, but should not because it is corrupting, demeaning, impoverished, shortsighted, simple-minded, unimaginative, or inconsistent with what would be far more satisfying now or in the future. Lives may fail to be good because they are led astray by mistaken beliefs about moral requirements, personal satisfactions, or both at once.

Let us suppose, however, that we avoid such mistakes. Our beliefs about moral requirements and personal satisfactions are reasonable, we live and act according to them, and no external obstacle stands in our way. Our lives may still not be good because reasonable moral requirements and personal satisfactions often conflict. Many moral requirements are onerous. Paying debts, keeping promises, telling the truth, accepting blame may be incompatible with personal satisfaction. And many personal satisfactions are self-indulgent, injurious to others, contrary to our responsibilities as parents, workers, citizens, neighbors, friends, lovers, and so forth. Such conflicts are part of most lives, and disrupt the routine activities of everyday life. Good lives depend on coping with such problems, as well as on avoiding mistaken beliefs about moral requirements and personal satisfactions. The question is how we should do that.

The time-honored answer is that we need a standard to which we can appeal to draw two crucial distinctions. One is between reasonable and unreasonable beliefs about moral requirements and personal satisfactions. The other is between reasonable and unreasonable ways of coping with conflicts between reasonable moral requirements and personal satisfactions. A standard to which we can appeal to draw these distinctions, of course, cannot assume that any of our existing moral or personal beliefs is reasonable, since that would obviate the need that the standard was meant to satisfy. So, it is supposed, we must go beyond our existing beliefs and look for the standard elsewhere. Where might we find it? A widely held assumption is that we will find it in a theory about what reasonable moral responsibilities and personal satisfactions are. But since part of the problem is that they may conflict, we need a more reflective approach to morality that enables us to identify reasonable moral requirements and another reflective approach that does the same for personal satisfactions.

Having such reflective approaches, however, does not lead to a reasonable way of drawing the required distinctions. For the two approaches prompt conflicting resolutions of the conflicts between reasonable moral requirements and reasonable personal satisfactions. And their conflicts lead us back to not having a reasonable way of resolving the original conflict. True, the question has been refined. We no longer ask about the conflict between any moral requirement and any personal satisfaction, but only between reasonable ones. That refinement, however, brings us no closer to a reasonable way of resolving their conflict than we had before we turned to these approaches for help.

It strengthens the doubts about relying on these reflective approaches that the specific content of the moral or the personal mode of understanding to which we looked for help makes no difference to there being a recurrent conflict between them. Regardless of whether the moral approach is consequentialist, contractarian, deontological, eudaimonist, or based on natural law, the requirements it regards as reasonable will from time to time conflict with personal satisfactions. Similarly, whether the personal approach is existentialist, neurological, psychoanalytic, psychological, or sociological, the personal satisfactions it deems reasonable will sometimes conflict with moral requirements. No matter how much progress defenders of these modes of understanding make toward strengthening their approaches, the conflict between them will remain.

These conflicts lead us back to the problems that stand in the way of the good life we want to have. They force us to seek some approach to resolving them. If we derive it from the moral mode of understanding, we will conclude that we should make do with fewer personal satisfactions. If we derive it from the personal mode of understanding, we will be inclined to be less scrupulous about honoring moral requirements. Neither will make our lives better. We are forced, then, to seek yet another approach to resolving the conflict between moral and personal modes of understanding. We can find what we seek, however, only by regarding one of the conflicting modes as overriding the other. But that would be arbitrary, because defenders of both modes claim that the one they favor should override the other. And this forces on us the philosophical problem of deciding which mode of understanding is really overriding. Thus, after all is said and done, we seem to be left with having to make an arbitrary decision. Since modes of understanding conflict, they give us no help in coping with the problem that our personal satisfactions and moral responsibilities conflict. Or we are forced to face and try to solve the philosophical problem of deciding which of two modes of understanding is overriding. That decision, however, would also be arbitrary, since defenders of both of the conflicting modes claim that the overriding one is the one they favor. And that is why finding a reasonable way of coping with this philosophical problem is difficult, recurrent, and controversial.

Is There a Providential Order?

The word "providence" is not much used nowadays, but the idea is alive and well. According to the *Random House Dictionary*, one meaning of the word is "God, esp. when conceived as omnisciently directing the universe and the affairs of humankind with wise benevolence." The philosophical problem I will now discuss is whether the scheme of things is indeed directed by such a wise benevolent order.

As all philosophical problems, this one is also prompted by a problem we encounter in everyday life. It is a widely shared frustration that we often do not get what we deserve and get what we do not deserve. We all know that this happens, and usually mind it, except perhaps when we actually benefit from it. We do not think that good people should suffer undeserved misfortune or bad people should enjoy undeserved good fortune. We think that the distribution of good and bad things in life should be proportional to what everyone deserves. We know that this often does not happen, it offends our sense of justice, makes us want to understand why life is so often unjust, and forces us to seek some reasonable approach to what we should do to make life at least a little less unjust.

If we turn to the religious mode of understanding, we are told that the explanation of this bad state of affairs is that we fail to live according to the providential order. Religious teaching makes clear what that order is, but we stupidly, weakly, or wickedly pit ourselves against it, and injustice is a consequence of our disobedience. If we are unconvinced by this explanation because it leaves unclear why good people who live according to religious teachings come to harm and why bad people who blatantly live contrary to it enjoy undeserved benefits, then we will look for a better explanation. The supposedly better explanation is that we do not always understand why things happen as they do, but we can be confident that in the long run, in this world or in the next, justice will be done, good people will enjoy deserved benefits, and bad people will suffer deserved harms. This is because the providential order is for the best, even if we do not understand what the best is, everything considered, in the total scheme of things. All the major religions agree that there is such a providential order, and its existence has been accepted by the vast majority of people holding very different world-views throughout history.

There has also been a dissenting minority whose size has been steadily growing during the last five centuries or so. The crux of their dissent is not to doubt that an order permeates the scheme of things, but to deny its benevolence. Some dissenters claim that the order is malevolent, or that it involves strife between malevolent and benevolent forces. These are also ancient traditions, but I ignore them in what follows. The more recent form of dissent I discuss holds that the order is not benevolent, malevolent, or mixed, but an indifferent, utterly imper-sonal natural order inherent in the nomological network of which everything that exists is a part. The best guide to the nature of this order is said to be the scientific mode of understanding. It is readily acknowledged by its defenders that scientific understanding is seriously incomplete and fallible, but they claim that on the basis of what we presently know, we have no reason to think either that the natural order is or that it fails to be for the best. If we follow the approach that emerges from the various sciences taken together, we can reasonably conclude that the natural order is the regularity inherent in the totality of all things, forces, and facts. Thinking about it in evaluative terms, such as good or bad, justice or injustice, is a sentimen-tal anthropomorphic fallacy that projects human concerns onto the indifferent scheme of things.

According to this scientific understanding, we should acknowledge that what happens to us certainly matters to us, but in the indifferent natural order nothing matters. The universe may expand or contract, ant heaps, galaxies, quarks, individ-uals, and species come and go, but none of this has any significance beyond being a minute link in a vast chain of causes and effects that has no beginning and no end. One of the things that certainly matters to us is injustice. We should do what we can to make human life more just, but for that we have to construct our own system of justice and conduct our affairs according to it. There is injustice because our system of justice is faulty, or because we act contrary to it, or, as it is most likely, because we fail in both ways. In any case, it is up to us to create and maintain a sys-tem of justice under which we could live.

Defenders of religious understanding may agree that there is a natural order to which the various sciences are the best guide and that we should do all we can to improve our system of justice, but they will say that it is not a coincidence that some man-made systems of justice are better than others. They are better because they are closer approximations of the providential order. Defenders of scientific understanding demand reasons for supposing that there is a providential order and, if there is, then for supposing that we could know enough about it to ena-ble us to improve our faulty system of justice. Their demand is met by defenders of religious understanding who cite all the good things in life as evidence for the existence of a providential order. Defenders of scientific understanding respond by citing all the bad things in life as evidence against the existence of a providential order. And so defenders of these two modes of understanding follow the well-worn grooves of long-familiar arguments prompted by the philosophical problem about whether the world as we know it provides reasons for believing in the existence of a providential order.

My interest is not in defending either mode of understanding, but in pointing out that the deeper defenders of the conflicting modes get into their arguments about which should override which, the more remote becomes the problem that prompted them to begin arguing, namely, that we do not get what we deserve and get what we do not deserve. We need some reasonable approach to guide our efforts to cope with injustice. It will not come from thinking about the overall scheme of things, which, both sides agree, we understand very imperfectly indeed, and, in any case, cannot alter. Instead of debating the relative merits of religious and scientific understanding, we should concentrate on doing what we can to make life more just. But to do that we would need to know in concrete terms what makes us deserving or undeserving, what specifically we deserve, and how to assure that what we get is proportional to what we deserve.

Defenders of religious and scientific understanding recognize the need for an approach to coping with injustice, but they propose conflicting approaches. Religious approaches conflict, because Buddhists, Catholics, Hindus, Jews, Moslems, and Protestants disagree with each other and among themselves about what the providential order is and what its practical implications are. Scientific approaches also conflict, because, although their defenders agree that there is no reason to suppose that there is a providential order, they disagree whether an improved system of justice would be Platonic, Aristotelian, Hobbist, Lockean, Kantian, utilitarian, Rawlsian, or something else. The solution of the philosophical problem of whether there is a providential order thus becomes ever more remote from the problem that we do not get what we deserve and get what we do not deserve. If we want to make human life more just, we should decide which of the many views of justice on offer is the best and act accordingly.

Defenders of the religious and scientific approaches will reject this conclusion. They will claim that how we resolve this philosophical problem has great practical significance. If there is a providential order, it follows from it how we should live and that in turn implies what system of justice we should have. If there is no reason to believe in a providential order, that too has the great practical significance that it is up to us to construct a system of justice that makes it more likely that we get what we deserve and not what we do not deserve. Both these claims are rendered practically useless, however, by the plurality of conflicting approaches to identifying the right system of justice. Defenders of both claims will say that this plurality exists because all but one of the proposed candidates for the right system of justice are mistaken. And this makes them fall back into the centuries old quest for the overriding system of justice that will put a final end to all the endless, recurrent controversies about what the right system of justice would be if we had it. As they hone their approaches, they leave unresolved the problem with which they began, namely, how to make life more just.

The conclusion I draw from understanding this quest for the overriding system of justice is that the conflicting modes of understanding have very little to do with it. For conflicts between proposals of the overriding system of justice that proceed on the basis of religious understanding cannot be resolved by affirming the existence of a providential order, since all the conflicting religious proposals affirm it. What they disagree about is how it should be interpreted and what it implies. Similarly, the conflicts between proposals that proceed on the basis of scientific understanding cannot be resolved by denying that there is a providential order, since all the conflicting proposals agree about that. The conclusion is that the attempt to resolve the philosophical problem about whether there is a providential order does not help to cope with the frequent injustice that stands in the way of improving our lives.

Can There Be an Ideal State?

A state is the political organization of a society, typically of a nation. In contemporary Western societies, the state includes the legislative, executive, and judicial institutions, the laws, customs, and traditions according to which these institutions function or are meant to function. We expect the state to provide certain benefits, such as reliable infrastructure, justice, liberty, protection of public health, security, system of education, and so forth, enabling us to live as we wish. But our reasonable expectations are often disappointed. This is another problem that threatens the improvement of our lives and makes us dissatisfied. We want the state to be better than it is. And so we naturally ask: why is it not better?

One possibility is that its institutions do not function as they should because public servants fail to meet their responsibilities. The remedy then is to correct their failures. Another possibility is that the state is threatened by enemies, criminals, natural or man-made disasters, or scarcity for which neither public servants nor institutions can be blamed. I will ignore these possibilities, and concentrate on problems caused by defects in some of the political institutions that partly constitute the state. We need to understand, then, what their defects are and how they might be corrected. There are two familiar modes of understanding to which we may turn for help in coping with this kind of problem: one looks toward the society's past to understand why present political institutions are as they are; the other looks toward the society's future to understand how closely its present institutions approximate an ideal.

The mode of understanding that looks toward the past is historical. It aims to understand the influences that have formed present political institutions, such as the founding documents, like a constitution, or a long series of gradually developing laws, traditions, customs, or precedents that have attracted the allegiance of successive generations. From these historical influences, slowly, over time, there has emerged a widely shared consensus about how the institutions ought to function. Such a consensus could be formed only because the institutions were responsive to the prevailing conditions and by and large served the interests of those who were governed by them. Conditions and interests, of course, are forever changing, and political institutions must be flexible enough to adjust to these changes.

According to the historical mode of understanding, if we want to correct defective institutions and remedy the resulting dissatisfactions, we need an approach to understanding what has changed from the past when the institutions were supported by a general consensus. It may be that the conditions and interests have not changed significantly, but the institutions have become enfeebled by complacency, poor public servants, or rigidity. Or, the conditions and interests have changed, but the institutions have not been flexible enough to respond to the changes. Whatever turn out to be the causes of present defects, defenders of historical understanding insist that it is essential for correcting them to understand the influences that have made the present institutions what they are. Only then can we understand what the standard is of which they are now falling short.

The other mode of understanding, the one that looks toward the future, is political. Not all political understanding is future-oriented, but I will concentrate on those that are. The future-oriented understanding is political in the sense that according to it the essential condition of coping with the problem caused by defective institutions is to appeal to an ideal. The ideal is of how political institutions ought to function so as to improve the lives of those who are governed by them. The ideal is formulated on the basis of political understanding, and the ideal becomes the standard with reference to which the defects of existing institutions ought to be corrected. This mode of understanding may take into account the history of the society, but not because it provides an ideal, as historical understanding claims, but because it may provide clues to what some elements of the ideal might be and what pitfalls the ideal ought to avoid.

It will perhaps be obvious that the historical understanding of politics tends to be conservative and its political understanding tends to be reformist. When the political condition of a society does not cause serious dissatisfactions, the conflict between these two modes of understanding is merely a difference in emphasis. But the deeper the dissatisfactions are, the more acute the conflict between these two modes of understanding becomes. I think it will be generally agreed that in the contemporary world, dissatisfactions with political institutions are widespread, and the conflict between the historical and the political modes of understanding is acute indeed. The crux of their conflict is whether there can be an ideal state. And when their conflict is as pronounced as it now often is in many societies, it stops being a matter of skillful political management amenable to compromise and negotiation, and becomes a conflict which defenders of the two modes of understanding attempt to resolve in incompatible ways.

Defenders of both modes are usually highly intelligent, respect the relevant facts, and are committed to giving reasons for or against the possibility of an ideal state. Their reasons are both constructive and critical. Conservatives argue constructively that we have nothing better to rely on than the history of institutions formed by a long process of gradual improvements that has eventually led to a consensus that reflected the allegiance of most of those governed by the institutions. And they argue critically that reformists pursue ideals that have been formulated by armchair theorists who tend to ignore the accumulated lessons of the past and follow instead unrealistic dreams that bear little relation to the historically formed conditions and interests that actually prevail.

Reformists argue constructively that human beings have constant permanent interests and the ideal they are proposing is based on the urgent requirements of satisfying those interests. And they argue critically that the supposed consensus that favored historically formed political institutions has been a myth perpetrated by those who benefited from them and who have forced or manipulated the rest of the population to live under them.

These familiar arguments go on and on without any prospect of a solution, because, although the approaches of both sides rest on facts and adduce reasons in defense of their description of them and in criticism of the opponents' view, the resulting arguments only appear to be about the reliability of the facts and reasons. The arguments are really about the significance of facts and reasons that defenders of both modes of understanding acknowledge, but which they evaluate in conflicting ways. Defenders of both modes of understanding acknowledge that the historical past and a better future matter, but they favor conflicting approaches to coping with the problems that disrupt everyday life. As a result, the problems fester because we lack a decisive way of coping with them. Defenders of the conflicting modes conduct their endless disputes claiming that their own constructive approach is overriding and criticizing their opponents for making the same claim for their own approach.

Can We Be in Control of Our Lives?

Everyday life partly consists in routine activities, some of which are at once neces-sary and instrumental. Engagement in them is dictated by our basic physiological, psychological, and social needs: for food, a sense of security, and earning a living, for instance. We aim to satisfy them in the conventional ways of our context. In seeking their satisfactions, we act much like countless others do around us. We have many similar needs and learn as we grow up to satisfy them in the same con-ventional ways. In civilized circumstances, the needs are not urgent and their sat-isfaction is not in danger. However, if life were not richer than this, we would have little control over it, and we would find it barely human and very boring.

Fortunately there is more to life. Many of our activities are not routine, bear the imprint of our individuality, and are important to us. We care about doing inter-esting work, enjoying beauty, nature, physical fitness, or loving relationships, pro-moting causes we value, making our house more to our liking, and so on. But these activities often pall: their novelty wears off and what used to be interesting and enjoyable become tedious habits, love may cool, lovers grow apart, tensions and irritations become frequent, we become disenchanted with causes we used to care about, our energy diminishes, leisure becomes more important, and we would rather go for a walk than do the laundry or deadhead our rhododendrons.

Familiarity need not breed contempt, but it tends to create tired habits, prompts questions, and makes us seek alternatives to what we have. As the initial frisson wears off, we become less wholehearted, at least about some activities that earlier filled us with enthusiasm. Few of us are fortunate or simple-minded enough not to reach a point when we ask why we should continue with the familiar activities that have calcified into habits as routine as the conventional activities by which we satisfy our basic physiological, psychological, and social needs. Once we start questioning what we used to find interesting and enjoyable, we may come to sus-pect that our preferences are unoriginal and conventional, and that we have as little control over them as we do over our basic needs and the conventional ways in which we were taught to satisfy them. We ask ourselves whether our preferences really express our individuality rather than follow conventional patterns into which we have unthinkingly or lazily fallen. Such doubts make us examine how we live and why we carry on in our familiar ways.

There are two modes of understanding to which we may turn for help in coping with such doubts. One is encouraging, the other is the opposite. The first insists that there are areas of our life we can control. If we have not exerted the control we might have, we could start doing it now. We could acknowledge that many of the possibilities we have and the limits that constrain us are created, maintained, protected, and enforced by the network of aesthetic, economic, legal, moral, political, religious, technological, and other conventions, which we must willy-nilly follow throughout our lives. We can opt out of that network, but only for another one that has its own conventions. There is no escape from conventions. Fortunately, in civilized circumstances they provide many more possibilities than we can choose to pursue.

Our control does not free us from conventions, nothing can do that as long we live. But the more control we have, the freer we are to decide which conventions to follow as expressions of our individuality and of the way we want to live. We can increase our control by deciding what relative importance we should attribute to the various conventions we have decided to follow and how deeply we become attached to them. That decision is not conventional, but personal, and we can make it, rightly or wrongly, on the basis of our judgment of what would improve our lives. Such judgments may be mistaken of course, even grotesquely, as a result of ignorance, irrationality, self-deception, stupidity, wishful thinking, and so forth, but whether mistaken or not, they are our own, the expressions of our individuality. In making such judgments, we exercise some control over how we live and what activities we engage in. This is the encouragement we may get if we proceed from the personal mode of understanding.

According to the other, discouraging, mode of understanding, control is a sentimental illusion that flatters us by ignoring the significance of the facts. Their significance is that whatever we do or fail to do, whatever judgments we make, however we want to live, we are parts of a chain of causes and effects in which our actions, judgments, and preferences are merely some of the minor links. Certainly, some of the causes are conventions, but conventions are themselves the effects of causes. If we trace the causes back far enough, we must recognize that they are a vast amalgam of astronomical, biological, chemical, climatic, demographic, epidemiological, evolutionary, genetic, geographical, physical, and other causes that stretch backwards and will continue forward forever. It is incredibly naïve to fasten on to an infinitesimal segment of this vast process and claim that we are in control of it. We can certainly think so, but what we think is itself the effect of causes that make us think what we do and make our brain, consciousness, and social and individual condition what at the moment of thinking they temporarily are. We glom on to our judgments and ignore the causes whose effects the judgments are. We are no more in control of any of our activities than volcanoes are of their eruptions, species of their mutation, quarks of their duration, and so forth. The naïveté of the defenders of personal understanding is that they attribute significance to fleeting impressions while forgetting the mass of reality that causes the impressions. Or so it appears from the scientific mode of understanding.

Defenders of personal understanding point out that scientific understanding presupposes the reliability of personal judgments because scientific understanding cannot get off the ground unless its initial data, instrument readings, and observations are reliable. And these unavoidable starting points are precisely those personal impressions whose reliability defenders of scientific understanding question. If all personal impressions were unreliable, so would be the scientific understanding that presupposes their reliability.

Defenders of scientific understanding reply that part of science is to test and if necessary correct initial personal impressions. Personal impressions are relied on only temporarily and then accepted or rejected on the basis of additional evidence. To which defenders of personal understanding reply that obtaining additional evidence also presupposes the reliability of the personal impressions of those who obtain the evidence. Their reply is countered by pointing out that the additional evidence is accepted only after rigorous scientific testing. To which defenders of personal understanding respond by repeating their earlier point, and defenders of scientific understanding do the same, and so it goes on and on.

The conflicts between these modes of understanding eventually lead to the philosophical problem of whether we can control how we live. Reason requires us to accept two undeniable and relevant facts. One is that our personal impressions are fallible. The other is that whatever scientific view we form of any segment of the world is initially formed by us on the basis of our personal impressions. Defenders of one of the conflicting modes of understanding stress the unreliability of personal impressions; defenders of the other stress our unavoidable reliance on personal impressions. Neither deny the relevance of these facts, but they sharply disagree about their evaluation, and consequently about their significance. Their reasons for the different significance they attribute to the relevant facts, however, are derived from their commitment to one or another of the conflicting modes of understanding being overriding. And so their arguments go on and on, and the problem caused by our doubts about whether we can be in control of how we live recedes into the forgotten background out of which both modes of understanding have emerged.

What Can We Reasonably Hope?

I am sure there is a sociological explanation of why the news that gets reported in the media is so often bad, but I am not sure what the explanation is. The fact is that crimes, accidents, natural disasters, wars, the outrages of dictators and terrorists, starvation, epidemics, ethnic and tribal massacres, and the abuse of helpless people are newsworthy. Rising living standards, decreasing infant mortality, the dedicated services of teachers, public officials, and nurses, conflicts settled by negotiation, the growth of religious and sexual toleration, the decent lives of hard-working people, loyal and affectionate families, happy love affairs, successful small businesses, and intimate lifelong friendships rarely, if ever, get into the news.

If we stand back for a moment and reflect on the implications of the bad news we are bombarded with, it will occur to us that on the whole life is a pretty sordid and uncertain affair in which innocent people suffer terrible injuries and endure great hardships. The unreported good news, by contrast, holds out the possibility of rea-sonable hope that some things at least are getting better, that there is also decency, good will, and toleration in the world. The reasonable response to the flood of con-trary impressions that comes our way is ambivalence and uncertainty about what we can reasonably hope for in general, for ourselves, and for those close to us. We do not know whether the future will be better than the past or the present; whether it is reasonable to be optimistic or pessimistic about it; or indeed whether on the whole human life has been getting better, worse, or persisting in a mixed state. It matters to us what we can reasonably hope for the future, because the plans we and those we care about can reasonably form depend on it.

The future, of course, is uncertain, yet we have to plan, choose goals, and try to adjust our good and bad feelings about it in a state of uncertainty. We natu-rally seek some way of alleviating our uncertainty. One of the great attractions of the religious mode of understanding is that it responds to our uncertainties and helps us overcome them by giving us hope for a better future. The main religions have not glossed over the enormity of hardship and suffering that have been part of human lives. Their proposed remedy is to cultivate faith, hope, and charity, or something like them, as the necessary virtues that help us live even if it is hard. Faith and hope make us believe that the future will be better than the past, and charity makes us respond to all those whose hard condition—the human condi-tion—we share. Religious belief gives us hope that eventually all manner of things will be well. Even if life here and now is a vale of sorrow, there is a future life that will be better, provided we are guided by faith, hope, and charity.

Religious understanding, however, is rejected either sharply as pernicious or mod-erately as naïve by those who favor a secular political mode of understanding. Some of its defenders think that religious understanding is pernicious, because it advocates resigning ourselves to the hardship and suffering around us instead of doing our best to overcome them. Others think that it is naïve, because it nurtures unreasonable hope about an afterlife in whose existence there is no reason to believe. According to secular political understanding, the remedy is to improve political arrangements in order to ameliorate the causes of man's inhumanity to man and to enforce the limits that prevent or at least reduce the resulting hardship and suffering. Reasonable hope must be based on putting our house in better order here and now, not on nurturing hope in an uncertain and remote better future. If we want to make life better, we need prudent policies and the reform of existing political arrangements, rather than the cultivation of unfounded religious faith, hope, and charity.

The religious response is to point out that in the long history of humanity count-less policies and reforms have been proposed, but they have not overcome the widespread hardship and suffering present in all societies known to us. The hope that humanity can be improved by political means only is false. All hope based on the assumption that we can raise ourselves by our own efforts is misguided. The only reasonable hope that we can have must begin with the realization that salva-tion is not in our hands. To which defenders of political understanding respond by pointing out the enormity of the crimes that have been caused by the irrational beliefs of religious fanatics who claimed to possess the key to salvation. The rejoin-der of defenders of religious understanding is that the corruption of religious fanaticism casts as little doubt on reasonable religious hope as the corruption of political fanaticism does on the possibility of improved political arrangements. The crux of the matter is whether reasonable hope for a better future is ultimately based on our own unaided efforts or on faith in divine help.

Both modes of understanding are old. Once again, it is common ground between their defenders that we need to cope with the problems caused by the hardship and suffering we endure. They also agree that we need reasonable hope to sustain us, hope that is based on more than wishful thinking. But they think that these facts have very different significance. Their conflict leads to the philosophical problem about what we can reasonably hope. Their attempts to solve the problem combine constructive and critical elements. Their constructive aim is to provide reasons on which either religious or political hope can be based. The critical one is to provide reasons why either religious or political hope is unreasonable. And then defend-ers of the conflicting modes charge each other with wishful thinking and mistak-ing the significance of agreed upon facts. According to defenders of the religious mode, we cannot improve the human condition without divine help. According to defenders of the political mode, we cannot improve the human condition if we rely on divine help. Both agree that we should do our best to improve our condition, but they disagree about whether the best is if political hope overrides religious hope, or whether the best is the reverse.

Are There Moral Absolutes?

Everyday life in contemporary Western societies, especially in America, is full of moral controversies, for instance about abortion, capital punishment, euthanasia, and war. Many people are passionately engaged in defending or attacking the morality of these practices. My interest is not in entering into these heated controversies, but in pointing out the oddity that the opposing sides both appeal to human life as an absolute moral value. Abortion is immoral according to pro-lifers, because it involves killing human beings, while their opponents hold that killing human beings is indeed immoral, but abortion is not an instance of it. Opponents of capital punishment claim that it is morally unacceptable to kill a human being, while its defenders claim that it is morally justified as a means of deterring potential killers and punishing those who have taken a human life. According to defenders of voluntary euthanasia, it is morally justified if a life is so full of pain and ravaged by illness as to have ceased being a recognizably human life, but its critics say that the protection of even a bad human life is of absolute moral value. Pacifists insist that war is always immoral, because it involves killing human beings, while defenders of just wars argue that it is morally justified as a means of defending the many lives that would be lost if the aggressors were not resisted.

Alongside these impassioned avowals are many conventional practices that obviously lead to the preventable loss of human lives. Traffic accidents cause thousands of deaths every year. If the speed limit were lowered by 20 miles per hour many of these lives would be saved. Overeating, sunbathing, spelunking, and rock climbing lead to the premature loss of many lives, as do diving, mining, policing, soldiering, logging, and fire fighting. Outlawing such activities and jobs would be unacceptable to most people, it would be unenforceable, and the foreseeable loss of life is readily accepted by those who claim that human life is an absolute moral value. The inconsistency of these attitudes is part of everyday life and it should give pause to those who reflect on it, which most people do not do. But some do, and they give conflicting answers to the question of whether there are moral absolutes.

On one side we find moral absolutists who are committed to there being an absolute moral value, a *summum bonum*, such as duty or happiness, or an absolute moral principle, like the categorical imperative or the common good. If a value or a principle is absolute, it should prevail over whatever conflicts with it. Acting according to it is an unconditional moral requirement. And the absolute value or principle is said to hold regardless of what anyone thinks. Even if most people in a society deny that it is absolute, they are all mistaken. The failure to act as it prescribes may be excused in special circumstances, such as ignorance of relevant facts or inadvertence, but it is always an act that the absolutist understanding of morality requires either condemning or excusing. If the act is not excusable, it is immoral.

On the opposing side we find the historical mode of understanding whose defenders argue constructively that the requirements of morality always depend on the moral outlook that prevails in a society and responds to its circumstances. Different societies in different times and circumstances have different moral outlooks. Morality, according to historians, is always conditional and changing. And they argue critically that moral absolutists have not succeeded in identifying a value or principle that all or most reasonable people find acceptable. Even if people in a society were to agree about the absoluteness of a value or a principle, they would routinely disagree about when actions contrary to it are excusable, or perhaps even justifiable.

Historians point at the inconsistency of those who think that the prohibition of killing another human being is absolute and yet defend activities and jobs that obviously lead to the loss of human lives. They also point at the deep disagreements in our society about whether and when abortion, capital punishment, euthanasia, or war are justifiable or excusable. Historians say that morality is not a matter of absolute values or principles, but a matter of which values or principles are widely accepted and which are controversial at a certain time and place.

Moral absolutists respond by arguing that human lives can be good only if some conditions are met, and morality is the attempt to identify and meet those conditions. Moral disagreements and immorality do not show that these conditions do not exist, but only that we are fallible, venal, and often make mistakes for a variety of usually bad reasons about what those conditions are. Moral absolutists may even grant that they themselves may be mistaken about what they regard as a moral absolute. They deny, however, that their fallibility shows that there are no moral absolutes and that making our lives better depends on following their requirements. To which historians reply that the only reason moral absolutists can have for whatever they regard as a moral absolute is derived from what they take to be the conditions of human lives, but those conditions continually change. Moral absolutists, then, assert that some conditions of human lives do not change. And historians counter by saying that many of the conditions do change and the changing conditions surely affect the unchanging conditions, if there are any. And so the argument goes back and forth, much as a Ping-Pong ball does between skilled players.

Moral absolutists and historians do not disagree about the facts. They both accept that there is continuity and change in human affairs, that values change in response to changing conditions, that the prevailing morality is always changing, usually gradually in small incremental steps. What they disagree about is the extent to which continuity and change affect the moral outlook of a society. Moral absolutists stress continuity; historians stress change. And the source of their disagreement is that they judge the significance of agreed upon facts from the point of view of different modes of understanding.

Historical understanding focuses on changes that make epochs, societies, and world-views morally different from one another. Moral understanding focuses on the respects in which human beings and their requirements remain the same even as conditions change. And when the opponents come to some specific and undeniable human value, like life, then one stresses its necessity, and the other stresses the variety of circumstances in which it is reasonable to put some lives at risk, as may be the case here and now about abortion, capital punishment, euthanasia, and war. Just so long as moral absolutists and historians are locked into their conflicting modes of understanding, they will have conflicting views that lead to the philosophical problem about whether there are moral absolutes.

The Pattern

Drawing on the preceding discussion of six philosophical problems, it is now possible to enlarge the pattern that I think characterizes all of them. At the beginning of the process that eventually leads to philosophical problems are problems of everyday life. Some of them are relatively simple and competent adults know how to cope with them. It is no more than a nuisance if our blood pressure is borderline high and we have to change our diet and exercise more. But other problems are much more serious because the resources of everyday life are insufficient for coping with them. If the conventional life we have been living is wretched, meaningless, hopeless, or our society unjust, or we are at the mercy of forces we cannot control, or we are beset by natural obstacles to the improvement of our lives, then we must look beyond everyday life to historical, moral, political, religious, scientific, or personal modes of understanding for help to make life better. We routinely find, however, that from these modes of understanding conflicting approaches follow about what we should do to cope with our more serious problems. These conflicting approaches compel us to seek some way of deciding which of the conflicting approaches that follow from modes of understanding we should accept. We have to decide which approach of which mode of understanding is overriding. But making this decision is formidably difficult.

It is arbitrary to decide that one mode of understanding is overriding and accept the approaches that follow from it, because defenders of all the modes of understanding claim that for their mode. It is no less arbitrary to accept the approaches that follow from the mode of understanding that happens to be conventionally favored in a particular context, because the conventional favorite may be mistaken and in accepting its approaches we reject the conflicting approaches that typically yield benefits we want to have. Why should we think that any one of the historical, moral, political, religious, scientific, or personal modes of understanding is overriding if doing so requires us to ignore the others that promise no less important benefits? And it is also arbitrary to throw up our hands, refuse to struggle with the problems, and try to manage as well as possible using the resources of everyday life, because its resources are insufficient. When we reach this point and recognize the difficulty of coping with problems that stand in the way of improving our lives, then we are ready to face just how formidably difficult these philosophical problems are.

4

Problems and Contexts

Every culture seems, as it advances toward maturity, to produce its own determining debate over the ideas the preoccupy it: salvation, the order of nature,
money, power, sex, the machine, and the like. The debate, indeed, may be said
to *be* the culture, at least on its loftiest levels; for a culture achieves identity
not so much through the ascendancy of one particular set of convictions as
through the emergence of its particular and distinctive dialogue.

R.W.B. Lewis[1]

It will deepen the understanding I have been proposing of philosophical problems if we distinguish between different kinds of problems and identify the different contexts in which they occur. These distinctions will make it possible
to compare and contrast philosophical problems with other kinds of problems,
and thus understand them better. In Part Two I will go on to discuss problematic
approaches to coping with philosophical problems, and in Part Three propose a
more promising approach.

Distinctions

We may distinguish between everyday, modal, philosophical, and epochal problems. Everyday problems occur in the context of common sense; modal problems
in the context of one or more modes of understanding; philosophical problems,
as we have seen, occur in the context of a world-view of which all resources at
problem-solving and all modes of understanding are parts; epochal problems
occur not within but about a world-view, and their context is formed of deep dissatisfactions with the prevailing world-view and of conflicts with other world-views
that seem to be more satisfactory than one's own. Since all available modes of
understanding and practical approaches are within a world-view, epochal problems indicate that the prevailing world-view may be deficient, not merely in some

of its parts but as a whole. This could happen, and if it does it is one of the most seri-ous threats that a society at a certain age could face.

In each context, problems are solvable, manageable, or intractable. A solved problem ceases to be one, like breaking a code or seeing the point of a joke. If a solved problem recurs, we need only to remember its solution. A managed prob-lem does not cease to be one. It persists and managing it is an ongoing process, like controlling the flow of traffic or maintaining order. An intractable problem can be neither solved nor managed in the context in which it occurs. It may be intractable because the necessary resources are unavailable in that context, as pre-venting polio was before the discovery of the vaccine, or because the would-be problem-solvers are unable or unwilling for some reason to make use of available resources, as France and England were before WWII to stop Hitler's aggressive policies. I will concentrate on the first kind of intractability, which indicates the deficiency of the available practical approaches, and ignore the second, which is caused by the deficiency of problem-solvers.

Problems solvable and manageable in a context are internal to it. Those that are intractable in a context may become external to it, and may be solvable or manage-able in another context whose practical approaches are better in general or more suited to deal with a particular problem. The problem of how to limit the power of rulers had been for a very long time intractable to common sense, but the political mode of understanding made it manageable by the policy of dividing and balanc-ing the powers of the executive, legislative, and judicial branches of government. In such cases, problems external to one context become internal to another. If a problem is intractable and external to all contexts, then it can be neither solved nor managed, given all the available practical approaches, as is, for instance, making us invulnerable to the contingencies of life. Contexts and problems become more complex as they go from everyday problems internal to common sense, to modal problems internal to a mode of understanding, to philosophical problems internal to a world-view, and to epochal problems external to the context of the prevailing world-view.

Within each of these contexts two approaches are distinguishable, although often not separable because they are usually followed by the same people at the same time. One is practical, the other is reflective. The aim of the practical approach is to solve or manage the problems that occur in a particular context. This is often difficult because it is uncertain whether the resources are adequate or more urgently needed for solving or managing other problems, or because there are conflicting practical approaches and it is unclear which would be more rea-sonable to follow than the others. Such difficulties call for a reflective approach whose aim is to find a way of overcoming the difficulties. It may happen that the difficulties prove too serious and all practical and reflective approaches fail, given the available modes of understanding and practical and reflective approaches in a context. Reasonable reflection then leads to the conclusion that the problem is intractable in that context and problem-solvers should rely on the more ample resources of a more complex context. I will discuss how these distinctions apply to different problems, but it might be helpful first to sketch an initial view of the contexts in which they occur.

Everyday problems are internal to common sense as it appears to those who live in a society at a certain age. The problems are solvable or manageable if the readily available, non-technical resources are adequate to it. We know how to keep clean, be polite, vote, balance the checkbook, go to work, drive a car, make amends, and so forth. And if unhandicapped mature adults who live here and now do not know such things, they have only themselves to blame. But a little reflection makes it obvious that common sense lacks the resources to cope with terrorism, maintain world peace, prevent cancer, prove or disprove the existence of God, solve quadratic equations, or treat psychosis. If we want to solve or manage such problems, we need to go beyond common sense and turn to modes of understanding.

Modal problems are so called because they are problems internal to one or more modes of understanding. As we have seen, each mode has methods, standards, and values by which various approaches to solving or managing problems can be evaluated. Identifying the best approach is often controversial within a particular mode. If the controversies prove intractable, they give rise to problems that are external to the mode in which the controversies occur. But modal problems may turn out to be intractable and external, if all available modes of understanding lack the resources to solve or manage them. One type of intractable external modal problem is that of coping with conflicts between modes of understanding about how to solve or manage problems that are internal to both. Different modes of understanding will lead to conflicting ways of solving or managing problems like age-old hostilities between two nations, the high crime rate, or diminishing natural resources. Such conflicts are intractable within particular modes of understanding and external to all of them. They are the philosophical problems I have been discussing. They are internal to the world-view of a society and an age. I have so far not discussed whether they are solvable or manageable by relying on the resources of our world-view. I will do so in Parts Two and Three.

All these approaches may be unsuccessful. Philosophical problems, then, would be intractable by the practical and reflective approach of any mode of understand we have and thus external to our world-view. I call them epochal to indicate both their enormity and that they are the problems of an epoch. If philosophical problems were indeed external to our world-view, then we would not know how to solve or manage them, because our world-view contains all our resources. We may be helpless then in the face of epochal problems, or we may turn to another world-view that perhaps has the resources that might make the epochal problems tractable. But world-views are not easy to come by. Nor is it easy to recognize that our own world-view is basically flawed, give it up, and try to form another.

Everyday Problems

Berkeley inveighs against "the prejudices of philosophers, which have so far prevailed against the common sense and natural notions of mankind" and thinks that the "return to the simple dictates of nature, after having wandered through the wild mazes of philosophy...is like coming home from a long voyage."[2] G.E. Moore is of the same opinion. He begins what is perhaps his most famous essay "by enunciating...a whole long list of propositions, which [are]...such obvious truisms as not to be worth stating: they are, in fact a set of propositions every one of which...I *know*, with certainty, to be true." And then he gives the excruciatingly pedantic list that he says is not worth giving. I consign it to the Notes.[3]

All the items on Moore's list, and countless more, are common sense beliefs. They are the kind of beliefs, which, borrowing a term of art from English jurisprudence, a reasonable person, the prospective juror, would unhesitatingly hold.[4] The beliefs of the reasonable person would be unanimously accepted by any 12 randomly selected, mature, and normally intelligent adults in contemporary Western societies. They need not articulate these beliefs, but they will show in their daily conduct that they accept them. Accepting them, however, is one thing, justifying them is quite another. Moore thinks he can do that as well: "I can prove now, for instance, that two human hands exist. How? By holding up my two hands, and saying... 'Here is one hand', and adding... 'and here is another.'" And he writes elsewhere that: "I do want to insist that...the proof which I gave was a perfectly rigorous one; and that it is perhaps impossible to give a better or more rigorous proof of anything whatever."[5]

Moore is right, I think, in claiming that we all hold the beliefs he lists, that any justification we might offer for holding them will at some point rest on some assumption we find much less plausible than the beliefs we are trying to justify, and that any justification, or indeed criticism, of common sense beliefs will presuppose at least some common sense beliefs. What I am accepting in all this is the primacy of common sense. We feel certain about common sense beliefs and practices and follow them confidently on the appropriate occasion, but that does not constitute as conclusive a justification as Moore supposes. Perhaps our common sense beliefs and practices are ways in which we have adapted to evolutionary pressures, but our ways may turn out to be maladaptive with consequences that have not yet caught up with us. Species rarely become extinct overnight. But in the context of common sense we have no reason to worry about this possibility, nor to seek a conclusive justification.

The primacy of common sense partly consists in holding the type of beliefs that appear on Moore's list. I say partly, because common sense includes much else beside beliefs, and the beliefs may just be tacit, non-conscious, and never expressed. All human beings believe that they have a head and act accordingly, but when would anyone have occasion to say "I have a head"? That we hold common sense beliefs transpires largely from our practices, from what we do, and much less frequently from what we say. Just think of the number of unexpressed beliefs implied by the simple act of having breakfast or keeping a dental appointment.

In accepting the primacy of common sense, I am not supposing that it is possible to specify clearly where its boundaries lie. Its boundaries change. A millennium ago belief in God was probably part of common sense in Christendom, but it no longer is. The rough and ready test of what is part of common sense is whether reasonable people would unanimously accept it without having to consult books, experts, or dredge their minds for barely remembered lessons learned in school many years ago. It is clear that eating, sleeping, and the simple beliefs implied by them are part of common sense; that the conjugation of Latin verbs is not; and that there are borderline cases where the answer is unclear. I doubt that we need greater clarity than unanimous agreement about very many beliefs and practices that are clearly part of common sense.

My point is, then, that the unanimously agreed and unquestioned beliefs and practices of normally intelligent and mature people in our society are those with which we all start. We just take them for granted. They are what I mean by the primacy of common sense. Its primacy is accepted by defenders of the Scottish philosophy of common sense[6] and the ancient tradition of Pyrrhonian skepticism.[7] Hume combines elements of these two lines of thought in the following passage:

A correct *Judgment*...avoiding all distant and high enquiries, confines itself to common life, and to such objects as fall under daily practice and experience; leaving more sublime topics to the embellishment of poets and orators, or to the arts of priests and politicians....Philosophical decisions are nothing but reflections of common life, methodized and corrected. But they will never be tempted to go beyond common life, so long as they consider the imperfection of those faculties which they employ, their narrow reach, and their inaccurate operations.[8]

This is a rich passage that contains much that is right and also much that is wrong. What I take to be right is that Hume recognizes the primacy of common sense, and that it includes both beliefs and practices. He believes, rightly I think, that we begin with common sense and philosophers go on from there to order and correct what they take from it. He rightly stresses the fallibility of the judgments philosophers make about common sense beliefs and practices. He is also right to want to avoid "distant and high enquiries," by which he means metaphysical speculations, about "the origin of the worlds [note the plural!], and the situation of nature, from, and to eternity."[9] But not all distant and high inquiries are speculations by metaphysicians, poets, orators, politicians, and priests, all of whom Hume scorns. And this brings me to what I think is wrong in this passage.

Surely, there is a large area including the various much-needed modes of understanding and their practical and reflective approaches that go far beyond common sense, and yet avoid undisciplined speculations. Think, for example, of the uses we make of arthroscopic surgery, calculus, the theory of relativity, pharmacology, risk assessment, symphony orchestras, medieval iconology, code breaking, translating poetry, explaining ancient tragedies, settling international conflicts by diplomatic means, and so on and on. It is quite true that the understanding required for these activities originates with the beliefs and practices of common sense, but our modes of understanding go beyond them, and often, recursively, result in substantial improvements of our lives. The many and various approaches that follow from modes of understanding need not be contrary to the beliefs and practices of common sense, but they rapidly ascend to a level more complex than common sense. And ascent means here greater complexity, not a different plane of existence. As we become familiar with the available modes of understanding and what they enable us to do, it becomes obvious that they clearly enable us to solve or manage many problems that are intractable in the context of common sense.

If the primacy of common sense is understood as warranting what seems to me the justified psychological claim that common sense beliefs and practices are the unavoidable starting points of even our most complex modes of understanding, then we have good reason to accept it. But if it is understood as implying the unjustified epistemological claim that all reasonable modes of understanding are merely "common life, methodized and corrected," then we have good reason to reject it. In the passage I have cited, Hume makes the unjustified claim. But he is not consistent, and many passages in his writings can be read as making the justified psychological claim. Whatever may be true of Hume's overall view, however, it is clear, I think, that Pyrrhonian skeptics are committed to the unjustified epistemological claim.

Here is Sextus: "We say, then, that the standard of the Sceptical persuasion is what is apparent.... attending to what is apparent, we live in accordance with everyday observances," and "It is enough, I think, to live by experience and without opinions, in accordance with common observations and preconceptions, and to suspend judgement about what is said with dogmatic superfluity and far beyond ordinary life."[10] It emerges from these passages and the others cited in Note 10 that Pyrrhonian skeptics aim at peace of mind that is free of uncertainty and conflict. They believe that the key to it is to remain within the beliefs and practices of common sense, make no judgment about the relative merits of different modes of understanding, and ignore the philosophical problems to which conflicts among them lead. They think that confining ourselves to common sense beliefs and practices is the key to the improvement of our lives, and in this they are mistaken. They fail to recognize the enormous benefits we derive from the modes of understanding and their various practical and reflective approaches. These benefits contribute to making our lives better. They are not dispensable lagniappe, but much-needed enrichments of the possibilities of life and means to overcoming limits imposed on us by ignorance. The price we pay for this is uncertainty and conflict in many areas of life. I doubt, however, that it can be reasonably denied that the price is worth paying.

Where, then, does this leave us about the primacy of common sense? My answer follows from the distinction between the reasonable psychological and the unreasonable epistemological claim about the primacy of common sense. The reasonable psychological claim is that common sense is the unavoidable starting point from which we venture out to seek understanding and ways of coping with everyday problems, and to which we return to enjoy the restored smooth flow of life, the riches we may have found along the way, and to recover from the hardships we have endured. Defenders of common sense and Pyrrhonian skeptics do make this claim, and this far I think they are right. But many of them make the further and unreasonable epistemological claim that common sense is the standard to which we must appeal in order to decide whether the practical approaches that take us beyond common sense are reasonable, including the efforts of our modes of understanding and of the various practical and reflective approaches that follow from them. And insofar as they do make this further claim, they are, in my opinion, mistaken.

Modal Problems

Problems that are intractable in the context of common sense may become internal problems in one or more modes of understanding in which the practical and reflective approaches for solving or managing them are available. These are the problems I am calling modal. Some modal problems may be simply solved or managed in a mode of understanding, but others are complicated by conflicts within it. Should historians aim at timeless objectivity, a psychologically perceptive narrative, a description of the problem-situation of decision-makers, or look for lasting trends? Should moral judgments focus primarily on character, actions, motives, principles, or consequences? Should politics be based on economics or should it be the other way around? Should the prevailing conventions and customs set limits to acceptable policies? And how far does or should political power extend? Should religious authorities be primarily advisers, teachers, interpreters, guides to soul-searching, law-givers, or intermediaries between the faithful and God? What is the relative importance of experimentation, problem-solving, reductive explanation, repeatability, and quantification in scientific research? To what extent should the development of individuality be based on self-knowledge, prudence, the pursuit of self-interest, loving relationships, or loyalty? What are the features that justify the inclusion or exclusion of possible contributions to a mode of understanding?

Reflective people committed to a mode of understanding may agree that how they should proceed and what they should aim at depends on several considerations about whose relevance they agree. They nevertheless often hold conflicting views about the relative importance of admittedly relevant considerations. Such conflicts are persistent features of all modes of understanding. Adapting W.B. Gallie's felicitous phrase, modes of understanding are essentially contestable, and, I now claim, often contested.[11] Such conflicts stand in the way of finding a reasonable way of solving or managing modal problems and may make them intractable. The problems, then, become external to modes of understanding, internal to a world-view, and are thus transformed into the philosophical problems I have been discussing.

Consider first conflicts internal to modes of understanding about what approach should be taken to solving or managing an agreed upon modal problem. The difficulty of these conflicts cannot be minimized by saying that those who favor incompatible approaches agree about their aim and disagree only about how to reach it. Their conflicts are not only about means, as we will see in a moment, but also about aims. It may be supposed that they all aim to solve or manage a particular problem, but that is not so. They often disagree about whether something is a problem at all; even if they agree about it being one, they often disagree about whether it is internal to their mode of understanding, rather than to another mode; and if they agree about that, they may still disagree about how it would be reasonable to solve or to manage it.

Historians may disagree about whether the periodic unprovoked massacres of innocent people require a historical explanation rather than a moral or political one. If they agree that the needed explanation is historical, they may disagree about whether one explanation is likely to fit all the massacres. If they agree about that as well, they are likely to go on to disagree about whether the explanation should focus on political ideologies, aggressive psychological drives, economic conditions, or religious or quasi-religious fanaticism. And even if they agree that all these considerations should be part of the explanation, they are all too likely to disagree about the relative weight that should be attached to them. Moral agents disagree about whether suicide, proportional taxation, or the frequency of divorce are moral problems at all, and if they agree that they are, they routinely disagree about their moral evaluation and about what, if anything, morality requires doing about them. Politicians disagree about whether AIDS is a political, as opposed to a moral or scientific, problem, and if they come to agree that it is political, they are likely to disagree about how it should be managed, to what extent should scientific research into its causes and cure be funded, whether its incidence could be reduced by legislation, or whether its cost should be covered by raising taxes or reducing other expenditure. Similar conflicts will divide religious believers about what articles of faith are indispensable, scientists about treating unorthodox approaches as imaginative explorations or pseudo-science, and subjectivists about the extent to which they should rely on their intellect, emotions, will, or imagination.

Such conflicts about what approach should be followed to solve or manage modal problems could be defused if there were a standard that those who are committed to a mode of understanding would agree to holding. The problem is that there often is no agreed upon standard. Each mode of understanding has several standards and their relative importance is no less subject to conflicts than those of the practical approaches. Historical explanations may be judged by the standard of whether knowledgeable experts accept them, or by narrative coherence, or by supporting statistical figures, or by the most thorough archival research. Moral standards may be any one of the supposedly highest values, such as happiness, duty, virtue, or any one of the principles claimed to be canonical, like the categorical imperative or the greatest happiness. Political standards may be the national interest, conformity to a constitution or to the prevailing laws, the consent of the majority of citizens, or the balancing of conflicting interests. And there will be similar conflicts about religious, scientific, and personal standards.

The problem caused by the multiplicity of standards cannot be avoided by saying that there is an ultimate standard about which all who are committed to a mode of understanding will agree. It may be thought that the ultimate standard in history, religion, and science is truth, and in morality, politics, and individuality it is the good. But even if this were accepted, it would not help. For the problem is to provide reasons for believing that one of the conflicting approaches is more likely to lead to the true or to the good than the others, as well as for believing that the various conflicting approaches really aim at the true or the good, rather than at something they mistake for it. Furthermore, the needed reasons would have to be persuasive enough to convince defenders of contrary reasons that their own evaluations of conflicting accounts of the true and the good are mistaken. This may happen on rare occasions, but as the persistence of conflicts in the history of all modes of understanding so amply shows, in most cases it does not happen. Controversies about historical or scientific method, the reasonable requirements and acceptable limits of moral prescriptions, political prudence, religious belief, and personal conceptions of how one should live have not diminished over the ages. And, it is crucial to remember, these controversies are most acute when they ultimately concern the relative merits of conflicting approaches to coping with the everyday problems we face now, not merely those that took place in the history of modes of understanding.

There are conflicting approaches to modal problems within each mode of understanding. They divide us between favoring reform or revolution, prudence or risk-taking, orthodoxy or heterodoxy, tradition or innovation, autonomy or authority, discipline or imagination, and so on. A large part of the reason why we find it so difficult to solve or manage these and other similar modal problems is that we are guided not merely by the problems and the available resources within our mode of understanding, but also by the larger context of which the mode, its resources, and its problems are only parts. The difficulty of modal problems, therefore, is not just that the approaches of that mode conflict, but that most of us, except a few fanatics, are committed to more than one mode of understanding. Most of us quite reasonably have moral, political, or personal commitments; and it is virtually impossible for us here and now to live in a society and not be directly or indirectly, constructively or critically, consciously or otherwise, influenced by the prevailing historical, religious, and scientific views. And even if we think that history is bunk, religion a scam, and science a sexist plot, we will still have multiple commitments to different modes of understanding—although perhaps not to all of them—to which we turn for solving or managing the problems we face.

The problem of multiple commitments, therefore, is not merely the epistemological one of making a reasonable decision about which of the conflicting approaches within our mode of understanding is the best, but also the psychological problem of how we can make reasonable decisions about which of our conflicting commitments we should honor. This is not only a cognitive problem, but also an emotional and motivational one. For how we evaluate problematic aspects of the world, and what we should do about them, unavoidably engages our emotions and influences our motivation. History, morality, politics, religion, science, or individuality tend to make us see and respond to the world in different ways. However, since most of us are committed to more than one mode of understanding, we tend to be divided about how we should evaluate and respond to the problem. We are simultaneously predisposed to follow their different, often incompatible, practical approaches.

The problems of conflicting approaches and standards, on the one hand, and the problem of multiple commitments, on the other hand, are not merely different, but make one another even more acute than they would be without the other problems. Conflicts among practical approaches are exacerbated by our ambivalence, and our ambivalence is reinforced by there being genuinely different and incompatible approaches to solving or managing modal problems. The problems caused by conflicting approaches, standards, and commitments, therefore, are not just philosophical puzzles that engage those who are interested in such matters, but also acute practical and personal problems that the improvement of our lives depends on solving or managing. As we reflect on these problems and deepen our understanding of their causes and consequences, we are compelled to recognize that many modal problems are intractable within and external to modes of understanding. We will recognize that many of them are in fact perennial. And then reflection compels us to face the question of whether our world-view has the resources we need for solving or managing them.

Philosophical Problems

The context of philosophical problems is the world-view of a society at an age. I said in the Introduction that a world-view is something like the mentality, sensibility, form of life, culture, spirit of an age, prevailing climate of opinion, or *Weltanschauung*, and left it at that, but now it is important to describe it in greater detail.

First, here are some examples: one is implicit in Plato's corpus taken together; another is Augustine's attempt to combine Platonism with Christian teachings; yet a later Christian outlook emerges from the three volumes of Dante's *Divine Comedy*; Confucianism, Buddhism, the Islam are others; then there is the Cartesian one that eventually turned into a scientific world-view; further examples are those of the Aztecs, the Enlightenment, and of Hegel and his historicist successors; and there is also our own, a mixture that combines various elements drawn from its Greek, Christian, and Enlightenment predecessors. There are other examples, but these perhaps will suffice to indicate the sort of thing a world-view is.

The contents of different world-views are different of course, but there are some structural similarities among them. They have, I think, four distinguishable components, although the relative importance attributed to these components often varies with world-views and times. There is, first of all, an ontology of what are taken to be the most basic types of existents. They include natural objects that range from microscopic entities to galaxies; often also God and perhaps other supernatural entities; human beings with psychological properties; as well as forces, laws, space, time, events, processes, and what used to be called primary and secondary qualities. They include all substances, properties, and relations. Historically, the ontology of our world-view has been formulated by the religious and scientific modes of understanding, which, of course, have clashed and are still clashing in ways that lead to philosophical problems. Ontology is intended to be a view of the world *sub specie aeternitatis*: an objective, descriptive, all-embracing view, such as God is thought to have, or would have if there were one.

The second component is *sub specie humanitatis*: an anthropocentric view of the significance the ontology has for human beings, of how it affects us, and of how we fit into the scheme of things. It is a view about our importance or unimportance within it, and about whether its effects on us are benign, indifferent, malign, or mixed. If the design and purpose of the scheme of things is part of the ontology, then the anthropocentric view is an attempt to understand what they are, and how we should live given our understanding of them. Or, if there is supposed to be no design and purpose, the question still is how we should live in the light of that. We struggle to form this understanding by relying on a system of values derived from the available modes of understanding. And we use these values to understand the significance of the facts that we believe jointly constitute the human condition.

All systems of values, however, are riven by conflicts, inconsistencies, and deep disagreements about whether our values are wholly or partly discovered or invented by us; whether they are derived from what is taken to be our nature; or follow from the accumulated historical reflections of our predecessors; or are bequeathed to us by the supposed wisdom of a sacred text or of a great man. The resulting values and conflicts permeate all aspects of life. They affect how we distinguish between good or bad and better or worse in the various modes of understanding. They provide conflicting guidance to how reason requires us to live. We evaluate our lives in the terms our system of values provides. But the values we derive from various modes of understanding and the conflicts that occur among them give rise to philosophical problems about how the conflicts should be resolved.

The third component of a world-view is an explanation of why life does not go as well as it might or as we hope. The various no less conflicting explanations may be based on our irrationality, weakness of will, undisciplined emotions, fantasies, or self-deception. Or the conflicts may be attributed to one or more obstacles, such as the difficulty of following our values, natural adversities, the incoherence of our system of values, the scarcity of necessary resources, hostilities between groups or individuals, the merciless struggle for survival, or our innate destructive tendencies. Whatever the explanation is taken to be, it may lead us to conclude, optimistically, that the difference between how things are and how we believe or feel they should be can be overcome or at least decreased. Or we may conclude, pessimistically, that there is little we can do about it, and must live with it as well as we can. It is characteristic of world-views that one of their philosophical problems is caused by the conflicts between idealistic optimists and pessimistic realists, who may agree about the relevant facts, but disagree about their evaluation and what should be done about them.

The fourth component of world-views are the various practical approaches beyond the resources of common sense that are provided by the available modes of understanding. Their immediate aim is to solve or manage particular problems internal to a world-view. If the problems are relatively simple, the resources of modes of understanding are usually sufficient. But if the problems are caused by conflicts between modes of understanding and the values we derive from them, then solving or managing them becomes difficult. The key to overcoming such difficulties may be to try to improve one or more of our modes of understanding, or parts or the whole of our system of values, or our individual conceptions of how we want to live, as well as our characters and efforts so that they enable us to solve or manage these more difficult problems. The difficulties, however, may be severe, and the problems may prove intractable, given the resources of our world-view. The problems, then, become external to the world-view. Since all the resources of a society in a certain age, all its modes of understanding, values, and practical approaches are embedded in its world-view, the problems become external to the world-view, intractable within it, and thus, as far as that society at that time is concerned, epochal. Those who live then and there will be unable to solve or manage problems that stand in the way of improving their lives.

In these regrettable circumstances, unreflective people who do not realize the truth will simply continue to try, futilely, to use the available resources to try to solve or manage the problems. Reflective ones who understand what is happening are likely to propose radical reforms of their modes of understanding and values. Or, in rare cases, they may come to accept gradually, over time and after repeated unsuccessful attempts at reform that their world-view is doomed. They will then see the intractable problems within a world-view as epochal problems external to it.

World-views, however, are resilient and it rarely happens that they are without resources to solve or manage problems that may seem temporarily intractable. What makes this possible is that world-views are not monolithic systems that stand or fall in their totality. They continually change, because defenders of the modes of understanding and the values derived from them are responsive to changing conditions. This has happened to our historical perspective (by paying more attention to non-Western influences), moral sensibility (as a result of the sexual revolution and expanded foreign travel), political arrangements (growing resistance to dictatorships), religious beliefs (greater toleration of dissent), scientific outlook (the development of genetics and artificial intelligence), and what we regard as our personal possibilities (the increasing pursuit of autonomy). If in doubt, compare how the world looks now to reflective people with how it looked two, three, and four centuries ago to those who lived then. And do not focus only on scientific and technological changes, which are the most obvious cases in point, but also on how our values, judgments, and what we regard as possible and impossible have changed.

The change need not be for the better. World-views can regress, not just progress. Rome and Byzantium declined for centuries before they finally disintegrated, and contemporary Iran seems to be returning to a medieval condition. The problems of a world-view can multiply or become more complex and more difficult, as did those of Ptolemaic cosmology. And a world-view can disintegrate fast, as the Aztec's did after the onslaught of the conquistadores. World-views can also improve over time. The spurs for improvement are the problems themselves and the changing conditions in which they have to be solved or managed. But not all components of world-views are equally likely to change: their core is more enduring than their periphery. Ontology is the slowest to change, next to it are changes in the anthropocentric component, followed by the far more flexible system of values, and then the constantly shifting practical approaches. World-views have capacities for both continuity and change. Typically, continuity is at the core, change at the periphery.

The changes are made possible by revisions in the modes of understanding that take account of new facts, lead to new evaluations or re-evaluations of the significance of both new and old facts. And these progressive or regressive changes do not always come from within a world-view. Buddhism changed Confucian China and Marxism did it again. The rediscovery of the culture of classical Greece has changed Christendom. Secularization changed Turkey. And contemporary Western science has been changing the Islamic world. The possibilities of a world-view may be enlarged by contacts with another world-view. And this too may happen for the better or the worse.

I stress the resiliency of world-views to leave room for the possibility that seemingly intractable problems within a world-view at a certain time, need not be so in fact. A world-view, therefore, may have the resources to solve or manage philosophical problems and thus stop them from turning into epochal problems that signal the deficiency and perhaps the coming end of a world-view. This is an important possibility for my purposes, and I will come back to it in Part Three.

Epochal Problems

Apparently intractable philosophical problems, however, may be intractable in fact. If they are isolated and the practical approaches of a world-view are otherwise effective, then they may be, as it were, bracketed in the hope that they can be solved or managed at a later time. Europeans did this with the Black Death that killed close to half the population, until, fortunately for them, the epidemic ran its course. But if it had not, it would have been the end of the prevailing European world-view. Or the problem may be religious wars, as was the one between Moslems and Christians over several centuries, that threatened, as the fortunes of war have shifted, first the survival of one world-view and then of the other, until both sides were forced to scale down their efforts as a result of internal tensions. If, however, the problems persist, and if they are serious threats to our lives, then they become epochal. The world-view then may be disintegrating because it cannot cope with its own problems and is judged by its own system of values as deficient. If such judgments are frequent, widely shared, and persistent, then it becomes unreasonable for people to remain committed to the world-view.

Diehards may continue to adhere to a disintegrating world-view, as 2nd-century Epicureans in Rome may have done as they reflected on the spread of what they saw as barbaric Christianity, but the vast majority of unreflective people, who have a life to live and a family to maintain, slowly begin to shift their allegiance from the unsustainable old to the emerging new world-view. A world-view rarely comes to an end suddenly. It dies slowly because people lose confidence in it, its serious problems become more and more numerous, its practical approaches become more and more convoluted and less and less effective, and the explanations of its repeated failures are rendered ever more implausible by a thousand qualifications and excuses. This is perhaps the worst thing that can happen to a people who for a long time have adhered to the system of values of a world-view that made their lives meaningful, and allowed them to make judgments about good and bad, better and worse possibilities among which they had to choose. It is, therefore, a matter of great interest whether a world-view can solve or manage its philosophical problems. And it is not just of philosophical interest, but a live issue for us here and now as we face the philosophical problems I have been discussing.

Alarming as this possibility is, it is not the end of matter. What fails if a world-view fails are the available resources for understanding and coping with problems. The facts and the problems they cause us, however, are what they are independently of how well we understand or cope with them. If a world-view fails, it is because it lacks the resources to accommodate the facts and cope with the problems. The facts and the problems, however, are independent tests of the acceptability of a world-view. And this opens up the crucial possibility that if the resources of a world-view are inadequate, then its defenders may turn to another world-view that appears to be doing better at understanding and coping than their own. This need not consist in abandoning one and embracing another. It may involve only adopting a new mode of understanding or radically revising an existing one by modeling it on another. The Chinese are trying to do this with their economy, India with the caste system, Russia with authoritarian government, and perhaps we ought to be doing it by learning from other world-views about ways of improving the bankrupt educational system, controlling rampant crime, and imposing some order on the news media that seeks profit at the expense of truth, privacy, and elementary standards of ethics. I offer these remarks merely as speculations about possibilities. But I do think that the important possibility exists that a failing world-view unable to cope with its epochal problems may be improved by drawing on the resources of another world-view that does better in those respects in which the failing world-view does worse.

The Pattern Completed

I have been describing the pattern of how philosophical problems arise, given modes of understanding and their practical and reflective approaches. I have tried to show that the more difficult problems of everyday life compel us to turn to modes of understanding; that conflicts internal to modes of understanding and external conflicts among modes of understanding compel us to reflect on how such conflicts can be reasonably resolved; and that reflection compels us to recognize that it is unreasonable to resolve these conflicts by supposing that one of the modes of understanding is superior to the others. This leaves us either with having to resign ourselves to accepting that epochal problems doom our world-view, or to seeking a reasonable way of resolving the conflicts that lead to philosophical problems.

Before leaving Part One I want to correct an impression that my concentration on the conflicts and the problems may have created. It is certainly true that as conflicts come closer to causing epochal problems so they become more formidable and threatening. But it is also true that few conflicts lead to epochal problems. Everyday, modal, and philosophical problems are often signs of the health of a world-view. The tensions they create may be creative tensions that give impetus to defenders of various practical approaches and modes of understanding to improve what they have as a result of criticisms by those who defend a different approach or proceed from a different mode of understanding. Conflicts and problems are antidotes to dogmatism, to the hardening of cognitive and imaginative arteries.

They may inspire more and better work than was done before. This is one of the considerations that John Stuart Mill so eloquently impressed on his readers:

The whole strength and value, then, of human judgment depending on the one property, that it can be set right when it is wrong, reliance can be placed on it only when the means of setting it right are kept constantly at hand. In the case of any person whose judgment is really deserving of confidence, how has it become so? Because it has been his practice to listen to all that could be said against him; to profit by as much of it as was just, and expound to himself, and upon occasion to others, the fallacy of what was fallacious....No wise man ever acquired his wisdom in any mode but this.[12]

In the chapters of Part Two that follow, I will discuss one type of widely favored approach to finding a reasonable way of resolving these conflicts and thus avoiding philosophical problems. I will argue that it fails. In Part Three I will propose a better approach to show that our world-view has the resources to resolve conflicts both within and among modes of understanding and thus cope with philosophical problems.

PART II

Problematic Approaches

5

History and Genealogy

The notion that human history could be turned into a natural science by the extension to human beings of a kind of sociological zoology…[is] a denial of the evidence of direct experience, a deliberate suppression of much of what we know about ourselves, our motives, purposes, choices, perpetrated in order to achieve by hook or by crook a single unitary method in all knowledge…one complete all-embracing pyramid…one method; one truth; one scale of rational 'scientific' values. This naive craving for unity and symmetry at the expense of experience is with us still.

Isaiah Berlin[1]

"Historicism" is a translation of the German "Historismus," which began life as a technical term around the middle of the 19th century. The first English uses of it date to around the end of that century.[2] Allowing for deviant uses, Mandelbaum defines it as follows: "Historicism is the belief that an adequate understanding of the nature of anything and an adequate assessment of its value are to be gained by considering it in terms of the place it occupied and the role it played within a process of development." He adds that it is "a methodological belief concerning explanation and evaluation." This is how I will understand historicism throughout this chapter.

Historicism has what I will call an old and a new version. The old one explains and evaluates the process of development in terms of historical laws or patterns, which may be linear, cyclical, progressive, regressive, or of some other metaphorical form. Old historicism is as dead as a doctrine can be. Perhaps a few diehard historians or philosophers are still committed to it, but the overwhelming consensus is to consign it to the graveyard of ideas. I will not discuss it. There is, however, also a new version of historicism: genealogy, and it is the main subject of this chapter. A subsidiary subject is relativism, which I began considering in Chapter 1 when I claimed that it is one of the problematic approaches to solving philosophical problems. I will give further reasons in support of this claim by discussing the connection between relativism and genealogy.

What Is Genealogy?

Historical understanding is an important part of our world-view. We would be seriously impoverished if we were ignorant of the origin and development of our institutions, beliefs, values, and practices, of the influences that have made us what we are, and of the causes and consequences of life-transforming events and processes in the past. Genealogists, however, go far beyond this and claim that history is the most important mode of understanding and the key to resolving philosophical problems. They claim that conflicts between the beliefs, values, and practices of historical and non-historical modes of understanding should be resolved in favor of those of the historical mode. According to them, historical understanding is deeper than any other, because it explains why non-historical modes of understanding are what they are now and why they are now committed to their beliefs, values, and practices. They claim that understanding the true significance of moral, political, religious, scientific, or personal commitments depends on understanding the historical conditions that have formed them. And they claim further that defenders of non-historical modes of understanding take these conditions for granted, often without being aware that they are contingent products of contingent conditions. Genealogists thus seem, at least initially, to subvert what we believe, value, and practice by explaining that they reflect shifting conditions that happened to have influenced us, rather than objective facts that exist independently of our evaluations.

As Bernard Williams puts it:

genealogy is a narrative that tries to explain a cultural phenomenon by describing a way in which it came about, or could have come about, or might be imagined to have come about. Some of the narrative will consist of real history.... A truthful historical account is likely to reveal a radical contingency in our current ethical conceptions. Not only might they have been different from what they are, but also the historical changes that brought them about are not obviously related to them in a way that vindicates them against possible rivals. This sense of contingency can seem to be in tension with something that our ethical ideas themselves demand, a recognition of their authority.[3]

How would genealogy affect how we live and act? One answer is Isaiah Berlin's:

It may be that the ideal of freedom to choose ends without claiming eternal validity for them, and the pluralism of values connected with it, is only the late fruit of our declining capitalist civilization: an ideal which remote ages and primitive societies have not recognized, and one which posterity will regard with curiosity, even sympathy, but little comprehension.

This may be so; but no sceptical conclusion seems to me to follow. Principles are not less sacred because their duration cannot be guaranteed. Indeed, the very desire for guarantees that values are eternal and secure in some objective heaven is perhaps only a craving for the certainties of childhood or the absolute values of our primitive past.

And he quotes with approval Schumpeter's remark that "To realise the relative validity of one's convictions...and yet stand for them unflinchingly, is what distinguishes a civilised man from a barbarian."[4] Berlin thus believes that genealogy leads to relativism, but denies that this has subversive consequences.

This is surely an odd answer. Why would we stand unflinchingly for our beliefs, values, and practices if we realize that they are contingent products of contingent circumstances? Why would that realization not weaken our commitment to them? Why would it not have skeptical implications if we were to accept that between objective facts, on the one hand, and our beliefs, values, and practices, on the other hand, lie layers of evaluations that we accept because we are subject to influences that temporarily prevail in our context? Why is it a mark of civilization rather than dogmatism to hold principles as sacred if we recognize that they are contingent? Berlin does not ask these questions, but genealogists do. Do their answers lead to relativism? Is genealogy really subversive? Is the historical mode of understanding more basic than the other modes? And how does this affect philosophical problems?

Consider by way of answering these questions some examples of genealogies: Thrasymachus on justice as the rule of the strong over the weak, Hobbes on the Leviathan as the means of escaping from the barbaric state of nature, Hume on religion as the product of fear and on justice as the protection of private property, Rousseau on civilization as the corruption of innocence, Nietzsche on Christianity as the product of *ressentiment* and on morality as the revenge the weak take on the strong, Marx on history as the dialectic of class conflict, and, more recently, Craig on knowledge and Williams on truthfulness as requirements of human nature. It is important to understanding what makes these examples of genealogy that they are philosophical, not simply historical, accounts. If they were intended as contributions to history, they would be rightly dismissed by historians as not worthy of serious attention. What, then, makes them philosophical? I will patch together an explanation by relying on the methodological parts of the genealogical works of Bevir, Craig, Geuss, Nehamas, and Williams.[5]

Genealogical explanations may be merely factual, or imaginative constructions, or philosophical, or some mixture of them. A merely factual explanation is based on historical evidence of the origin and development of its object and of how people engaged in the appropriate activities, or their sympathizers and critics, evaluated what they were doing. This is where the works of genealogists and historians coincide. But if genealogists were interested only in providing a purely factual explanation, they could not reasonably suppose that even the most complete one would enable them to justify or criticize the contemporary state of the object of their explanation. For its justification or criticism does not depend on how it came about, but on how it now is. Reasonable justification or criticism of practices like chastity, campaign financing, treating Sunday as a holiday, interpreting dreams, or spelunking is entirely independent of the history of morality, politics, religion, science, or personal preference, which has led to them. It is far more reasonable to try to justify or criticize recursively the contemporary state of modes of understanding on the basis of the practices that follow from them than to justify or criticize the practices on the basis of the history of the modes of understanding whose products they are. The origin and development of practices is one thing; their justifiability is quite another. To think otherwise is to commit the rightly criticized genetic fallacy.[6] If genealogists wanted to propose only factual explanations, they should stick to history and stop trying to justify or criticize contemporary practices.

Genealogists, however, often mix factual explanations based on some historical evidence with imaginative constructions that go beyond the supporting evidence. They construct, for instance, an imaginative account of what the state of nature was like and how we got from it to civilized life. Hobbes thought that the benefits of this process far outweighed its costs, whereas Rousseau thought the reverse. If we ask genealogists what reason there is for preferring one imaginative construction to the others that have been or, with a little ingenuity, could have been proposed, they typically offer further elaborations of their preferred imaginative construction by adducing some additional facts that fit into it.

This procedure, however, is haphazard and takes no account of facts that do not fit. Hobbes ignores altruism, sympathy, and love. Rousseau forgets about aggression, fear, and ignorance that we have no reason to suppose absent from the state of nature. When charged with their cavalier approach to facts, they acknowledge it, but fail to notice how damaging that is. Hobbes says about the state of nature that "it may peradventure be thought, there was never such a time, nor condition of warre as this; and I believe it was never generally so."[7] And Rousseau begins "by putting aside all the facts, for they have no bearing on the question. The investigation that may be undertaken concerning this subject should not be taken for historical truths, but only for hypothetical and conditional reasonings."[8] And yet, led by counterfactual reasoning, Hobbes defends authoritarian government and Rousseau condemns what he sees as the corruption of the world that surrounds him.

Nehamas and Williams think, however, that such imaginative constructions are nevertheless important. According to Nehamas, they have "direct practical consequences because, by demonstrating the contingent character of the institutions that traditional history exhibits as unchanging, it creates the possibility of changing them."[9] And Williams says that "the power of imaginary genealogies lies in introducing the idea of function where you would not necessarily expect it, and in explaining in more primitive terms what the function is."[10]

Why should we think that a mere possibility, even if it is of an unexpected function, would contribute to the evaluation of a mode of understanding or of its constituent beliefs, values, or practices? The answer is that if the possibility is more than a mere fiction, if what it is taken to show is not how morality, politics, religion, science, or an individual might have developed a specific function, but how they must have developed it, then we can reasonably evaluate their present state by asking how well or badly they function. If it is the function of morality to make people treat each other better; of politics to devise arrangements that foster peaceful coexistence; of religion to make life meaningful; of science to understand the natural world; of the personal mode to live according to one's preferences; then the possibility has the practical consequences of allowing us to understand what they aim at, to justify or criticize them on the basis of how well they approximate their aims, and of asking whether their aims are worth pursuing at all, or worth pursuing in that way. Such imaginative constructions of the aims of modes of understanding transform genealogical accounts from mere fictions into philosophical explanations, which are perhaps the strongest form of genealogy.

What kind of necessity might it be that compels modes of understanding to have these aims? It is certainly not logical, since its denial makes perfectly good sense and involves no error in logic. It is not nomological either, since it is possible to pursue contrary aims and no one is prevented from doing so by any law of nature. Nor is it axiological, imposed on us by our commitment to a legal, moral, political, or some other principle, since we can and often do violate such principles. I will say that the necessity is conditional on elementary facts about our nature and conditions. Given these facts, our elementary understanding of ourselves and our world must have certain aims dictated by beliefs and values we either hold and act on or perish.

It is a conditional necessity that we aim to satisfy our basic needs, cooperate, seek meaning in our existence, try to understand our environment, and strive to follow our preferences. Our moral, political, religious, scientific, and personal modes of understanding must recognize and help us pursue these aims. They may do it at a certain time and place well, badly, or unreliably, but do it they must, otherwise human lives in that context will individually and collectively soon come to an end. The contingent beliefs, values, and practices of the various modes of understanding, therefore, can be justified or criticized by asking how well or badly they serve these aims. And genealogy is the method that makes it possible to explain why we do what we do, what good or bad reasons we believe we have for doing it, and to evaluate how well or badly we do it.[11] This is why the initial appearance that genealogists deny that there are objective facts needs to be qualified. Philosophical genealogists actually presuppose that there are some objective facts, although they aim to subvert our belief in the objectivity of some other facts.

Philosophical genealogists will say that the reason why their historical mode of understanding should override any non-historical understanding that conflicts with it is that the true significance of our beliefs, values, and practices emerges from their genealogy. It alone leads to a sufficiently deep understanding of the aims that the other modes must, consciously or otherwise, have. And it alone provides the means for evaluating the success or failure of non-historical modes of understanding by the equally necessary and equally conditional considerations provided by genealogy. These conditionally necessary aims are ones human beings must have, given elementary and enduring features of our nature and environment. Their significance for us is deeper and more important than the significance of any particular moral, political, religious, scientific, or personal belief, value, or practice, because we understand their real aims only with the help of genealogy. The key to coping with philosophical problems, therefore, is to resolve the conflicts between the modes understanding by recognizing that the genealogical form of the historical mode of understanding is overriding.

Philosophical Genealogy

From now on I will simply refer to genealogy and omit the qualification that I am discussing its philosophical, as opposed to factual or imaginative, version. Genealogists claim, then, that the true significance of the beliefs, values, and practices of a mode of understanding emerges from the best genealogical description and evaluation of its aims and of how well it pursues it.

The description is a historical account of the relevant facts, including the context and the beliefs, values, and actions of moral agents, politicians, religious believers, scientists, and individuals trying to satisfy their personal preferences. The historical description slides into evaluation when genealogists ask why those involved hold particular beliefs and values, and participate in particular practices, when there are readily available alternative possibilities. Part of the evaluation is to identify the aims (Williams says functions) these people, consciously or not, have. And, since they may not be aware of their aims, evaluation goes beyond mere history and adds to it conjectures that infer from what they say and do what their aims are likely to be. The evaluation, then, leads genealogists to question the conjectured aims and their pursuit: why pursue a particular aim in a particular way when other aims and other ways of pursuing any one of them are available? The evaluation may yield the conclusion that a particular aim is one that human beings will have in any context, like living in a stable and secure society in which at least their basic needs are met; or that the aim is pursued only in the context of a particular society, such as converting infidels, outlawing child labor, or protecting privacy.

More searching evaluations, however, will lead genealogists to ask about the reasons for the aims and for pursuing them in that particular context by moral, political, religious, scientific, personal, or other means. After all, what we believe, value, and do may or may not be reasonable, or may be more or less reasonable. We may be, individually or collectively, mistaken, misled, indoctrinated, ignorant, distracted by emergencies, obsessed, or defeated by adversity. The evaluation of aims and ways of pursuing them, therefore, requires drawing a threefold distinction between reasons for and against the relevant beliefs, values, and practices; reasons for or against them that are recognized in a society at a certain time; and reasons for or against them that are recognized by particular individuals. It often happens that societies and individuals are unaware of available reasons. Evaluation will lead genealogists to ask whether they could or should be aware of them. When did the reasons for and against the idea of sin, primogeniture, or individual autonomy become available? If they were available at a certain time, why was no one or only a few aware of them? What stood in their way? And if they were aware of the reasons, but ignored them, why did they?

The significance of the beliefs, values, and practices of a mode of understanding, then, emerges from the overall result of the description and evaluation of the origin and development of their aims and ways of pursuing them. One clear implication of this account is that genealogy makes it possible to justify or criticize its object.

Consider two examples of each. One justificatory genealogical attempt is Hume's account of justice as necessary for the protection of private property and thus for civilized life. Another is Kant's little known but no less extraordinary claim that "mankind's earliest history reveals that . . . this path of the species leads to *progress* from the worse to the better" that for this reason "it is of the greatest importance . . . *to be content with providence*" and "this is the outcome of a philosophical attempt at setting out man's primordial history."[12]

Critical genealogies, by contrast, show that the real, as opposed to the supposed, aim, say of justice or morality, is not dictated by human nature and conditions but serves very different interests. Thrasymachus claims that the real aim of justice is not to do what is right, but to enable those in power to rule over the rest, and Nietzsche claims that the real aim of morality is not to foster good lives, but to allow the weak to revenge themselves on the strong.

Justificatory genealogies attempt to show that pursuing a particular aim is necessary for good lives and that it is pursued in the right way for the right reason. Critical genealogies attempt to show that the real, not the supposed, aim is pursued and that it is pursued for the wrong reason. But whether justificatory or critical, genealogists regard modes of understanding and their beliefs, values, and practices as instrumental and contingent. They are instrumental to the pursuit of their real or supposed aims. And they are contingent, because whether the aims are pursued at all, by what means they are pursued, whether the means used are the best ones available, what reasons are available for the aims and for the ways of pursuing them, and how seriously these reasons are taken vary with contexts, times, and places.

There is a sense, therefore, in which both justificatory and critical genealogies are subversive: they show that all beliefs, values, and practices are contingent, not necessary. Even those that are conditionally necessary remain contingent because, reasonably or not, the beliefs and values may not be held and the practices may not be followed. It is also part of our nature and condition that we sometimes act in ways that make our lives worse. If this were not so, our history would not be as disheartening as it is. If we understand the subversive implications of genealogies, we will recognize that they give us no reason for optimism.

John Stuart Mill, who can hardly be accused of pessimism, recognized that:

it is a piece of idle sentimentality that truth, merely as truth, has any inherent power denied to error.... Men are not more zealous for truth than they are for error, and a sufficient application of legal or even social penalties will generally succeed in stopping the propagation of either.[13]

Or, as Williams writes, echoing Mill:

the hope that a truthful story on a large scale will not cause despair is already hope. Doubtless people will continue to make sense of the world in terms that help them survive in it. But the question is how truthful those terms can be, and how far they can sustain the more ambitious ideals of truthfulness that we possess.... As Nietzsche served to remind us...there are very compelling accounts of the world that would lead anyone to despair who did not hate humanity.[14]

Williams might have added Nietzsche's words that "there is no pre-established harmony between the furtherance of truth and the well-being of mankind."[15]

The subversive implication of genealogies goes far beyond how we think of the historical origin and development of the modes of understanding from which we derive our beliefs, values, and practices. It affects our present condition and undermines the confidence of those who understand and accept what genealogists claim. They claim that our beliefs, values, and practices are not objectively valid but instrumental to the pursuit of contingent aims, that we are often unaware of readily available reasons because our understanding is subverted by influences we cannot control, and we mistakenly take to be justified what is in fact unjustified. The view emerging from genealogies is that we are adrift in a sea of uncertain beliefs, values, and practices, our vessel is frail, there is no safe harbor in sight, and we do not have a destination. That is why genealogists claim, contrary to Berlin and Schumpeter, that if we understand the subversive consequences of the contingency of our beliefs, values, and practices, then we will not stand unflinchingly for whatever convictions we happen to have. And this brings us to the difficult questions of exactly how genealogists understand their contingency and whether their understanding commits them to relativism.

Contingency

Some genealogists understand contingency as the claim that there are no true descriptions of objective facts, either because there are no objective facts, or because there is no truth. I cannot take this claim seriously. It is a true description of an objective fact that those who read these lines have words in front of them, that men cannot get pregnant, and that we cannot drink mountains. It is absurd to deny that there are some true descriptions of the elementary facts of our nature and conditions.

Nietzsche, who calls himself a genealogist, denies that there are objective facts:

All philosophers have the common failing of starting from man as he is now and thinking they can reach their goal through an analysis of him. They involuntarily think of "man" as an *aeterna veritas*, as something that remains constant in the midst of all flux, as a sure measure of things. Everything the philosopher has declared about man is, however, at bottom no more than a testimony as to the man of a *very limited* period of time. Lack of historical sense is the family failing of all philosophers. ... There are *no eternal facts*, just as there are no absolute truths. Consequently what is needed from now on is *historical philosophizing*.[16]

Rorty thinks that there is no truth, not because all we believe is false, but because the idea of truth makes no sense:

To say that we should drop the idea of truth as out there waiting to be discovered is not to say that we have discovered that, out there, there is no truth. It is to say that our purposes would be served best by ceasing to see truth as a deep matter, as a topic of philosophical interest, or "true" as a term which repays "analysis."[17]

Neither Nietzsche nor Rorty, however, can reasonably deny the truths that human beings need nutrition and rest in order stay alive, or that they cannot fly by flapping their arms. No one can reasonably deny the truths that at all times and places human beings are incarnate and that this makes some things humanly possible and others impossible. This way of understanding contingency is absurd and it leads to an equally absurd form of relativism.

Contingency may be more plausibly understood as the claim that above the most basic level defined by the elementary facts of our nature and conditions, what we take to be objective facts depends on the evaluation of our experiences, which, in turn, depends on our upbringing, the language we speak, on the customs we follow or against which we rebel, on the habits we form, on the beliefs, values, and practices of everyday life in our context, and on the modes of understanding we happen to have. All these are contingent products of contingent circumstances, all could have been different, and if they had been, we may well evaluate differently what we take to be objective facts.

If this is what genealogists claim, then their claims are undoubtedly true. Our beliefs, values, and practices are contingent. But this is a truth about us, not about the facts we take to be objective. We may all believe for good or bad reasons that something is an objective fact and we may all be mistaken. And something may be an objective fact even if everyone denies it. It needs at most a reminder, but hardly an argument, that we are subject to influences we cannot control and that we are fallible. If genealogists are merely reminding us of these truisms, then all reasonable people are committed to genealogy and to this form of relativism. That commitment, however, leaves open the crucial questions of what the objective facts are, whether our descriptions of them are true or false, whether a genealogical account of some purportedly objective fact is justified or unjustified, and how disagreements about whether it is one or the other could be settled.

Genealogists may argue far more challengingly, however, that it is only a small part of the truth that our descriptions of what we take to be objective facts are fallible and that we are not fully in control of the influences that affect our descriptions. It is also part of the truth that how we evaluate what we regard as objective facts and how we respond to them partly depends on our evaluation of them as, in some sense, good, bad, mixed, relevant, irrelevant, or indifferent. Genealogists may be understood, then, as claiming that these evaluations always proceed from the point of view of one or another mode of understanding, which has itself been formed and developed by contingent conditions. The beliefs, values, and practices of all modes of understanding, therefore, are contingent products of contingent conditions, and if the conditions had been different, so would be their products.

Genealogists may claim, then, that the true significance of facts emerges from the contingent historically conditioned state of the mode of understanding from whose point of view we describe and evaluate what we take to be the objective facts. Reasonable defenders of different modes of understanding will agree in their descriptions of the elementary facts of our nature and conditions, but disagree about the evaluation of both elementary and more complex facts, because they presuppose the different beliefs, values, and practices of their different modes of understanding. If we understand in this way what genealogists say about the significance of facts, we will conclude that their significance varies with the changing state of the modes of understanding from whose point of view the purportedly objective facts are evaluated. In order to understand the true significance of facts, we have to understand the contingent beliefs, values, and practices on which their evaluations are based. And that is a matter of understanding their historical origin and development.

This is why genealogists are historicists, why they are committed to regarding history as the overriding mode of understanding, and why they are also committed to the view that the key to resolving philosophical problems is to understand that the conflicts between modes of understanding that lead to philosophical problems are not disagreements about what is true or reasonable to believe or do, but the symptoms of different contingent conditions that have shaped the moral, political, religious, scientific, or personal beliefs, values, and practices of the defenders of different modes of understanding. Their real aim is not to arrive at objective truths about the justification of their beliefs, values, and practices, but to serve, consciously or not, what they take to be good from a moral, political, religious, scientific, or personal point of view. In their different ways, therefore, they arrive at explanations whose true significance is not what moral agents, politicians, religious believers, scientists, or individuals pursuing their preferences take them to be. This is what makes all genealogies subversive and what leads to what seems to me as the strongest form of relativism. They unmask the real aims of the defenders of all modes of understanding, aims that those who pursue them deliberately or unwittingly disguise. Genealogists expose the contingency of the defenders' beliefs, values, and practices, and shatter their illusion that reason requires everyone to share what the defenders happen to believe, value, and practice.

This is perhaps what Nietzsche had in mind in saying that "what is needed from now on is *historical philosophizing*."[18] And also Rorty when he writes that:

We pragmatists, following Hegel and Dewey, are very much interested in finding psycho-historical accounts of philosophical impasses. We particularly enjoy reading and writing dramatic narratives which describe how philosophers have backed themselves into the sort of corner which we take contemporary realists to be in. For we hope that such narratives will serve therapeutic purposes, that they will make people so discouraged with certain issues that they will gradually drop the vocabulary in which those issues are formulated.[19]

The Problem of Reflexivity

Turning now to criticism, I begin with acknowledging that genealogies can be and often are important for understanding their significance of our moral, political, religious, scientific, and personal beliefs, values, and practices, and that understanding may subvert them. The problems I will now discuss are meant to give reasons against the much stronger claim that both justificatory and critical genealogies are bound to be subversive, and that they alone can lead to understanding the true significance of our beliefs, values, and practices.

Let us suppose, if only for the moment, that the genealogies of all beliefs, values, and practices reveal their contingency and thereby subvert them. If this were so, then, since genealogies involve beliefs, values, and practices, genealogies would also have to have genealogies that reveal their contingency and subvert them. Some genealogists acknowledge this. Bevir writes, for instance, that:

> genealogists may question their own narratives, and accept that the genealogical stance is a particular one that arose historically, without thereby rejecting their narratives or the genealogical stance. In short, [genealogists] . . . will typically incorporate a self-reflexivity in their beliefs such that they situate them by reference to a particular tradition or narrative, but this self-reflexivity may not undercut the beliefs so much as contribute to the attempt to establish that historicism is the best account of the world currently on offer.[20]

Whether or not genealogists join Bevir in this acknowledgment, they all face an insuperable dilemma. Suppose they accept that genealogies have genealogies. If a genealogy subverts a belief, value, or practice by showing its contingency, then the genealogy of a genealogy subverts the genealogy by showing its contingency. Furthermore, the genealogy of a genealogy, of course, will also have a genealogy, and that leads to an infinite regress of one genealogy subverting another. And that, in turn, leads to the conclusion that we have as little reason to accept any genealogy on its face value as genealogists say we have of accepting at face value any belief, value, or practice. We may reasonably conclude, then, that genealogists have a moral, political, religious, scientific, or personal ulterior aim for subverting our beliefs, values, and practices. And we can as reasonably unmask their ulterior aim and demand that they justify it as they unmask our supposedly ulterior aims and demand of us to justify them. We may or may not be able to do this, but it is a consequence of the genealogists' commitment to genealogy that they cannot do it, since, according to them, all views are subverted by unmasking their contingency. In that case, however, we would be perfectly justified in ignoring their unjustified subversive efforts and go on holding our beliefs and values and continuing our practices.

If, however, genealogists deny that genealogies have genealogies, then they must still explain what reason they have for appealing to them to reveal the true significance of all beliefs, values, and practices. They will say that the reason is historical. But of course beliefs, values, and practices also have moral, political, religious, scientific, and personal significance, and genealogists must give some reason for deriving the reason they need from the historical rather than from non-historical modes of understanding. Their earlier reason was that genealogy subverts these other modes by showing that they are instrumental to contingent aims. That reason, however, is no longer available to them, because, whether or not they acknowledge it, the genealogy of a genealogy subverts the genealogy exactly in the same way in which genealogy is supposed by genealogists to subvert the beliefs, values, and practices that follow from non-historical modes of understanding.

It seems, therefore, that, regardless of whether genealogists accept or deny that genealogies have genealogies, they end up with bewildering logical problems. They either subvert their own position or arbitrarily declare that the historical mode of understanding is overriding because it subverts non-historical modes, while exempting the historical mode from exactly the same charge of being subverted that they apply to non-historical modes.

Is there a way of avoiding these logical conundrums? Of course there is. It is to accept the glaringly obvious assumption that what appears to be the real significance of beliefs, values, and practices is often, although not always, their real significance. The real significance of the moral judgment that murder is bad is to condemn it; of the political judgment that democracy is better than dictatorship is to defend the first and oppose the second; of the religious judgment that prayer is good is to encourage it; of the scientific judgment that hypotheses ought be tested is to seek to test them; and of the personal judgment that it is good to satisfy one's preferences is to try to satisfy them. Such judgments may be mistaken and their real significance may be other than the apparent one, but the reasonable assumption is to accept their significance at their face value and doubt them only if we have some reason for it. In the normal course of events, things are as they appear to be. That is just what makes them normal. As Wilde memorably remarked, "it is only shallow people who do not judge by appearance."[21] Genealogists begin with the shallow assumption that nothing is as it appears to be, and that is what leads to the insuperable dilemma I have described.

The Problem of Subversion

I come now to a second problem with genealogy. Let us suppose that reasonable genealogies have been given and they show that the real significance of beliefs, values, and practices is not what those who are committed to them suppose. Say that Christians are persuaded by Hume's genealogy of religion, moral agents by Nietzsche's genealogy of morality, and liberals and conservatives by Marx's genealogy of their political views as expressions of their economic interests. The supposition is that this will subvert their Christianity, morality, and political views. This may happen, but it is more likely that it will not happen. Genealogies provide reasons both for and against religious, moral, and political commitments.

If the real source of religious belief is fear, if morality is an expression of resentment, if the politics of liberals and conservatives serves their economic interests, then unmasking their real reasons will not dissolve their fear, resentment, and interests. It will make Christians, moral agents, and liberals and conservatives perhaps for the first time aware of the real reasons why they are committed to their beliefs, values, and practices. But the realization that their real reasons are fear, resentment, and interests may strengthen rather than subvert their reasons for acting on them. They may just continue to act in the same way as before, but now in awareness of their reasons for doing so, whereas before they acted on them without awareness.

This is not just logically possible, but psychologically likely. For serious commitment to Christianity, morality, and liberal or conservative politics is demanding, and those who are so committed must have strong reasons for it. Their reasons, if genealogists are right, are the strength of their fear, resentment, or interests. If they become aware of them, they will feel their strength and will be moved by it. They will think that it is right to fear life without God, to resent the immorality of the strong, and to pursue their interests if that involves defending liberty or tradition. They may be chagrined by not having been aware of their real reasons before genealogists made them realize what they were, but it will not make them all of a sudden less afraid, resentful, or attached to their interests. They have reasons for their commitments, genealogists helped them to become aware of their reasons, but this is likely to reinforce rather than subvert their reasons.

Of course, genealogies may also provide subversive reasons, especially if the real reasons of Christians, moral agents, liberals, and conservatives turn out to be weak. If they discover that they really do not fear all that much a life without God, or if their resentment of the strong is weakened by the suspicion that strength is admirable, or if they think that their real interests are private, not political, then the reasons genealogists help them to discover may subvert their commitments.

The question genealogists and their subjects need to answer is whether the strength or weakness of their reasons is proportionate to their importance. They need to ask whether they should hold their reasons as strongly or as weakly as they do, whether their aims warrant the strength or weakness of their reasons. The answers to such questions, however, cannot be genealogical, because genealogies reveal, at best, the origin and development of their reasons, not whether their strength or weakness is commensurate with their aims. Whether or not genealogies are subversive does not depend on the reasons they reveal, but on whether or not the strength they attribute to them is warranted. Genealogies may serve the useful purpose of increasing our self-knowledge, but there is no reason to suppose that increased self-knowledge of our commitments will subvert them.

Justificatory genealogies, like Hume's of justice, Craig's of knowledge, Williams' of truthfulness, do not change our commitment to these worthwhile aims. If they change anything, it will only be to strengthen our commitment to them. By contrast, critical genealogies, such as Hume's of religion, Marx's of politics, and Nietzsche's of morality are supposed to be subversive and lead to momentous changes. As Marx and Engels succinctly put it: "philosophers have only interpreted the world in various ways; the point, however, is to change it."[22] And Bevir, Nehamas, and Williams concur.[23] But they are mistaken. Critical genealogies may change our knowledge of the reasons that lead us to act as we do, but they need not change what we do. The realization that genealogies may have no subversive consequences ought to deflate the rhetoric that suggests that critical genealogies will lead to the radical transformation of our world-view. It may be that "we shall not cease from exploration/And the end of all our exploring/Will be to arrive were we started/And know the place for the first time."[24]

The Problem of Relativism

This problem arises even if we accept all that genealogists, justificatory or critical, claim, and even if we ignore the first two problems. Genealogists focus on the causes that lead us to believe, value, or practice what we do. It is far more important, however, for the smooth flow of everyday life to ascertain whether our beliefs, values, and practices are justifiable than to discover their causes. The origin and development of our various commitments are one thing, their justification or criticism is quite another. The failure to recognize that there is a sharp distinction between their causes and their justifications leads to the mistaken tendency of justificatory genealogists to suppose that if they show that the causes of our beliefs, values, and practices are aims that our evolutionary inheritance compels us to have, then our commitment to them is justified. Or it leads to the similarly mistaken tendency of critical genealogists to suppose that if they show that their real causes are aims that presuppose questionable cultural influences of which we are not aware, then that makes our commitments to them also questionable.

It may be true that many of our moral values have causes that the values themselves would lead us to condemn if we became aware of them; that our political practices grew out of the rejection of the very traditions that make the practices possible; that the roots of religious beliefs are pagan superstitions; that the driving force of science is not the search for truth but the curiosity, ambition, or status-seeking of scientists; or that what we think of as our personal preferences are reactions to those of our parents. But whether our moral values, political practices, religious beliefs, scientific views, or personal preferences are justifiable depends on reasons for or against them, not on the causes whose effects they are. Genealogists focus on causes, not on reasons. There is nothing wrong with this, unless they suppose that the discovery of their causes preempts the need to justify them. But they do suppose it.

They suppose that if human nature and our circumstances make it a conditional necessity that we value justice, knowledge, or truthfulness, then we have a reason for valuing them. We are no doubt saddled with our evolutionary inheritance, but it is, at least to some extent, at our discretion to value some parts of it more, others less, and others not all. We need better reasons for regarding justice as essential for social life than that our nature and circumstances demand the protection of private property. Perhaps property should not be private but communal; perhaps what is more important for social life is compassion, loyalty, or conscientiousness, and perhaps justice is less important. Perhaps we have inflated the importance of knowledge at the expense of love, or imagination, or beauty. Perhaps the high value we put on truthfulness leads to intolerance and religious, ethnic, and racial conflicts. Perhaps knowledge and truthfulness make us much too critical of friends and lovers who are as flawed as we are; or they make us turn inward and lead to loathing our unworthy selves. The questions such possibilities raise demand better answers than pointing at our evolutionary inheritance. But how good the answers are depends on the reasons we have for valuing parts of our inheritance more than other parts. The conditional necessity of some of our beliefs, values, and practices is only a first step toward their justification. Genealogists are right to claim that it is an important step, but they fail to recognize that other steps are also needed. Why are they needed and what are they?

They are needed, in the first place, because our evolutionary inheritance is a mixed bag. It gives us not only beneficial aims, like justice, knowledge, and truthfulness, but also harmful ones, like aggression, fear, and ignorance. Beneficial and harmful aims routinely conflict, and the conflicts cannot be resolved merely by appealing to our evolutionary inheritance, because both aims are part of it. We need to justify or criticize the aims. Secondly, it is not just that beneficial and harmful aims conflict. We have many different beneficial aims that are also part of our evolutionary inheritance, such as fellow-feeling, loving our children, and taking pleasure in achievement. Beneficial aims also conflict, and we need to find reasons for or against resolving their conflicts in particular ways. Thirdly, our aims are formed not merely by evolutionary but also by cultural forces. Our evolutionary inheritance underdetermines our modes of understanding and the beliefs, values, and practices that follow from them. The outer limits of our possibilities are set by our biological nature and physical environment, but within those limits we have many possibilities, and we need to make reasonable choices about which of them we aim to realize. These needs are not met by appealing to the conditional necessity of some of our aims: that is not enough for justifying the choices we make. Nor is it enough for criticizing the aims we pursue without awareness, or for concluding that if we became aware of our real aims, we would disavow them.

These considerations lead to another dilemma that genealogists need somehow avoid, but I doubt they could. Their efforts go either too far or not far enough. If they go too far, they get to the form of relativism that denies that our beliefs, values, and practices can be justified by appealing to some standard. Relativists of this persuasion claim that all standards ultimately rest on assumptions that cannot themselves be justified by appealing to further standards. As Wittgenstein put it, "if I have exhausted the justifications I have reached bedrock, and my spade is turned. Then I am inclined to say: 'This is what I do.'"[25] But his metaphor is misleading. What we reach is not bedrock but a swamp. And, to speak plainly rather than metaphorically, saying that this is what I do is not enough, because what I do may be vicious, stupid, superstitious, or life-diminishing. Reasonable genealogists would want to avoid going too far in this direction.

The other dilemma is that they do not go far enough in their attempt to justify or criticize the beliefs, values, and practices whose genealogy they investigate. As we have seen, pointing out their evolutionary or cultural, worthy or unworthy causes is not enough to show that it is reasonable or unreasonable to be committed to them. Everything we believe, value, or do has causes, and the causes have causes, but we need to go beyond their genealogy to justify or criticize our commitments to them.

Suppose, however, that genealogists avoid relativism and find a non-arbitrary basis for the justification or criticism of our beliefs, values, and practices. But that basis, if indeed there is one, will not be historical, since history leads only to causes, not to reasons. The reasons may be moral, political, religious, scientific, personal, or something else. But whatever they may be, they will be incompatible with historicism that claims that the historical mode of understanding should override any mode of understanding that conflicts with it. And that, in turn, has the consequence that reasonable genealogists will not be historicists.

The dilemma of genealogists, then, is that if they embrace relativism, then all their claims, justificatory or critical, turn out to be arbitrary, and no one has any reason for accepting them. If they reject relativism and accept that there is some basis for the justification or criticism of our beliefs, values, and practices, they must acknowledge that the basis is not genealogical. Genealogy, therefore, fails to show that history is the overriding mode of understanding, it will not resolve conflicts between modes of understanding, and consequently it will not resolve philosophical problems caused by their conflicts.

History without Genealogy

Nothing I have said should be construed as doubting the importance of the historical mode of understanding. It is of indispensable help toward understanding ourselves and the conditions in which we live. It shows how our predecessors have contended with their conditions, how they understood themselves and what they were about, how they conceived of the possibilities open to them, and how they coped with their problems. Historians may or may not intend the understanding they provide to help us here and now. We can nevertheless learn from what they give us by comparing and contrasting our world-view, our conceptions of our possibilities, and our efforts to cope with our problems with those that prevailed at different times and places. What we can learn in this way is not obvious because the differences between the past and the present are substantial, but so are the continuities. History helps us recognize both the differences and the continuities. That is a great benefit that we would be foolish to deny or ignore.

For the enjoyment of this benefit, however, we do not need genealogy. If genealogy were merely an account of the origin and development of some of our more important beliefs, values, and practices, it would not in any way be objectionable. But then genealogy would be only another name for history, and it is hard to see why we should substitute a pretentious term for the perfectly serviceable one we already have. Genealogists, however, aspire to more than description. They propose justificatory or critical evaluations, and that is where they go wrong. For even if they show that our evaluations are faulty and theirs are not, it would neither justify nor criticize our evaluated beliefs, values, and practices. For their reasonable justification or criticism depends on the rightness or wrongness of the aims of our beliefs, values, and practices, and on how well or badly they serve those aims. And that is not a matter of their genealogy, but of their success or failure in improving our lives here and now, given the contingencies of our world-view and conditions.

6

Morality and Moralism

When we leave the domain of the purely logical we come into the cloudy and shifting domain of the concepts which men live by—and these are subject to historical change. This is especially true of moral concepts.... We should, I think, resist the temptation to unify the picture by trying to establish, guided by our own conception of the ethical in general, what these concepts *must be*. All that is made clear by this method is: our own conception of the ethical in general—and in the process important differences of moral concepts may be blurred or neglected.... Man is a creature who makes pictures of himself and then comes to resemble the picture. This is the process which moral philosophy must attempt to describe and analyse.

Iris Murdoch[1]

What Is Moralism?

Moralism is the misguided tendency to exaggerate the moral importance of what has little or none. Led by this misplaced emphasis, moralists arrogate to themselves a spurious authority to judge others. They cultivate a hyperactive sensitivity that finds serious moral problems behind ordinary, customary practices, and condemn those who resist their bullying for colluding in immorality. They pontificate about how we should live, but their inflated claims actually give morality a bad name.

Here are some egregious examples. According to Kant "by a lie a human being throws away and, as it were, annihilates his dignity as a human being. A human being who does not himself believe what he tells another...has even less worth than if he were a mere thing."[2] If this were true, the kingdom of ends would be severely underpopulated. Mill says that morality requires that "between his own happiness and that of others, utilitarianism requires him to be as strictly impartial as a disinterested and benevolent spectator"; that education should "establish in the mind of every individual an indissoluble association between his own happiness and the good of the whole"; and that a "feeling of unity... [should] be taught as a religion."[3] This is just the kind of sanctimonious absurdity that turns reasonable people against morality. It is moralism that leads Singer to condemn as murderers hundreds of millions of people who live beyond the level of absolute poverty on the grounds that: "by not giving more than we do, people in rich countries are allowing those in poor countries to suffer... malnutrition, ill health, and death" and since, "allowing someone to die is not intrinsically different from killing someone, it would seem that we are all murderers."[4] With one fell swoop, Singer declares as null and void the distinction between Hitler, Stalin, Mao, and their murderous henchmen, on the one hand, and, on the other hand, law-abiding citizens who managed to rise above poverty. Dworkin joins this chorus of moralists by declaring that

no government is legitimate that does not show equal concern for the fate of all those citizens over whom it has dominion and from whom it claims allegiance. Equal concern is the sovereign virtue of a political community—without it government is only tyranny.[5]

It does not faze Dworkin that the preposterous claim follows from his moralism that in human history there has never been a legitimate government because all fell short of what he thinks of as the sovereign virtue.

What has gone wrong in all these cases is that moralists generalize from some contexts in which moral claims are justified to others in which they are unjustified. Lying is wrong, but not when it saves lives; impartiality is a moral requirement in law courts, but not in our relations with those we love; we should help others, but taking a vacation does not make us murderers; equality has become a political value, but past societies are not remiss for failing to conform to a value that has not yet come into existence.

Moralists are sometimes just ridiculous nuisances, as in designing speech codes for how invitation to sex must be phrased, forbidding 20-year-old combat veterans to buy a beer, or treating ethnic jokes as hate crimes. But sometimes moralism is much worse than ridiculous. It has often led to the murder of religious or ideological dissenters; to the persecution of ethnic minorities, infidels, and foreigners; to terrorism, crusades, holy wars, and show trials; and to many other all too familiar horrors committed in the name of morality. The perpetrators of these atrocities typically believe that they are acting in the best interest of humanity, and regard their crimes as not merely morally justified but obligatory. Moralism is prevalent now, and it has been so throughout human history, even when, and especially when, defenders of some orthodoxy succeeded in silencing their critics. To deplore moralism, of course, is not to deplore morality, but to defend it against those who use it to justify their dogmatic and often vicious prejudices.[6]

Moralism in a less extreme form has many more reasonable contemporary defenders as well.[7] They differ in various ways, but they agree about the central claim of moralism that morality is overriding. When what they regard as moral requirements conflict with non-moral requirements, then, they claim, practical reason requires that the conflicts be resolved in favor of moral requirements. Practical reason is thought to require this because morality, alone among the various modes of understanding, is supposed to provide the correct evaluation of all relevant considerations. The evaluations that follow from non-moral modes of understanding are more or less deficient because they fail to ascribe the right weight to relevant considerations, since their main concerns lie elsewhere. Thus, according to moralists, morality is overriding because it conforms to the requirements of practical reason, while non-moral modes of understanding do not, and that makes morality the best approach to improving the human condition. The failure to recognize this is a failure of practical reason, the failure to solve or manage as best as possible in particular circumstances the everyday, modal, philosophical, or epochal problems that stand in the way of good lives. Moralists, then, claim that morality, practical reason and good lives jointly require that the moral mode of understanding should override any other mode of understanding that may conflict with it. I will argue that just as historicism is an unreasonable extension of relativism to history, so moralism is an unreasonable extension of absolutism to morality.

Four Distinctions

Moralism is clarified and strengthened by four distinctions. The first is between the wide and narrow senses of morality. In the wide sense, morality includes all evaluations that bear on the good. Any such evaluation, then, is a moral evaluation. This makes moralism true by definition and transforms it into the trivial claim that morality is overriding because all evaluations having to do with the good are moral and consequently could not conflict with moral evaluations. But conflicts between moral and non-moral evaluations cannot be resolved by defining them out of existence. And even if this definition were accepted, it would not resolve the conflicts between what it arbitrarily defines as moral evaluations. The familiar conflicts between historical, moral, political, religious, scientific, and personal evaluations would reappear as conflicts between evaluations that are now called moral. The wide sense of morality is an obfuscating distraction from facing the serious question of whether practical reason indeed requires that moral evaluations should always override conflicting non-moral evaluations.

In the narrow sense, moral evaluations are directly concerned with the improvement of lives. Historical, political, religious, scientific, or personal evaluations have other concerns and they affect the goodness of human lives at best only indirectly. Their evaluations could, in the narrow sense, conflict with moral evaluations. Moralism is interpreted then as the claim that practical reason requires that moral evaluations should always override conflicting historical, political, religious, scientific, or personal evaluations. This is a clear and substantive moral claim, one that moralists should try to justify.

The second distinction is between a strong and a moderate interpretation of the supposed requirement of practical reason that moral evaluations, narrowly interpreted, should always override conflicting non-moral evaluations. According to the strong interpretation, it is irrational to perform any action that is contrary to practical reason. There can be no reason for such an action, and thinking otherwise is absurd, like trying to grow a third arm. The moderate interpretation allows that there may be some reasons for actions contrary to practical reason, but claim that the balance of reasons clearly tells against them. Such actions are not irrational, because there are some reasons for them, but they are nevertheless unreasonable, because there are much stronger reasons against them, as there are against refusing to undergo a life-saving surgery because one dislikes hospitals.

The strong interpretation of the claim that it is a requirement of practical reason that moral evaluation should always override conflicting non-moral evaluations leads to indefensibly excessive moralistic judgments. The examples cited earlier from the writings of Kant, Mill, Singer, and Dworkin illustrate this excess. The claims of these authors ignore plain facts of psychology and seem to write about a species other than our own. They require us to ignore our conception of how we want to live, a conception formed on the basis of our experiences, values, and social conditions, act contrary to what gives meaning and purpose to our life, and follow a principle that requires us to go against most of what matters to us. They say that this is a requirement of practical reason and morality, and they condemn those who fail to recognize and act according to it for being irrational and immoral. It is to them that Bernard Williams rightly says that

there can come a point at which it is quite unreasonable for a man to give up, in the name of the impartial good ordering of the world of moral agents, something which is a condition of his having interest in being around in that world at all.[8]

Moralists, however, need not accept the strong interpretation from which such excessive claims follow. They may hold that the failure to resolve conflicts between moral and non-moral evaluations in favor of the moral ones is unreasonable, but need not be irrational. There may be some reasons against moral evaluations, but the reasons for them outweigh the reasons against them. This is the moderate interpretation of the claim that practical reason requires that moral evaluations should always override conflicting non-moral evaluations. Moralists can thus acknowledge that when non-moral evaluations, which follow from historical considerations, personal preferences of how we want to live, political interests, religious faith, or scientific research, conflict with moral evaluations, then there may be some reasons in favor of these non-moral evaluations. They will argue, however, that practical reason requires that moral evaluations should override non-moral evaluations. This is not an absurd claim, and the case for moralism is more convincing if it is based on the moderate, rather than the strong, interpretation of the requirement of practical reason. The claim still needs to be justified, but the distinction between the strong and moderate interpretations makes clearer what needs to be justified.

The third distinction is between unconditional and conditional interpretations of moralism. The unconditional interpretation is Kantian. Morality is overriding because moral evaluations are universal and impersonal requirements of practical reason. If something is a moral requirement, it is an absolute requirement that allows no exceptions. Whatever is morally wrong is wrong always, everywhere, for everyone, in all circumstances. No matter what historical, political, religious, scientific, or personal requirement may incline us to act contrary to a moral requirement, it is an unconditional requirement of practical reason that we should act as the moral requirement dictates. This makes it irrational and immoral ever to tell a lie, break a promise, be unkind, not to punish a criminal, fail to pay a debt, and so on, regardless of the circumstances. No reasonable person can accept this, and moralists need not be committed to it. They can adopt the far more reasonable conditional interpretation of moralism.

The conditional interpretation is Ross's.[9] According to it, moral requirements are prima facie, not absolute, requirements of practical reason. They allow for reasonable exceptions, but in one kind of case only: when prima facie moral requirements conflict. In such cases, a prima facie moral requirement may be overridden by another but stronger prima facie moral requirement. It may be reasonable to tell a lie, break a promise, and so forth, if some more important moral requirement, like saving a life, conflicts with it. On this interpretation, moral requirements in general are still overriding, but particular moral requirements are conditional on not being in conflict with more important moral requirements. It may be difficult to tell in particular circumstances which of two conflicting moral requirements is more important, but that just means that we have to stop and think, which may be hard to do. Making moral decisions is often complicated, difficult, and we may make mistakes; that, however, is hardly news. Given the conditional interpretation, moralists still hold that moral requirements should always override conflicting non-moral requirements, not on the ground that moral requirements are always overriding, but on the ground that they are overriding provided they do not conflict with a stronger moral requirement.

The fourth distinction is between two interpretations of what we should do when we override non-moral evaluations. According to one, we should assimilate historical, political, religious, scientific, and personal evaluations to moral ones. Non-moral evaluations are reasonable insofar as they conform to moral requirements. If they do not, they should be dismissed as unreasonable. The resulting view is that morality has veto power over the form and the direction historical, political, religious, scientific, or personal understanding may reasonably take. This interpretation is too restrictive. Civilized life depends on minimal interference with research and the pursuit of a plurality of reasonable but different modes of understanding. Moralists need not burden themselves with becoming censors.

A more reasonable interpretation is that moral evaluations set limits that must be observed by reasonable and plural modes of understanding and the non-moral evaluations that follow from them. Moral evaluations, then, constrain rather than dismiss non-moral evaluations. Moralism is thus more plausibly interpreted as the view that moral evaluations should override non-moral evaluations if non-moral evaluations are contrary to reasonable moral requirements.

In the light of the four distinctions, we can say that the most plausible case for moralism is to interpret morality in the narrow, not wide, sense; the requirement of practical reason as moderate, not strong; moralism as making a conditional, not an unconditional, claim; and moral evaluations as constraining, not dismissing, non-moral evaluations. I think that moralism thus understood is indefensible. I stress, however, that this is not an argument against morality, but against excessive claims made for it. I share this view with many others,[10] but I stop far short of the views of those who are led by the absurdities of moralism to reject morality itself.[11]

The Pluralism of Practical Reason

Essential to moralism is the claim that practical reason requires that there be a principle on the basis of which moral and non-moral evaluations can be distinguished. As Kant puts it, his aim is "nothing more than the search for and establishment of the *supreme principle of morality*."[12] Mill shares this aim:

There must be some standard by which to determine the goodness or badness, absolute and comparative, of ends, or objects of desire. And whatever that standard is, there can be but one: for if there were several ultimate principles of conduct, the same conduct might be approved by one of those principles and condemned by another; and there would be needed some more general principle, as umpire between them. Accordingly, writers on moral philosophy have mostly felt the necessity...of referring...to some one principle;

some rule, or standard, with which all other rules of conduct were required to be consistent, and from which by ultimate consequence they could all be deduced.[13]

Kant and Mill of course propose incompatible supreme principles, and their followers and critics propose a great variety of defenses and criticisms of the refinements of the purported supreme principles. Uncommitted observers of these controversies may reasonably ask why must there be a supreme principle of morality? They will be told that otherwise there could not be a reasonable resolution of conflicts about what makes actions good or bad. It is certainly important to resolve such conflicts reasonably, but why do we need a supreme principle for that? Why must that principle be moral? Why must it be a principle? Why could it not be reasonable to resolve one conflict in one way and another conflict in another way? Why must a resolution that is reasonable in one context also be reasonable in a different context?

Kant, Mill, and those who agree with them in seeking a supreme moral principle will say that we need it to tell us what reason requires us to aim at when we are concerned with the good, just as reason requires us to aim at what is true in all contexts, when we are concerned with the facts. But what is good is not like what is true. If something is true, it is true always and for everyone. If something is good, it need not be good always and for everyone. It may be good for a society at one time to foster scientific research, even if it threatens the prevailing religious orthodoxy; or to cultivate a historical perspective, even if it offends dogmatic moral certainties; or to foster personal projects, even if they lead to disengagement from politics. But it may not be good for that society at another time. And if in another society scientific research demands resources needed elsewhere; if personal projects endanger the political order; or if a historical perspective undermines religious belief, then it is open to argument whether it would be good.

We know that such arguments sometimes can be reasonably settled, because the procedures for settling them are available in civilized societies, and at least occasionally they are successfully followed—indeed, that is in part what makes societies civilized. But the key to that is not appeal to a supposed and usually contested supreme principle, but careful attention to the relevant facts, informed judgment about their likely consequences, and aiming at a consensus acceptable to most reasonable people in that society. Coping with problems in civilized societies often aims at finding a *modus vivendi*, rather than appealing to a supreme principle that all reasonable people in a society accept. In contemporary Western societies there is no such supreme principle, and it is doubtful that there ever was one.

What is good in one context, however, need not be good in another. The good varies with contexts, the truth does not. The good is many, the truth one. Practical reason requires aiming at the good, theoretical reason requires aiming at the truth. Practical reason, therefore, is unlike theoretical reason, because aiming at the good is different from aiming at the truth. The search for a supreme principle of morality, however, rests on the assumption that the requirements of practical and theoretical reason are the same. As Kant puts it, his program requires "the unity of practical with speculative reason in a common principle, since there can, in the end, be only one and the same reason, which must be distinguished merely in its application."[14]

This assumption is fundamentally challenged by a problem Sidgwick had arrived at—one that led him to despair: the dualism of practical reason. Sidgwick was familiar with the supreme principles Kant and Mill proposed, but he recognized that there is an insuperable difficulty in the way of defending any such principle. He was centrally concerned with showing that the requirements of virtue and self-interest coincide. He recognized

the vital need that our Practical Reason feels of proving or postulating this connexion of Virtue and self-interest, if it is to be made consistent with itself. For the negation of the connexion must force us to admit an ultimate and fundamental contradiction in our apparent intuitions of what is Reasonable in conduct; and from this admission it would seem to follow that the apparently intuitive operation of Practical Reason, manifested in these contradictory judgments, is after all illusory.

He concluded with "the profoundest problem in Ethics" which is that—after his ever so conscientious examination of the claims of egoism and utilitarianism—he had to admit that both were reasonable and incompatible.[15] He wrote honestly and with great regret that

hence the whole system of our beliefs as to the intrinsic reasonableness of conduct must fall...the Cosmos of duty is thus really reduced to Chaos: and the prolonged effort of the human intellect to frame a perfect ideal of rational conduct is seen to have been foredoomed to inevitable failure.[16]

What Sidgwick saw as "the profoundest problem in Ethics," however, is even more profound than he had supposed, because there is not only the dualism but also the pluralism of practical reason. There is no good reason to suppose that practical reason requires that morality, interpreted in the narrow sense, should always override the conflicting claims of history, politics, religion, science, and personal concerns.

Historical considerations may show that what used to be regarded as moral requirements, such as humility, chastity outside of marriage, church attendance on Sundays, and avoiding the abominations of money-lending, masturbation, and theater attendance are very far from universal and impersonal requirements of practical reason. We know that vital political interests, such as the survival of one's society, may require actions that are contrary to moral requirements. Devout religious believers are celebrated for saying to prevailing moral authorities that "Here I stand, I can do no other" as they refuse to comply with prevailing moral requirements, as did Abraham in preparing to sacrifice Isaac, Job in accepting what appeared to be God's injustice, and Jesus in commanding his followers to turn the other cheek rather than punish wrongdoers. No one can reasonably suppose that practical reason required Galileo not to lie to inquisitors, or that defecting scientists should not break the promises various dictatorial regimes extracted from them, or that as a matter of kindness an experimental vaccine believed to be effective should be given even to the control group, or that scientists on the brink of an important discovery should give up their research and take a lucrative industrial job in order to meet the repayment schedule for personal loans they have received.

There is also the decisive personal consideration that without a

conscientious man's commitment to ... seek out and weigh what cogent reasons would lead him to do, and to submit himself without self-deception or evasion to their determination ... one may never confront any of one's special obligations. ... All principled conduct which is reasoned practice ... turns on this commitment as its pivot. ... And this commitment has the most intimately personal reason. It rests on an individual's inmost concern to preserve himself intact as a living and functioning self: mentally in possession of himself and of his world, able to look at himself and what he is doing without having to hide himself from himself.[17]

To live this way is not to legislate for all of humanity, but only for ourselves. Nor is it to pursue the good of everyone equally, but only of our own. We can legislate for others and pursue the common good only if we have committed ourselves to "the principled mode of life as such." And "if no commitment may count as 'moral' unless one has it on account of others [that is in the narrow sense of morality], then the commitment to the practice of non-evasive living cannot properly count as a 'moral' commitment at all."[18]

I conclude that if morality is interpreted in the narrow sense, then, for the preceding reasons, it is not true that practical reason requires that moral requirements should be always overriding. Furthermore, the commitment to non-evasive living may take a plurality of forms. It may be to historical understanding, conscientious moral conduct, political practice, religious faith, scientific research, or the pursuit of personal projects. The commitment to conscientious moral conduct is merely one among others. Moralists have not shown that practical reason requires that in weighing cogent reasons, being non-evasive, and living a principled mode of life we must regard moral requirements as overriding. We may just think, as countless reasonable and decent people do, that many moral requirements are important but so are many non-moral requirements. And when the various requirements whose force we recognize conflict, as they will, then, depending on the circumstances, reason does not require, but allows, that sometimes one, sometimes another of the requirements should override the others. If, however, morality is interpreted in the wide sense, then all requirements become moral. As we have seen, however, the conflicts between moral and non-moral requirements will then recur as conflicts between different types of moral requirements, and no one type will be always overriding.

It may be supposed that moralism can still be defended by combining its narrow and conditional interpretations. The conditional Rossian interpretation claims that moral requirements are prima facie. This allows that moral requirements may conflict, whereas the unconditional interpretation does not. Ross argues, however, that conflicts between moral requirements can be resolved reasonably because more important moral requirements should override less important ones. Doubts about which of the conflicting moral requirements is more important can be resolved by considering the context in which the conflict occurs. Moralism, then, is the apparently reasonable view that reason and morality require that if moral requirements conflict, then the more important moral requirement should override the less important one.

I say that this view is only apparently reasonable, because, while it is reasonable within the limits it recognizes, the limits are set so as to assume what needs to be shown, namely that moral requirements are overriding. Of course more important moral requirements should override less important moral requirements that conflict with them. But why does Ross consider only conflicts between moral requirements? What about conflicts between admittedly important moral requirements and important requirements that follow from historical, political, religious, scientific, or personal modes of understanding? Why do reason and morality require that moral requirements should override whatever non-moral requirement conflicts with them? I have found no answer in Ross's work to this question.

In two excellent articles, however, Copp and McLeod consider the question.[19] They recognize that what would be needed to answer the question in favor of moralism and in support of Ross's view is that there be what McLeod calls a "just plain 'ought,'" that is an ought that does not assume any particular mode of understanding. Only if it followed from the just plain ought that important moral requirements ought to override conflicting important non-moral requirements would moralism be the correct view. The question, then, becomes whether there is such a just plain ought. It seems to me that Foot's answer is still exactly right (even though she came to doubt it):

This "ought"—the one in the sentence "One ought to be moral"—is supposed to be free floating and unsubscripted, and I have never found anyone who would explain the use of the word in such a context.... My own conclusion is that "One ought to be moral" makes no sense at all unless the "ought" has the moral subscript, giving a tautology, or else relates morality to some other system such as prudence or etiquette.[20]

This conclusion is strengthened by recognizing that defenders of the claim that reason requires that moral requirements should override conflicting non-moral requirements is either arbitrary or leads to infinite regress. A supposedly overriding moral requirement must rest on some standard that is independent of morality and does not assume what is at issue. If there is no such standard, then the claim is arbitrary. If there is one, then it must also rest on some standard independent of it, and that standard, if it is not arbitrary, must also rest on some standard independent of it, and so on ad infinitum.[21] It seems, then, that the conditional interpretation of moralism is in the last analysis no more defensible than the unconditional interpretation.

The All Things Considered View

Practical reason requires doing what seems best after we have considered all that is relevant. We can do that, however, only after we have decided what is relevant. Part of making this decision is not very difficult if we leave behind generalities and concentrate on concrete situations. We have to decide what to do in order to solve or manage an everyday, modal, philosophical, or epochal problem that stands in the way of improving our lives. The relevant facts are those that aid or hinder our practical approaches. If there is disagreement about the relevance of some consideration, then those who disagree need to explain why they think that it aids or hinders our specific efforts. There is no reason why such disagreements could not be reasonably settled, even if it is sometimes difficult to reach agreement. After all, disagreements within history, morality, politics, religion, science, and personal preferences are frequently and reasonably resolved. And if they persist in a particular case, we still have to act, and do as well as we can even if we are uncertain about what is the best.

The really serious difficulty in the way of considering all relevant things is disagreement about the significance of the facts, not about what they are. The source of this disagreement is that those who evaluate the significance of the facts from the point of view of different modes of understanding rely on different practical and reflective approaches, and on different standards of success and failure. I have stressed this point again and again, but I do so once more because one of its implications is that the search for all relevant considerations is futile. The difficulty in the way of solving or managing a particular problem will make this clear. The problem is what to do about the current wave of terrorism by Islamic fanatics.

If the problem is approached from a historical point of view, then the significance of the facts will emerge from understanding the longstanding Islamic tradition of jihad, from the persistent hostilities between Sunnis and Shiites that runs through Islamic history, from how centuries of domination by Christian Western powers appears to Islamic thinkers, and from the Western tradition of responding to threats directed against the very foundation of Western societies, such threats as were represented, among others, by Nazism and Communism.

If the significance of the facts is sought from a moral point of view, it will be thought to depend on what the morally acceptable responses are to terrorists whose conscious policy is to outrage Western moral sensibilities and who feel justified to use any means at their disposal to undermine Western societies. The significance of the facts will depend on our evaluations of whether morally justified responses should be based on compassion, justice, an impartial concern for the welfare of everyone affected by our actions, including terrorists and the security forces who defend us from them, or whether our responses should be guided by the common good or by the good of Western societies.

If we seek to cope with terrorism by relying on a political point of view, our evaluations will focus on what defensive and aggressive measures would be consistent with the best interest of Western societies, cause the least damage to the prevailing ways of life, and would be acceptable to the electorate whose cooperation and general consensus are necessary for finding a reasonable response. We will be concerned with how much of our economic resources should be devoted to countering the threat and the funding of what programs should be reduced in order to finance whatever measures are thought to be necessary.

If it is a religious understanding we seek, we will be concerned with distinguishing between Islamic faith and fanaticism, forming a reasonable view of what Islamic theologians have in mind who encourage the faithful to be indifferent to common human concerns and how they justify attacks on innocent people. We will ask whether our own religious tradition is best protected by waging a contemporary version of a Crusade, whether Islam and Christianity are just different ways of seeking the same God so that a dialogue leading to mutual understanding might be possible, whether the neighbors we are enjoined to love include those who want to kill us. And as we ask these and other questions, we will come to see the significance of the facts in the light of the mode of understanding that lead us to ask the questions.

If we consider terrorism from a scientific point of view, we will be concerned with developing effective defensive measures, including surveillance, screening travelers and immigrants, detecting of nuclear and biological weapons, as well as effective offensive measures that will cause the least loss of life and injury. We will wonder whether there is a reliable scientific approach to understanding the psychology and sociology of terrorists and suicide bombers who are quite willing to lose their lives in service of their cause.

If it is a personal understanding of terrorism we seek, then our main concern will be with evaluating the facts on the basis of how they affect our present and future lives and the lives of those we care about. We will wonder how seriously we should take the threat; what, if anything, we should do to help coping with it; whether we have to revise such understanding of the world as we have managed to arrive at; and what we ourselves should make of the various historical, moral, political, religious, and scientific understandings that have been proposed in our society.

It must be obvious by now that the recommendation to consider all that is relevant is useless, unless it tells us what the point of view is from which we should do so. Defenders of the recommendation might say that what practical reason requires is the consideration of the significance of all relevant facts from all the available points of view put together. According to them, practical reason requires the consideration of all things in a way that combines the accounts of significance that emerge from all the various modes of understanding. If this were possible, then practical reason would indeed require doing it, but it cannot be done, because it is impossible to combine conflicting accounts of the significance of all the relevant facts.

Historical, moral, political, religious, scientific, and personal evaluations of the significance of the relevant facts are not merely different—they are mutually exclusive. Their defenders evaluate the facts in conflicting ways. Such conflicts will not be about what the facts are, but about their relative importance to arriving at a reasonable way of solving or managing the problem at hand. A historical understanding will focus on the past influences that have formed terrorism, to which our present moral, political, religious, scientific, and personal responses will have little relevance. The main concern of the moral approach will be to evaluate the facts in the light of whatever the supreme moral principle is thought to be, and all else will be subordinated to that concern. And the same will be true of the political, religious, scientific, and personal modes of understanding. Modes of understanding are what they are because they are committed to the evaluation of the significance of the facts in accordance with their own practical and reflective approaches, but they differ from mode to mode.

It will seem from the point of view of each mode of understanding that defenders of the other modes are misjudging the significance of the facts. And defenders of each mode will claim that their own account of significance should override the accounts that follow from the other modes. The all things considered view was meant to resolve the resulting philosophical problems by claiming that what should be overriding is the view that emerges from the combination of all the modes of understanding, rather than any of the particular views that follow from any of the modes of understanding. But such a view cannot be constructed because it would have to be formed of mutually exclusive accounts of significance.

Let us suppose, however, that a view could be constructed that would somehow manage to combine the accounts of significance that follow from the historical, moral, political, religious, scientific, and personal modes of understanding. This would be as serious an objection to moralism as the objections are that I have so far discussed. For it is a consequence of this view that moral requirements could not be overriding. They could be merely one of many different kinds of requirements that follow from the different modes of understanding that have been combined, none of which would be always overriding, since each would be only one of the many requirements that have to be combined. Moralists, therefore, cannot reasonably identify the moral point of view with the all things considered one. They may resort to the desperate measure of defining the synoptic view as the moral point of view, but this will do nothing to help their case. For it is open to the defenders of the claim that their own mode of understanding is overriding to propose an equally arbitrary definition of their favored mode as the all things considered view, and then all the philosophical problems will have to be faced again in the now corrupted form of warring arbitrary definitions.

There remains a last consideration that moralists may advance in favor of their position. They may concede that it does not follow from the all things considered view that moral requirements should always override all conflicting non-moral requirements, but claim that moral requirements should always constrain conflicting non-moral requirements. It is of moral concern what effect acting on historical, political, religious, scientific, or personal practical approaches would have on the improvement of our lives. No one can reasonably regard this as a matter of indifference. It may be that some of these approaches unavoidably cause some harm to innocent people, but it is also true that much harm is avoidable. It is always a reasonable question to ask whether the likely harm that follows from an approach is avoidable. If it is, then reason requires avoiding it. Moralism, then, would not be the claim that reason requires that moral requirements should always override conflicting non-moral requirements, but that reason requires that moral requirements should always constrain conflicting non-moral requirements.

This claim is true, but it does not show that moral requirements are more important than historical, political, religious, scientific, or personal requirements. Moral requirements should constrain non-moral ones, but each of these non-moral requirements should constrain the others. Reason requires that moral requirements should take into account the historical and political conditions of a society, the religious beliefs of the people who live in it, the possibilities and impossibilities vouchsafed for by the current state of science, and the extent to which personal projects whose pursuit makes our lives worth living would be affected by moral constraints. Reason requires that each of these types of requirements should constrain each of the other, and that all practical approaches should be constrained by them. Conformity to such constraints is part of what makes an approach reasonable. But reason does not require, it in fact forbids, that any one type of requirement should always override any of the others. They all have veto power over the others. The necessity of solving or managing everyday, modal, philosophical, or epochal problems may require overriding the veto, but normally reason requires solving or managing problems by taking into account the prevailing historical, moral, political, religious, scientific, and personal conditions and commitments of the people living together in a society. As we do that, the conflicts whose resolutions give rise to the philosophical problems come flooding back.

Overriding Moral Considerations

Moralists may respond to the preceding objections by citing cases in which moral considerations are indeed overriding. Here is Dostoyevsky:

Imagine that it is you yourself who are erecting the edifice of human destiny with the aim of making men happy in the end, giving them peace and contentment at last, but to do that it is absolutely necessary, indeed quite inevitable to torture to death only one tiny creature, the little girl who beats her breast with her little fist, and found the edifice on her unavenged tears—would you consent to be the architect on those conditions?[22]

William James writes in a remarkably similar passage, that

if the hypothesis were offered us of a world in which . . . utopias should all be outdone, and millions kept permanently happy on the simple condition that a certain lost soul on the far-off edge of things should lead a life of lonely torture, what except a specifical and independent sort of emotion can it be which would make us immediately feel . . . how hideous a thing would be its enjoyment when deliberately accepted as the fruit of such a bargain?[23]

These cases may be rejected on the ground that the imagined situations could not occur, but it is not hard to think of realistic cases in which all decent people would find moral requirements overriding, such as not to cut off someone's limb for fun; not to silence noisy infants by frying them; or not to blow up an orchestra because it plays badly. Any reasonable person will recognize that in some cases moral considerations are overriding. Defenders and critics of moralism can agree about that.

What moralists claim, however, is not that moral considerations are *sometimes* overriding, but that when moral and non-moral considerations conflict, then practical reason requires that moral considerations should *always* override non-moral ones. And that is the claim that critics of moralism reject. It can be said of each mode of understanding that practical reason requires that the claims that follow from it should sometimes override conflicting claims that follow from the other modes. Of course there are cases in which conflicting evaluations of the significance of facts should be resolved in favor of historical, or moral, or political, or scientific, or personal considerations. The claim I am rejecting is that practical reason requires that conflicts between modes of understanding should always be resolved in favor of any one of the modes. Practical reason favors a particular way of resolving such conflicts in all contexts, but what that way is varies with contexts and conflicts.

It is not true that the requirements of morality and practical reason always coincide. It is not true that morality is more concerned with the good than any of the other modes of understanding. And it is not true that moral values or principles are always overriding, not even that they are always more important for the improvement of lives than non-moral values or principles.

Morality without Moralism

I have stressed throughout this chapter, and I do so again, that the rejection of moralism is not the rejection of morality. Morality is an important mode of understanding and we cannot do without it. Civilized life depends on peaceful coexistence with others who have different beliefs, values, commitments, interests, and projects. Morality is one of the most important ways of making this possible—but it is only one of them. It sets reasonable limits to how we might act and it provides reasonable possibilities we may try to realize—but each mode of understanding does this. It is an ever-present temptation to believe that the limits and possibilities of the mode of understanding we value most are more significant than those of the others. The temptation, however, should be resisted, because giving in to it leads to the mistake of supposing that what we value most is most valuable. Nothing is most valuable always, everywhere, in all conditions and contexts. There may be something that is most valuable in every condition, but conditions change and what is most valuable in one need not be most valuable in another.

There are permanent human interests, but the forms in which they present themselves, the problems that threaten their realization, the available means of protecting the interests and coping with the problems, the conditions in which we have to employ the means, and the severity of the problems forever change. Reason requires balancing these conditions as well as we can, given their contingencies, and our fallibility and disagreements. That we must live under such conditions is the human condition, and we cannot alter it. Moralism is one form of the attempt to transcend our condition, but the attempt cannot succeed because it is subject to the condition it attempts to transcend. Philosophical problems indicate the futility of such attempts.

Moralists believe that if we abandon the search for a supreme principle of morality, unconditional moral values, and the commitment to take into account all relevant considerations, then we end up without a reasonable way of resolving conflicts among the plurality of values we hold. If the proposed conflict-resolutions do not assume that one of the conflicting values should always override the others, then, moralists think, we will end up with reciprocal charges of arbitrariness and dogmatism. The underlying assumption is that the alternative to moralism is relativism.

The source of this assumption is the belief shared by both moralists and relativists that conflict-resolutions can be reasonable only if we can appeal to some unconditional value or supreme principle whose authority is recognized by all reasonable approaches to conflict-resolution. Moralists think that such a value or principle can be found, while relativists deny it. But they agree that reasonable conflict-resolution depends on it. I have been arguing throughout this chapter that this shared belief is mistaken. Conflicts among a wide plurality of values can be reasonably resolved without appealing to a supposedly unconditional value or supreme principle. Of course, we still need something to which we can reasonably appeal, something that allows us to avoid the ultimate arbitrariness of both moralism and relativism, and I must say now what that something is.

It is our shared concern with solving or managing the particular problems we face in our particular circumstances. Our concern, however, is not merely with our problems, but with coping with them in a way that leaves as intact as possible the world-view formed of the particular historical, moral, political, religious, scientific, and personal values on which the identity of our society and the meaningfulness of our lives to a large extent depend. A society deserves our support if we can count on it to provide the possibilities we want to pursue and to protect our efforts to pursue them by setting and enforcing limits to how that may be done. We habitually pursue some of these possibilities and adhere to the limits because we draw from them the values that make our lives worth living. It is to this system of values, and to the world-view of which the values are parts, that we can reasonably appeal to in order to resolve conflicts among the values whose legitimacy we recognize.

Our appeal, then, is not to an unconditional value or to a supreme principle, but to a valued way of life we want to perpetuate. There is for this no blueprint or a priori theory that provides a universal and impersonal procedure that would tell us what we must do when we face a particular problem and conflicting values guide us regarding how we should cope with it. We need to cope with the problem and we need to resolve the conflicts between various practical approaches to it, but how we might do it varies with the system of values and world-view in the background and the particularities of the circumstances, the problem, and the conflict. Our task is analogous to raising our children well, doing our part to sustain a good marriage, or being conscientious in discharging the various aesthetic, intellectual, moral, personal, political, prudential, religious, and other responsibilities we recognize ourselves as having. There is no set way of doing any of this. Nevertheless, some ways are more reasonable than others, and if we are guided by practical reason we can distinguish between them, explain why they are more or less reasonable, and act accordingly—but only in particular circumstances, not once and for all as dictated by morality or any other mode of understanding.

7

Politics and Ideology

The man of system...is often so enamoured with the supposed beauty of his own ideal plan of government, that...he seems to imagine that he can arrange the different members of a great society with as much ease as the hand arranges the different pieces upon a chess-board; he does not consider that...in the great chess-board of human society, every single piece has a principle of motion of its own, altogether different from that which the legislature might choose to impress upon it....To insist upon establishing...in spite of all opposition, every thing which that...[ideal plan] may seem to require, must often be the highest degree of arrogance. It is to erect his own judgment into the supreme standard of right and wrong.

Adam Smith[1]

In Chapters 5 and 6 I aimed to show that historicism and moralism are unsuccessful approaches to coping with philosophical problems. The historical and moral modes of understanding are certainly important components of our world-view, but it is a mistake to inflate their importance by claiming that the true significance of the facts emerges from historical or moral evaluations, which should always override any other consideration that may conflict with them. In this chapter, I will argue that the same is true of the political mode of understanding. Many philosophical problems have political causes and implications, but they also have non-political ones. It is a mistake to exaggerate the significance of political at the expense of conflicting non-political considerations.

It would be convenient if "politism" were a word that I could use—analogously with historicism and moralism—to refer to the mistake of inflating the significance of the political mode of understanding, unfortunately the dictionaries do not countenance it. But I do need a word to refer to this mistake and I have opted for "ideology." I considered and rejected "politicization" as a possibility on the grounds of euphony. I emphasize that I am not going to deny that political considerations sometimes should override conflicting non-political considerations. I claim only that they should not always do so.

If, however, ideology is to be more than the name for what I take to be a mistake, I need to explain what exactly I mean by it, why it is supposed to have overriding importance, why ideologies in one form or another appeal to so many people, and why all ideologies, wherever they stand on the political spectrum, rest on mistaken and dangerous assumptions.

What Is an Ideology?

Freeden's definition is a good beginning:

Ideologies are usefully comprehended...as ubiquitous and patterned forms of thinking about politics. They are clusters of ideas, beliefs, opinions, values, and attitudes usually held by identifiable groups, that provide directives, even plans, of action for public policy-making in an endeavour to uphold, justify, change or criticize the social and political arrangements of a state or other political community....Ideologies differ from one another in the particular meaning they allocate to every one of the main political concepts, in the priority they accord each concept, and in the particular position and interrelationship between each concept and other political concepts contained within the given ideological field.[2]

Some examples of contemporary ideologies are communism, conservatism, fascism, feminism, liberalism, nationalism, Nazism, and socialism. Each has numerous versions, and some of them are not ideological.

Ideologies are intended to defend, reform, or overthrow some or all of the political arrangements of a society. They are held by people in social groups, such as nations, political parties, ethnic or religious communities, majorities or minorities. They may be primarily religious or secular, egalitarian or anti-egalitarian, traditionalist or radical, parliamentary or revolutionary, economic or cultural, individualist or communitarian, and so forth. They aim to affect many aspects of life in a society, including criminal justice, defense, economics, education, foreign relations, immigration, law enforcement, legislation, privacy, public health, torts, trade, welfare, and so forth. Ideologies prescribe more or less coercively, depending on their beliefs and values, what political arrangements should govern these aspects of life within and often outside of a society.

This description is compatible with a wide and narrow sense of ideologies. In the wide sense, an ideology is what I have called a world-view. In that sense, every society has an ideology. But I will understand ideologies in the narrow sense in which they are meant to be specifically political and focus on the political arrangements that a society ought to have. Of course, the world-views of all societies strongly influence their political arrangements, but ideologies in the narrow sense influence them in a particular way: by aiming to transform the prevailing political arrangements in accordance with a hierarchical system of specifically political values.

Ideologies differ, partly because they are committed to different hierarchies of political values, and especially to one or a small number of them as the highest that should override whatever other political or non-political values conflict with it or them. Some, but by no means all, contemporary political thinkers are committed to an ideology in the narrow sense. They are the ideologues. They advocate different hierarchies of value in which different values, for instance equality, justice, liberty, national supremacy, prosperity, racial purity, religious doctrine, rights, or the rule of law are held to be the highest. Whatever the highest value is, it is the ideal in accordance with ideologues that aim to transform their society's political arrangements so that they would approximate more and more closely the ideal. The promise of ideologies is that the extent to which this transformation is effected is the extent to which the lives of people in their society will be liberated from coercion, conflicts, crimes, exploitation, frustrations, injustice, poverty, repression, scarcity, and other political problems that presently permeate the society.

The pursuit of this ideal requires the identification of the specific political problems that need to be solved and an explanation of their causes. Ideologies are practical. They do not merely defend abstract ideals, but propose ways of solving specific political problems. They say, for instance, that the problems are discrimination based on race, gender, or class; unequal access to education or to medical care; treachery by a minority living in their midst; poor diet or housing; the abandonment of tried and true traditions; the corruption, indifference, or stupidity of politicians, judges, and civil servants; the spread of irreligion; and so on. And the causes of the political problems are specific individuals or groups: the rich, the criminals, the police, the corporations, the party in power, the immigrants, foreign enemies, the freeloaders, the indifference of the public, and the like.

Ideologues, then, propose specific policies whose aim is to solve specific political problems. The policies will be, for example, nationalization, limiting the power of the group that abuses it, strict law enforcement, just tax laws, education that teaches the right values, holding officials accountable, and so forth. The justification of the policies is supposed to be that they are instrumental to the transformation of the political arrangements of the society in accordance with the ideal. The policies are needed to solve the problems, which are caused by the violation of the values embedded in the ideology's hierarchy of values. Policies that implement the values are the key to the realization of human potentialities. And the justification for doing all this is said to be the improvement of lives from what they wretchedly are to what they ought to be.

Ideologies, then, are intended to transform the political arrangements of a society. These arrangements are assumed to constitute both the framework within which all non-political aspects of life take place and the economic, legal, social, and other conditions that provide the possibilities and set the limits in accordance with people in a society live and act. Most people do not question the overall political framework and conditions of their society. They become concerned, if they do, with only a few of them that they find particularly unsatisfactory. But ideologues are centrally concerned with questioning the prevailing political arrangements. They regard such questioning as necessary for justifying or criticizing the political framework and conditions, and for protecting, reforming, or overthrowing them.

The reason why ideologies are supposed by their defenders to be overriding, why their account of the significance of the facts is thought to be deeper than those of conflicting accounts, whether or not ideologectal, is that the right ideology evaluates the prevailing framework and the conditions in which all other activities take place. The various modes of understanding provided by history, morality, religion, science, and our individuality lack depth if they do not evaluate the significance of political facts that makes these non-political modes of understanding possible. And the extent to which they do this, the extent to which they become aware of the conditions that enable them to understand anything, is the extent to which they will implicitly or explicitly recognize that ideological considerations are overriding.

The Appeal of Ideologies

The appeal of ideologies is that they offer an ideal for the improvement of lives. They propose a program that is at once intellectual, action-oriented, has great emotive appeal, and provides an imaginative view of how much better life would be if only the ideal inspired concerted action and its enemies were defeated. Their appeal is particularly strong for those who are directly or indirectly beset by the political problems of their society, who are at a loss to understand why the prevailing conditions are as bad as they are, and who seek in vain for something to do about it. Such people see themselves as helpless in the face of the massive power structures or bureaucratic systems that surround them and to which they are subject. They will be likely to find whatever ideology happens to come their way particularly attractive. Religious fundamentalism, oriental cults, utopian fantasies, magic, mysticism, numerology, and other visionary weeds of unreason have a similar appeal.[3]

As Geertz perceptively writes:

Ideology is a response to strain.... It is a loss of orientation that most directly gives rise to ideological activity, an inability, for the lack of usable models, to comprehend the universe of civic rights and responsibilities in which one finds oneself located.... It is a confluence of sociopsychological strain and an absence of cultural resources by means of which to make sense of the strain, each exacerbating the other, that sets the stage for the rise of systematic (political, moral, or economic) ideologies. And it is, in turn, the attempt of ideologies to render otherwise incomprehensible social situations meaningful, to so construe them as to make it possible to act purposefully within them, that accounts...for the intensity with which, once accepted, they are held.[4]

Although the ideological approach to politics is widespread, I do not claim that all contemporary conservatives, feminists, liberals, nationalists, socialists, and so forth are ideologues. Many people are strongly committed to political views without commitment to their ideological versions. Politics need not be ideological, although it often becomes so when non-ideological policies are consistently challenged. Then their defenders need to justify them, and this often, but not always, leads them to appeal to the ideological version of their previously non-ideological view.

Ideologues often combine their view with moralism and thereby reinforce the political appeal of the ideal embedded in their ideologies by the claim that following it is an overriding moral requirement. They routinely claim that their ideology's hierarchy of values is not just political but also moral, and that it is the key to the improvement of society and individual lives. If the policies that follow from an ideology are justified both by their necessity for solving pressing political problems and by being requirements of morality, then ideologues and their followers can see themselves as doing not only what needs to be done, but also what it is morally obligatory to do.

In the interest of keeping our feet firmly on the ground it may be helpful, by way of illustration, to recall how a contemporary ideology actually exemplifies the preceding description of ideologies and explanation of their appeal. I have in mind John Rawls' theory of justice.[5] It is perhaps the most influential contemporary statement of an ideology, and it has the great virtue of making explicit and attempting to justify the assumptions on which it rests. In its hierarchy of political values, justice stands highest. "Justice is the first virtue of social institutions...laws and institutions no matter how efficient and well-arranged must be reformed or abolished if they are unjust."[6] Justice consists in distributing benefits so as always to favor the least advantaged regardless of why they are in that position. Rawls explains political problems as resulting from a failure to follow the ideal of justice, and he advocates policies that are instrumental to the approximation of the ideal. He also offers a vision, which is "objective and expresses our autonomy," "it enables us to be impartial" and "to see our place in society from the perspective of this position is to see it *sub specie aeternitatis*," "it is a certain form of thought and feeling that rational persons can adopt," and "purity of heart, if one could attain it, would be to see clearly and to act with grace and self-command from this point of view."[7]

The quoted passages are likely to be familiar to readers. I hope, however, that they will ask, as I am led to ask, why we should think that justice is the first virtue of social institutions, rather than order, peace, prosperity, or security? Why must social institutions have a first virtue, rather than several equally important ones? Why should principles of justice primarily benefit the least advantaged, rather than those who deserve it, or who benefit society most, or who are victims of crimes, or who work hard? Why must purity of heart take the form of impartiality, rather than love of one's family, loyalty to a cause, conscientiously doing ones responsibilities, or being wholeheartedly committed to beauty, scientific research, or historical understanding?

I will now proceed to give reasons against ideologies. These reasons will not be directed against any specific ideology, but against the very idea that ideological considerations should always override whatever non-ideological considerations conflict with them. The idea rests on mistaken assumptions and it is morally dangerous and imprudent.

Mistaken Assumptions

The mistaken assumptions on which ideologies rest will become apparent if we examine their commitment to an ideal. Ideologues disagree, of course, about what the ideal is and how best to pursue it, but they agree that one way or another, pursuing one ideal or another, that is what politics ought to aim at. I think that this agreement is misguided regardless of what the ideal is and how it is pursued. It rests on two mistaken assumptions, which I will discuss in turn. The first is that without an ideal we would not know how to solve or manage political problems. The second is that if we had an ideal, we would pursue it.

Most ideologues are not explicit about holding these assumptions, but, as so often, Rawls is an exception. He writes about the first assumption that "the reason for beginning with ideal theory is that it provides, I believe, the only basis for the systematic grasp of these more pressing problems." Such an ideal is "a vision of the way in which the aims and purposes of social cooperation are to be understood" and the ideal "presents a conception of just society that we are to achieve if we can."[8] Is it true that unless we begin with an ideal we would not know how to grasp the political problems we face? No one with the slightest familiarity with actual past or present of approaches to political problems could believe this.

To begin with, some of the most influential political thinkers do not begin with an ideal but with the problems themselves. This is how Aristotle, Machiavelli,

Hobbes, Locke, Hume, Tocqueville, and, closer to our times, Popper, Oakeshott, Aron, Dunn, and Geuss proceed. Rawls and other ideologues could not be ignorant of the influential works of at least some of these political thinkers. And if, unlikely as it is, they are ignorant, they should not make claims about what can and cannot be done toward solving or managing political problems.

Furthermore, it is wildly unrealistic to suppose that without an ideal to dictate our policies, we would be helpless in the face of murder and mayhem, epidemics, deteriorating infrastructure, foreign aggression, pollution, adverse trade agreements, or inflation. We have public officials and organizations whose task is to cope with such problems, and sometimes they do so quite successfully without deriving their policies from an ideal. They certainly have an aim, which is to reduce the rate of violent crime, prevent the spread of a disease, repair highways and bridges, and so forth. For that, however, they need experience and expertise, not conservative, feminist, liberal, nationalist, or socialist ideology.

Scarcity of resources, conflicting interests, ignorance of causes, incompetence, or the reluctance to make hard choices may handicap practical efforts. But the various conflicting ideologies on offer merely exacerbate such problems by adding meddling ideologues to them, motivated by conflicting ideals rather than by the urgency of the problems and the need to overcome obstacles in the way of solving or managing them. The police, public health officials, civil engineers, diplomats, treasury officials, and so forth know perfectly well how to grasp the problems and what needs to be done to solve or manage them without appealing to an ideal. And they know also that the most effective way of doing so is rarely feasible because historical, moral, political, religious, scientific, and personal considerations routinely, and often rightly, set limits to what they can do. Politicians may reasonably accept or reject the recommendations of experts. The grasping of the problems and the offering of ways of solving or managing them, however, must come first, and the ideal, if indeed there is one, can only follow.

The obvious alternative to approaching political problems by relying on an ideal, therefore, is to concentrate on the problems themselves and try to cope with them as best we can given the available resources and the possibilities and limits recognized in the society in which we live. What we aim at is not to bring our society closer to an ideal, but to make it a little less difficult to live in it.[9] We want fewer deaths from diseases, fewer people living in poverty, fewer murders, fewer terrorist attacks, better roads, better trade agreements, better education, and so forth. Reasonable people can readily agree about the importance of proceeding in this way, even if they have sharp ideological disagreements, or indeed even if they have no ideological commitments. On the basis of these considerations, I conclude that the first assumption on which the supposed necessity of having a political ideal rests is mistaken. It is not true that without a political ideal we would not how to grasp and cope with our problems.

Turning to the second assumption, let us assume that we do have an ideal and have somehow been convinced that it is superior to its rivals and that we would be helpless without it. Make the ideal what you like: conservative, feminist, liberal, nationalist, socialist, or whatever. The second assumption on which they all rest is that if we have what we believe is an overriding ideology, then its ideal will be followed.[10] Ideologues of all stripes are committed to assuming that whatever the highest value of the hierarchical system of values they favor—equality, justice, liberty, national interest, rights, and so forth—will be followed by all who understand what is at stake. What reason is there for this assumption?

The supposed reason, to put it plainly, is that human beings are basically good. If they understand what the good is, as Plato's Socrates claimed a long time ago, they will act on it. Some highly influential ideologues are explicit about this. According to Rousseau, "man is naturally good; I believe I have demonstrated it" and "the fundamental principle of all morality, about which I have reasoned in all my works...is that man is a naturally good creature, who loves justice and order; that there is no original perversity in the human heart."[11] Kant writes that man is "*not basically* corrupt (even as regards his original predisposition to good), but rather...still capable of improvement" and "man (even the most wicked) does not, under any maxim whatsoever, repudiate the moral law.... The law, rather, forces itself upon him irresistibly by virtue of his moral predisposition."[12] Mill thinks that the "leading department of our nature," which is a "powerful natural sentiment," namely "the social feeling of mankind—the desire to be in unity with our fellow creatures, which is already a powerful principle in human nature, and happily one of those which tend to become stronger, even without express inculcation."[13] This optimistic view of Rousseau, Kant, and Mill is shared by many contemporary thinkers.[14]

Against this amazing optimism stand the hard facts of past and present politics. Perhaps ideologues can condemn the horrors of Nazi, communist, and some nationalist and religious ideologies. They may regard them as aberrations to which some ideologies, but of course not their own, may be liable. And they may rightly claim that ideologies in general should no more be condemned by the terrible uses to which they have been put than science or religion. But this defense still leaves serious political problems, even though there are well-intentioned ideologies that have not led to horrors. If such ideologies are readily available in the contemporary world, and if we are basically good, why is there widespread poverty, unemployment, drug addiction, fraud, violence, substandard education, domestic and foreign terrorism, warring gangs, murderous drug syndicates, and organized crime? Why is there rampant commercialism, recurrent economic crises, and political corruption?

The well-known ideological answer is that such problems are precisely the ones that exist in our present non-ideal conditions and make it necessary to transform society in accordance with the right ideal. But the ideologues who acknowledge the seriousness of the problems that beset us do not ask the obvious question to which they owe an answer: why are some existing political arrangements unjust, repressive, immoral, exploitative, illegal, discriminatory, corrupt, or, in general, bad?

Bad political arrangements are made and maintained by us. If they are bad, it is because we make or maintain them badly. It may be that we do it badly because we have been corrupted by bad political arrangements, but sooner or later this explanation comes to an end. It must eventually be acknowledged that we are the causes and the political arrangements we make and maintain are the effects. To try to explain why we make and maintain bad political arrangements by the arrangements we make and maintain is to try to explain causes by their effects. The conclusion is inescapable that if political arrangements are bad, it is because we are bad. And if we are bad, then our bad selves will prevent us from following the ideology. The amazingly optimistic second assumption on which ideologies rest—that if we understand their ideal, then we will follow it—is belied by the existence of the very problems that supposedly create the need for ideologies. I conclude that this assumption is also mistaken.

What, then, is the alternative to proceeding on the second assumption? It is to follow the more realistic recommendation of political thinkers who were far from likeminded about other matters. According to Machiavelli, "it is essential that anyone setting up a republic and establishing a constitution for it should assume that all men are wicked and will always vent to their evil impulses whenever they have a chance to do so."[15] Or as Hume put it:

> political writers have established it as a maxim, that, in contriving any system of government, and fixing the checks and controuls of the constitution, every man ought to be supposed a *knave*, and to have no other end, in all his actions, than private interest. By this interest we must govern him, and, by means of it, make him, notwithstanding his insatiable avarice and ambition, co-operate to public good. Without this, say they, we shall in vain boast of the advantages of any constitution, and shall find, in the end, that we have no security for our liberty and possessions, except the good-will of our rulers; that is, we shall have no security at all.[16]

Moral Dangers

The reasons why ideologies are morally dangerous emerge if we consider the frame of mind of ideologues who are convinced that they hold the key to coping with the political problems of their society. There is poverty, discrimination, crime, lawlessness, repression, exploitation, and so forth, because the existing political arrangements of the society are contrary to the ideal of equality, justice, liberty, order, rights, security, or whatever. What has to be done to overcome the problems is to transform the existing political arrangements so that they conform to the ideal. Ideologues are committed to believing that doing so will make both the society and the lives of individuals living in it better, and the failure to do so is to collude in the perpetuation of conditions that stand in the way of the ideal whose pursuit should take precedence over any other consideration that conflicts with it.

These commitments are expressed, for instance, by Berlin, "no power, only rights, can be regarded as absolute"; by Dworkin, "equal concern is the sovereign virtue of political community—without it government is only tyranny"; by Hayek, "liberty is not merely one particular value but that it is the source and condition of most moral values"; by Mill "the object of this essay is to assert one very simple principle, as entitled to govern absolutely the dealings of society with the individual in the way of compulsion and control"; by Nozick, "individuals have rights, and there are things no person or group may do to them (without violating their rights)"; and by Rawls "justice is the first virtue of social institutions...laws and institutions...must be reformed or abolished if they are unjust."[17]

Impassioned declarations about absolute rights, sovereign or first virtues, the source and condition of most values, and simple principles are the familiar rhetoric of ideologues. Their substance, beyond their emotive appeal, is that the political ideal that is claimed by ideologues to be the highest value should override any other value that conflicts with it. Ideologues are committed to pursuing the resulting policies, and if they fail to do so they are culpably inconsistent with their avowed beliefs.

The moral dangers of this way of proceeding become obvious if we ask what attitudes would ideologues have to have, assuming that they are consistent, toward those who disagree with them. They would probably begin with explaining and justifying the ideology to them. Suppose, however, what is more than a little likely, that people committed to other ideologies or who believe that ideologies are a menace would disagree with them even though they understand perfectly well the ideology they reject, and who advocate as strongly as they can policies contrary to the ones ideologues favor. Defenders of the rejected ideology must believe that such dissenters and their policies are obstacles to badly needed political improvements. They must, at least privately, condemn their opponents for acting immorally. For what else could those be doing who advocate policies that are contrary to what would benefit everyone, and who do so despite having been given convincing explanations of why the right policies are right? Spurned ideologues, then, must ask themselves how they should respond to what they must see as utterly misguided dissent. They will find it very difficult to arrive at a reasonable answer, because neither the toleration nor the repression of such dissent will be acceptable to them.

It is important to remember that what are at stake are not unconventional styles of life, like nudism, cross-dressing, or witchcraft, but actions that threaten the ideal whose defense is central to an ideology. Would conservatives tolerate breaking just laws? Would liberals tolerate racism? Would socialists tolerate untaxed wealth? Consistency requires ideologues to believe that although toleration is good, it has limits. And whatever the limits are, they are set by their ideal, and they must be committed to prohibiting their violations and punishing the violators. The punishment need not be as brutal as those that are meted out by fanatical ideologues, but it cannot avoid repressing dissent.

Some ideologues are fanatics, but many others in contemporary Western societies are morally committed, civilized people who unqualifiedly condemn the horrors committed in the name of Nazi, communist, and nationalist ideologies, and who are opposed to the repression even of wrongheaded dissent. Certainly, the ones I have cited in Note 17 would advocate toleration. In this, however, they seem to be inconsistent. For if they do indeed think that their ideal should override any value that conflicts with it, then it is hard to see how they could consistently make an exception for the lesser value of toleration, especially since the tolerated dissenters threaten the ideologues' political programs on which the improvement of their society supposedly depends. If non-fanatical ideologues tolerate dissent, they seem to be inconsistent; if they repress dissent, they violate what they see as a condition of a civilized approach to politics and a basic requirement of morality.

I have been careful to say only that ideologues seem to fall afoul of this dilemma, because they are aware of it and propose a way of avoiding it. Once again, Rawls is admirably clear about this. His way avoiding the dilemma is to regard toleration and some other conditions of civilized life and morality, not as values that may conflict with justice, but as parts of the circumstances of justice. He writes, following Hume, that:

the circumstances of justice may be described as the normal conditions under which human cooperation is both possible and necessary.... Although a society is a cooperative venture for mutual advantage, it is typically marked by a conflict as well as an identity of interests.... There is a conflict of interests since men are not indifferent as to how the greater benefits produced by their collaboration are distributed, for in order to pursue their ends each prefer a larger to a lesser share. Thus principles are needed for choosing among the various social arrangements which determine the division of advantages.... These requirements define the role of justice. The background conditions that give rise to these necessities are the circumstances of justice.[18]

Accordingly, toleration is not a value that may conflict with justice, but part of the background conditions that make the pursuit of justice possible. And, although Rawls does not say so, the other putative values, which I listed earlier as possibly conflicting with the highest ideal of an ideology, such as order, peace, prosperity, rule of law, or security, may also be regarded as part of the background conditions that form the circumstances of justice. Is this an acceptable way of defusing conflicts between the ideal of an ideology and other important values?

It is not. Although it is certainly true that any value can be pursued only in civilized circumstances and should be pursued only by observing at least the basic requirements of morality, it is an open question what should be included in and excluded from the circumstances. What Rawls has done is to deny that the values, such as toleration, whose conflict with justice may be particularly difficult to resolve always in favor of justice, are genuine values. He calls them instead part of the background conditions and relegates them into the circumstances of justice. Not only is this an arbitrary way of dismissing serious problems with his claim that justice is the first virtue of social institutions, it is also a way that is open to those who regard the values Rawls dismisses as the highest. They could say that justice—or equality, liberty, rights, and so forth—cannot conflict with order, peace, prosperity, the rule of law, or security as the highest value, because justice—or the others—are part of the circumstances in which order, peace, and so forth can be pursued.

I conclude that for ideologues to be consistent, they would have to follow the morally dangerous policy of repressing dissent, a policy that has led to the horrors painfully familiar from past and present politics. Or, if their commitment to morality and civilized life leads them to tolerate dissent, then they cannot consistently claim that whatever happens to be the ideal of their ideology should always override whatever value conflicts with it. To put this more positively, the minimum requirements of morality and commitment to civilized life are incompatible with ideological politics. Ideologies are morally dangerous precisely because they threaten morality and civilized life.

The Imprudence of Gratuitous Abstraction

Consider how ideologies fit into the pattern that leads from everyday to modal, and from there to philosophical, problems. The relevant problems in the present context are the political ones of a society at a certain time. For us, they include poverty, drug addiction, violent crimes, substandard education, deteriorating infrastructure, and so forth. The resources of everyday life are inadequate for solving or managing these problems, so we turn to history, morality, politics, religion, science, or to our personal point of view for a more adequate practical approach. But from these modes of understanding very different practical approaches follow, and people committed to one of these modes routinely favor incompatible approaches. Our problem, then, becomes one of making a reasonable decision about which of these practical approaches we should follow. Defenders of these approaches routinely question each others' assumptions, and they attempt to justify their own. But defenders of each mode of understanding do this, and this leads to the philosophical problems caused by conflicts between modes of understanding. The net result is that we do not know how to make a reasonable decision about which of the various incompatible practical approaches, assumptions, and modes of understanding we should accept.

We need to understand ideologies against this background. Ideologues say that coping with our political problems depends, not merely on the political mode of understanding, but on a particular interpretation of it in terms of a hierarchical system of values in which a favored ideal is the highest and should override any other value of their own or of any other mode of understanding that conflicts with it. So, according to ideologues, the best way of coping with poverty, drug addiction, violent crimes, substandard education, deteriorating infrastructure, and so forth is to be guided by the ideal of equality, or justice, or liberty, or rights, or some other highest and overriding value.

This raises obvious questions to which ideologues owe answers. Why is it reasonable to suppose that we should approach the problems of a society from a political, rather than a historical, moral, religious, scientific, or personal point of view? Why is it reasonable to suppose that if we approach the problems from a political point of view, then we have to assume that there is a highest political value, rather than a plurality of equally important political values? Why is it reasonable to suppose that if there is a highest political value, then it has to be the one a particular ideologue regards as an ideal, rather than any one of those that other ideologues favor? And if we do suppose all this, how exactly would it enable us to cope with the political problems of poverty, drug addiction, and so forth to be guided by whatever ideologues tell us is the highest value?

Ideologues typically answer these questions by appealing to a theory that describes a state of affairs that admittedly does not exist, but they think that the answers nevertheless follow from it. This non-existent state of affairs may be: an island on which mysteriously available resources are distributed equally, people buy insurance programs against the risks of life and pay for them by clamshells (Dworkin); a society where a principle called generic consistency is observed and everyone who understands it honors everyone else's rights (Gewirth); a speech community in which everybody respects everybody else and enters with them into a reasoned public discussion about how the affairs of the community should be arranged (Habermas); a classless society in which alienation and conflict could not occur (Marx); an enlightened people who always put the common good ahead of their own good (Mill); the minimal state that does no more and no less than it should (Nozick); decision-making in the original position and behind the veil of ignorance (Rawls); a pastoral society uncorrupted by culture and private property (Rousseau); a community whose members have consented to all the prevailing arrangements (Scanlon); and so on and on. How such fictions bear on the actual problems, incompatible approaches to coping with them, and the plurality of conflicting values, assumptions, and modes of understanding remains, as ideologues say, merely a question of the application of the principles that supposedly would be arrived at by rational and moral people in the non-existent state of affairs.

This is the approach I call gratuitous abstraction. Rawls, who acknowledges the problems and the conflicts, does not acknowledge that the abstractions are gratuitous and imprudent. He thinks that they are necessary:

> the work of abstraction, then, is not gratuitous: not abstraction for abstraction's sake. Rather it is a way of continuing public discussion when shared understandings of lesser generality have broken down. We should be prepared to find that the deeper the conflict, the higher the level of abstraction to which we must ascend to get a clear and uncluttered view of its roots.[19]

The way to understand problems and conflicts, then, is to construct a high-level abstract theory from which the problems and the conflicts have been deliberately excluded. That would supposedly give us an uncluttered view of the problems and the conflicts that were deliberately excluded from the theory, and with which we have to find a way of coping. The prescription is: if it is too difficult to cope with problems and conflicts, we should construct a theory from which the problems and the conflicts have been excluded. How could it enable us to solve or manage the political problems of poverty, drug addiction, violent crimes, and so forth to construct a theory of a non-existent ideal state of affairs in which such problems do not occur? It is useless to say that we can then explain why the ideal state of affairs is ideal, because that would not tell us anything about the actual state of affairs in which we have to cope with our problems.

It is remarkable that Rawls and other ideologues who are committed to abstract theories are serious about this, and that their many followers devote much time and energy to fine-tuning the theory from which the problems and conflicts they have to cope with are deliberately excluded. In the meantime, the problems and conflicts persist. That is why the abstraction is not only gratuitous but also imprudent.

Politics without Ideology

In this chapter I gave reasons against the mistaken view that there is an overriding mode of understanding, and that it is political. I called this mistake ideology. If the reasons against it are as compelling as I think they are, then how are we to cope with the political problems that stand in the way of improving our lives, and how are we to make reasonable decisions about which of the conflicting practical approaches we should follow? We can rely on a non-ideological approach to politics that has gradually emerged in affluent Western societies. This approach is not without ideological rivals, but it has resources that seem to me far superior to what any existing ideology can provide. Its basic assumption is that political values are plural and conflicts among them are an unavoidable part of the political life of civilized societies. The aim of politics is to find ways of coping with the resulting problems by balancing as well as we can the conflicting values that prompt incompatible approaches to the particular problems we face.

The acceptance of the plurality of conflicting political values does not mean that any political value becomes acceptable if enough people hold it. The political system of a civilized society is the standard to which we can appeal to recognize or to exclude particular values as having or not having a legitimate place in political life. Such a political system is not arbitrary or coercive. Of course, many societies are not civilized, their political systems are coercive, and power is wielded arbitrarily by the rulers. But the political system of a civilized society is the repository of conventions that have commanded the allegiance of a substantial number of people over a period measured in decades and sometimes centuries, not days. Their allegiance is voluntary, not coerced. They could and do question, reject, or aim to reform the prevailing conventions, or they could leave the society if they are deeply enough dissatisfied with it. But if they stay, follow the conventions, and put up with their unavoidable inconveniences, like paying taxes, having to have a passport for foreign travel, or a license for driving a car, then their allegiances are shown by their actions. Legitimate political values conform to the political system of a civilized society, and they are plural and conflicting.

There is and can be no ideology that could tell us how to resolve conflicts among political and non-political values, unless it question-beggingly assumes its own overriding status. What we need is prudent judgment informed by the history of our society, an understanding of the conflicting values, and a reasonable estimate of what people living in our society would find an acceptable way of coping. Having such judgment is difficult. It requires political experience and the ability and willingness to stand back from the clamor of narrow interests loudly proclaimed, and to weigh instead the long-term interests of the society. Few politicians have such judgment, but those few are statesmen who, if we are lucky, are listened to by their less experienced and less prudent colleagues. Political decisions are fallible, often mistaken, and the plurality of conflicting values makes political problems philosophical. And yet, as Dunn so well put it:

human beings have done many more fetching and elegant things than invent and routinize the modern democratic republic. But, in the face of their endlessly importunate, ludicrously indiscreet, inherently chaotic and always potentially murderous unrush of needs and longings, they have, even now, done few things as solidly to their advantage.[20]

8

Science and Scientism

Philosophers constantly see the method of science before their eyes, and are irresistibly tempted to ask and answer questions in the way science does. This tendency is the real source of metaphysics, and leads the philosopher into complete darkness.

Ludwig Wittgenstein[1]

By "science" I mean a synoptic view of the world that emerges from the findings of all the various physical, life, and social sciences taken together. Scientific understanding is rapidly growing both by the addition of new knowledge and the elimination of what was mistakenly thought to be knowledge. Its growth is one of the great successes of our world-view. It is true that

our age is often called an age of science, and with good reason: the advances made during the past few centuries by the natural sciences and more recently by psychology and the social sciences have vastly broadened our knowledge and deepened our understanding of the world we live in and of our fellow men; and the basic soundness of the insights achieved by science is eloquently attested to by the striking successes of their applications, both constructive and destructive, which have radically changed the quality of life on our planet and have left their characteristic imprint on every aspect of contemporary civilization.[2]

Scientism goes beyond this and claims that scientific understanding is deeper, truer, and more important than any other mode of understanding. If historical, moral, political, religious, or personal understanding conflicts with scientific understanding, then scientific understanding should override it. The importance of science is undeniable, but scientism is as mistaken as historicism, moralism, and ideology, and mistaken for the same reason. They all inflate the importance of one mode of understanding at the expense of other, no less important, modes. They all propose to resolve conflicts between modes of understanding by mistakenly claiming that the mode they favor should always override any mode that conflicts with it.

What Is Scientism?

One brief description of scientism is Wittgenstein's early view (later abandoned) that "we feel that even if all *possible* scientific questions have been answered, the problems of life remain completely untouched. Of course there are then no questions left, and this itself is the answer."[3] The implication is that all genuine questions are scientific and can in principle be answered by science. Another description is Hempel's. He asks "whether all questions about the world can ultimately be answered by scientific inquiry, or whether there are absolute limits beyond which scientific knowledge and understanding can never go?" His answer is that he has examined a variety of arguments "which appeared to prove that scientific knowledge and understanding are flawed by insuperable defects and limitations. I have tried to show that those arguments fall short." And he says that his "discussion is meant to apply to all branches of scientific and scholarly inquiry, from the physical sciences through biology and psychology to the social and historical disciplines."[4] The last two include the modes of understanding I have been discussing.

An older form of scientism is logical positivism and its successor logical empiricism. Both are now recognized as seriously defective.[5] A newer form of it, however, is very much alive. It is defended by numerous epistemologists, including among many others Carnap, both Churchlands, Davidson, Goldman, Grunbaum, Hempel, Popper, Quine, and Sellars. They disagree whether the right understanding of science is empiricist, holist, naturalist, pragmatist, or realist, but they agree that science is the paradigm of rationality and that history, morality, politics, religion, and personal concerns are rational to the extent to which they approximate scientific standards. I will concentrate on the claim that science is the paradigm of rationality and ignore their disagreements about how science should be understood.[6]

According to defenders of scientism, the main reason why science is the paradigm of rationality is the remarkable success of scientific explanation:

Science explains why a given event came about by showing that it occurred in certain particular circumstances...in accordance with certain general laws of nature or well-established theoretical principles.... Thus, the phenomenon is explained by showing that, under given particular conditions, it "had to" occur according to the specified laws. The explanatory account can accordingly be conceived as a deductive argument whose premises...consist of the relevant laws and of descriptions of the particular circumstances, while the conclusion...describes the phenomenon to be explained. The argument enables us to understand the phenomenon by showing that, given the laws and the particular circumstances, its occurrence "was to be expected" in the sense that it could have been inferred from the explanatory information.[7]

Scientific explanation may be either deductive or probabilistic. But in one or the other of its forms, science explains by fitting events into a causal sequence in which causes are connected with effects by laws that make it possible to predict that if the causes are present and the conditions are as specified, then the effects will occur. Science, then, is the paradigm of rationality because it provides nomological explanations of why events occur and makes it possible to predict what will happen if certain conditions are present.

The resulting explanations and predictions enable us to take more and more control over the conditions to which we are subject. Defenders of scientism accept that history, morality, politics, religion, and personal values may aim at "the welfare and happiness of mankind," but if they pursue these worthwhile aims rationally, then they must "proceed by the standards of *scientific* rationality," whether or not their defenders know or intend it. "Surely, one who is seriously concerned to enhance the welfare and happiness of mankind would still have to proceed by the standards of *scientific* rationality in search for knowledge about suitable means to achieve those ends."[8] This is because

the nature of understanding... is basically the same in all areas of scientific inquiry; and the deductive and probabilistic model of nomological explanation accommodate...explanations that deal with the influence of rational deliberation, of conscious and subconscious motives, and of ideas and ideals.[9]

Scientism is qualified by the recognition that many of the events that require explanation are not simple physical or physiological processes, but complex phenomena that can be explained only by taking into account the cultural significance they undoubtedly possess, such as "the meanings of words," "the morals of a story," "the significance of gestures and facial expressions," "the challenges and obligations and social opportunities," and "all the intricacies that make up a functioning culture." "But... these things are wholly consistent with a reductionist program for understanding the nature of human cognition. What the reductionist must do is explain how a physical system can come to address and manipulate such subtle and culturally configured features."[10]

The key to the reductive explanation of "culturally configured features" is cognitive psychology, artificial intelligence, and the neurocomputational model. It is acknowledged that "a naturalistic approach to human consciousness is not automatically and fundamentally opposed to the explanatory categories of our existing culture. On the contrary, it may vindicate them by providing a naturalistic explanation of them."[11] The last sentence is of particular significance because close to its surface is the assumption central to scientism that cultural explanatory categories need to be and can be vindicated by naturalistic explanations that provide a nomological account of the causes whose effects the cultural explanatory categories are. This account explains why our historical, moral, political, religious, and personal beliefs, values, and practices are what they are.

Rational Action

Turning now from the description of scientism to its criticism, I focus on Hempel's clear, lucid, and mistaken account of rational action.[12] I do not think that other defenders of scientism would have serious disagreements with his account. According to it:

whether a given action ... is rational will depend on the objective that the action is meant to achieve and on the relevant empirical information available at the time of the decision. Broadly speaking, an action will qualify as rational if, on the basis of the given information, it offers optimal prospects of achieving its objectives. (311)

What about the rationality of the objectives? Are we to think that an action can be rational in pursuit of an irrational end? Not quite:

Some of the courses of action which, according to the information basis, are available and are likely to achieve the end-state, may nevertheless be ruled out because they violate certain general constraining principles, such as moral or legal norms, contractual commitments, social conventions, the rules of the game being played, and the like.

"What I will call its *total objective*," says Hempel, "may then be characterized by a set of E sentences describing the intended end-state, in conjunction with another set, N, of constraining norms" (312–13). A rational action, then, is one that "offers optimal prospects of achieving its objectives," provided the objectives do not, as he says above, "violate certain general constraining principles."

This makes the account a little more plausible, but not by much, because it leaves open the question of the rationality of both the ends and of the constraining principles. This is not an oversight but a deliberate decision: "I will not," says Hempel, "impose the requirement that there must be 'good reasons' for adopting the given ends and norms: rationality of an action will be here understood in a strictly relative sense, as its suitability, judged in the light of given information, for achieving the specified objective" (313). According to this account, then, an action can be rational even if it aims at an irrational objective, provided it is constrained by norms, even if the norms are also irrational. If my information is that the growth of human population endangers the survival of several non-human species, my objective is to decimate the human population in order to protect the endangered species, and my constraining principle is to select the humans to be killed by lot and kill them painlessly, then my actions directed to this end will be rational. Countless other, no less absurd, consequences follow from this account of rational action. Something has gone terribly wrong with it.

What has gone wrong, of course, is that the rationality of actions depends also on the rationality of the ends they aim at, and on the rationality of the principles that constrain how the ends may be pursued. If these obvious conditions on which the rationality of actions partly depends are recognized, then it becomes unavoidable to ask the question that Hempel does not ask: who is to judge the rationality of ends and constraining principles? Is the judge the agent? Historians? Moral thinkers? Politicians? Religious authorities? Scientists? Individuals for themselves? Or someone else? And from what point of view is the judgment to be made? By appealing to what standards? Is the point of view historical, moral, political, religious, scientific, personal, or some other? And what is the standard of rationality that follows from these very different points of view?

It is precisely to avoid having to ask and answer these difficult questions that Hempel refuses to "impose the requirement that there must be 'good reasons' for adopting the given ends and norms" (313). His refusal leads to a dilemma that must be faced by all who accept this account. If they deny that the rationality of actions partly depends on the rationality both of their ends and the norms that constrain them, then they must accept the absurd consequence that obviously irrational actions are rational. If they accept that the rationality of actions partly depends on the rationality of their ends and the constraining norms, then all the questions they refuse to ask come flooding back. Why, then, do they refuse to ask what makes ends and constraining norms of supposedly rational actions rational? They do so because the answers unavoidably lead to the conclusion that scientism is indefensible. I will now try show why this conclusion would follow, if the obvious questions were actually asked.

I turn once again to Hempel's account. He summarizes his argument by saying that rational actions "conform to the general conception of an explanation as subsuming the explanandum under covering laws (the laws may be strictly universal or of statistical form, and the subsumption will accordingly be deductive or inductive-probabilistic in character)" (322). He does not ask about the rationality of ends and constraining norms because the answers could not be subsumed under covering laws. Why not? Because the answers could not consist in a nomological explanation of actions as the effects that follow if the causes are present and the conditions are as specified. Perhaps it is true that all actions—rational, irrational, and non-rational—have nomological explanations. But that is not the question. The question is whether the actions are rational, rather than irrational or non-rational, and the answer to that question cannot be nomological, because the question is about the rationality of ends and constraining norms, not about the nomological explanation of ends and norms. This becomes blatantly obvious if it is recognized that irrational ends and constraining norms also have nomological explanations.

The answer, if there is one, must explain whether the ends the actions aim at and norms that constrain them are rational. And whether they are rational depends, first, on whether they are judged to be rational from a historical, moral, political, religious, scientific, personal, or from some other point of view; second, on specifying who should make those judgments; and third, on deciding how conflicts between judgments made from different points of view should be resolved. There is no universal or statistical law to which we could appeal for the answers, for the question is whether the rationality of actions should be judged from a scientific point of view or from a historical, moral, political, religious, personal, or some other point of view.

Perhaps the answer will be that the rationality of ends and norms should be judged from a scientific point of view. But if that answer is rational, it can be reached only after reasons have been given why conflicting answers that follow from non-scientific points of view should be overridden by reasons that follow from the scientific point of view. These reasons, however, cannot be reasonably derived from the scientific point of view, since that would arbitrarily assume what is in question. If non-arbitrary reasons can be found, then those reasons cannot be scientific and what makes them reasons cannot be that they fit into the scientific view, not even if they do fit into it.

I do not know whether Hempel refused to ask the obvious questions about the rationality of the ends and constraining norms because he realized that the answers would lead beyond the scientific point of view. But that is where the questions lead, whether or not he realized it. Not asking them, however, leads to the absurd consequence that actions may qualify as rational even if they aim at irrational ends and are constrained by irrational norms. As Hume pointed out some time ago, on this view of rational action: " 'Tis not contrary to reason to prefer the destruction of the world to the scratching of my finger. 'Tis not contrary to reason for me to chuse my total ruin, to prevent the least uneasiness of an *Indian* or person wholly unknown to me."[13]

I have so far left unquestioned the surely implausible treatment of norms as merely constraining how objectives might be pursued. It is certainly true that we may have historical, moral, political, religious, or personal values that constrain how we go about trying to achieve what we want. But it is also true that what we want, our objectives, may be to live and act so as to approximate historical, moral, political, religious, or personal values. And it is no less true that our pursuit of these values may well be constrained by scientific considerations. It is highly misleading, therefore, to treat scientific considerations as alone dictating our objectives and historical, moral, political, religious, and personal considerations only as constraining how we might pursue them. Our objective may be to understand why revolutions so often lead to a period of terror; why courage and moderation can, but wisdom cannot, be excessive; why politicians must frequently compromise their genuinely held principles; why religious rituals unify participants in them; or why we so often deceive ourselves about our motives. Surely, answering these questions are rational objectives, and surely their rational pursuit should be constrained by the possibilities and limits that the best scientific opinion of the day reveals.

Why, then, do Hempel and other defenders of scientism think of non-scientific considerations as constraints and scientific ones as objectives? Why does Quine end the only essay he wrote on moral values with the lament that when we come to moral values "we have to deplore the irreparable lack of empirical checkpoints that are the solace of the scientist. Loose ends are untidy"?[14] Does science have no loose ends? Might historical, moral, political, religious, or personal checkpoints not prove to be solace to scientists as they pursue their researches? Why do moral agents suffer an irreparable loss of empirical checkpoint if their moral values lead them to say that benevolence is better than malevolence?

The answer to these questions is that defenders of scientism are steeped in science and view the rest of life from the scientific point of view. They may do that of course, but only at the cost of failing to recognize that there is an enormous amount of life that other people, or perhaps even scientists in their civilian capacity, regard as immensely important and life as greatly impoverished without some historical understanding, moral sensitivity, political acumen, religious hope, and the satisfaction of some personal preferences. These objectives are no less rational than those of science. It is a narrow and life-diminishing approach to the possibilities and limits of life to insist that their overriding significance emerges from the scientific point of view. The scientific view is important and illuminating, but so are the others. Defenders of scientism are as misguided as historical pedants, dogmatic moralists, political ideologues, religious fanatics, and self-centered individualists. They all cultivate a deliberately narrowed sensibility and misguidedly celebrate it as a token of their dedication to rationality.

Holism

These reasons against scientism are strengthened by the implications of the holistic interpretation of science.[15] It is one interpretation among others, but it is among the dominant ones. As Quine puts it: "Our statements about the external world face the tribunal of sense experience not individually but only as a corporate body" and he adds by way of characterizing this holistic view that "I espouse a more thorough pragmatism. Each man is given a scientific heritage plus a continuing barrage of sensory stimulation; and the considerations which guide him in warping his scientific heritage to fit his continuing sensory promptings are, where rational, pragmatic."[16]

The tribunal of sense experience and our sensory promptings give us facts. We disregard them at our peril, but sense experience and sensory promptings do not tell us what significance the facts have. Before we warp our scientific heritage to fit the facts, we have to understand whether the facts are important, reliable, dangerous, interesting, routine, groundbreaking, and whether they confirm or disconfirm our theories. We have to understand what bearing, if any, they have on seeing ourselves as continuing or departing from the historical conditions that have formed us, on the morality by which we live, on the reform of our political institutions, on the credibility of religious beliefs, and on how we pursue our personal projects. And we understand them in the only way we can: in terms of the modes of understanding we have. From these modes, however, conflicting accounts of the significance of facts follow, and it is stultifying to decide a priori that the significance of the facts must be understood in scientific terms.

The tribunal of sense experience judges not just the scientific mode of understanding, but also the historical, moral, political, religious, and personal modes. And it judges them as a corporate body that includes learning from the history of science; from the moral problems involved in experimentation with human subjects, nuclear energy, or biological weapons; from the political importance of allocating scarce funds to more rather than less promising lines of research or to ameliorating miseries; from the danger of letting religious dogma interfere with scientific work; and from the need to guard against personal considerations that intrude into understanding the significance of the facts.

Our world-view, in which our modes of understanding and their assumptions, beliefs, values, and practices are embedded, forms a whole whose parts are connected with one another in countless ways. Holists are right: when facts come our way that we find inconsistent, anomalous, unusual, doubtful, or suggestive, we have to accommodate them, if need be, by revising our existing modes of understanding, and eventually our world-view itself. And we make the revisions by relying on parts of our world-view that have remained unaffected by the new facts. As a result of such revisions, our world-view is at once continuing and changing. In all this, holists are right. But they go on, inconsistently with their announced position, to claim that reason requires that scientific considerations should be overriding in deciding what revisions are needed. In some cases, the overriding consideration may be scientific, but in others it may be one of the many considerations that follow from non-scientific modes of understanding. Reason does not require that one type of consideration should always be overriding. If holists think otherwise, they join historicist, moralist, ideological, religious, and subjectivist dogmatists in arbitrarily claiming the authority of reason for what are only their personal predilections. If, however, holists accept that non-scientific considerations may sometimes override scientific considerations, then they must abandon the claim that rationality must be scientific.

These considerations will not disarm holists. They will continue to insist that if the scientific understanding of the significance of facts comes into conflict with the historical, moral, political, religious, or personal understanding of it, then scientific understanding should override the conflicting ones. If critics ask why they should believe this, holists will say, as Quine does, that

extrapolation was always intrinsic to induction, that primitive propensity that is at the root of all science. Extrapolation in science, however, is under the welcome restraint of stubborn fact: failures of prediction. Extrapolation in morals has only our unsettled moral values themselves to answer to.[17]

It is hard to see what Quine could have in mind by supposing that moral values are not restrained by stubborn facts. The stubborn facts that restrain moral values are those that aid or hinder the improvement of our lives. Stubborn facts have made us change our minds about the moral value of slavery, masturbation, contraception, church attendance, child labor, and so forth. It is partly on the basis of stubborn facts that we argue about the moral value of capital punishment, the legalization of drugs, abortion, campaign financing, and so forth. It is true that science has special excellences that other modes of understanding lack: nomological explanations and predictions that enable us to predict, and at least to some extent control, future events, so that we can build bridges, cure diseases, and enjoy numerous other blessings. But it is also true that each mode of understanding has special excellences that the scientific mode lacks. History uses the past to illuminate the present; morality distinguishes between right and wrong, virtues and vices, and explains, albeit not nomologically, what makes one better than the other; politics balances interests and ameliorates conflicts by negotiation; religion consoles the faithful for their misfortunes and gives them hope for a better future; and the personal mode enables us to identify and pursue our individual preferences. Of course, all these modes of understanding, including the scientific one, are fallible, their pursuit of various excellences often fail, experienced participants in them often disagree with each other, and they all change over time, occasionally in basic ways. The defenders of each can truly claim that their favored mode has special excellences that the other modes do not have or have only to a much more limited extent.

It is against this background that the claim of defenders of scientism that scientific considerations are always overriding is shown to be as implausible as it would be to claim that any of the considerations that follow from other modes of understanding are overriding. Modes of understanding certainly conflict, and reason requires finding some way of resolving their conflicts. But there is no mode of understanding in whose favor reason always requires resolving the conflicts. If the conflict is about present facts, then we should turn to science. If it is about why past decisions that have led to how we live now have been made in one way rather than another, then history should be our guide. If we disagree about what does or does not excuse or justify an action that would normally be culpable, then morality is likely to be of most help. If we are struggling with how scarce resources should be distributed, then we should turn to politics. If we are dispirited, then religion may console us. And if we find ourselves lost in life's way, then understanding our personal values may help us discover what we really care about. We have many different problems, many different, often conflicting approaches to coping with them, and it is misguided to suppose that reason requires that the scientific approach to them should always override all the other approaches that may follow from non-scientific modes of understanding. It is, of course, no less misguided to suppose that we could understand the requirements of reason independently of science, which is a conspicuously successful exercise of reason.

What Reason Requires

Consider three quite different decisions to embark on three quite different courses of action that are particularly important from their agents' point of view. I sketch in their background, but only briefly. The first is from the *Old Testament* (2 Samuel 11–13). David, King of Israel, "saw from the roof a woman bathing; and the woman was very beautiful." David found out that she was Bathsheba, the wife of Uriah the Hittite. David summoned her, "she came to him, and he lay with her." David, then, sent Uriah off to fight in the war, and commanded his general to "set Uriah in the forefront of the hardest fighting, and then draw back from him, that he may be struck down, and die." Bathsheba mourned her husband, but David "brought her to his house, and she became his wife, and bore him a son."

[What] David had done displeased the LORD. And the LORD sent Nathan to David ... and he said to him, 'There were two men in a certain city, the one rich and the other poor. The rich man had very many flocks and herds; but the poor man had nothing but one little ewe lamb.... The rich man ... took the poor man's lamb.... David's anger was greatly kindled against the man; and he said to Nathan, 'As the LORD lives, the man who has done this deserves to die.' ... Nathan said to David, 'You are the man'. And David, realizing what he did, said to Nathan, 'I have sinned against the LORD'.

Before Nathan, David had seen his taking of Bathsheba as a royal prerogative. Nathan showed him that he should see it as grievous injustice. And this led David to recognize his offense, regret it, make such amends as he could, and change his ways.[18]

The second decision is Montaigne's (parenthetical references are to the pages of the *Essays*).[19] In 1570, after many years of public service, he retired to his estate "long weary of the servitude of the court and of public employments...where in...freedom, tranquillity, and leisure" (ix–x) he intended to read and reflect. He began to record his thoughts in a form that eventually became the *Essays*. He thought that "there is no one who, if he listens to himself, does not discover in himself a pattern all his own, a ruling pattern" (615). His main aim in life had become to discover this pattern in himself and live according to it. In order to discover it, "I recognized," Montaigne wrote, "that the surest thing was to entrust myself and my need to myself" (799). He thus opted for "a private life that is on display only to ourselves...[and has] a pattern established...by which to test our actions." And then we "now pat ourselves on the back, now punish ourselves." He aimed to "have my own laws and court to judge me, and I address myself to them more than anywhere else" (613). "The greatest task of all," he wrote, is "to compose our character...not to compose books, and to win, not battles and provinces, but order and tranquillity in our conduct. Our great and glorious masterpiece is to live appropriately. All other things...are only little appendages and props, at most" (850–1). He did live appropriately, and left us his wonderful *Essays*.

The third decision was told to me by a friend. Life was not going well for him. His career was stagnating, he had money problems, his marriage was unhappy, and his children were brats. He was depressed. He found himself in Houston, and to escape from the rain, he entered the Museum of Fine Arts, came across Caillebotte's painting of his brother in his garden, and found himself mesmerized by it. The painting is of a man sitting on a chair reading a book under an orange tree, his back is turned toward us, the sun gently suffuses the picture outside of the cool shade of the dark green leaves of two trees. A few feet away there is a woman, probably young, perhaps the sitting man's wife or daughter, also reading. And a little further on, in the sun, a dog is napping with his nose resting on his paws. There is an atmosphere of calm, quiet, enjoyment, evoking wonderful summer days when undisturbed by the world, unworried by disasters, we reflect in tranquility. The painting made vivid to my friend a possibility of what life may be like. It communicated to him what he knew but forgot, that rarely, all too rarely, life could be like the artist's brother's was that summer at least for some of us some of the time. It helped my friend to remember what he might hope to have in the future, what is worth struggling for. And he decided to try to do better with his career, finances, marriage, and children. The painting, of course, did not change the facts, but it did change his attitude to them. His depression lifted, he got a new lease on life, he acted on his decision, and his life got better.

It seems obvious that David, Montaigne, and my friend made rational decisions that led to rational courses of action. It seems equally obvious that their decisions and actions cannot be explained nomologically as effects connected to causes by scientific laws. I am not denying that the decisions and the actions were the effects of causes. I am denying that it makes sense to talk of a nomological connection between them. What happened in each case was that the person involved re-evaluated how he had previously seen his life. David resolved to subordinate his royal prerogatives to what he took to be God's law. Montaigne gave up public life in order to compose his character and the *Essays*. And my friend came to be inspired by an unexpected vision of how good life could be. Each had made a highly personal and individual decision and proceeded to rearrange his life accordingly. Their decisions and actions were based on how each viewed his past, his present circumstances, and what he hoped for the future. David wanted to be forgiven by his God; Montaigne wanted to live appropriately to the character he was forming; and my friend wanted his depression to lift and his career, finances, marriage, and children to improve. But making the decision and acting according to it were the highly individual acts of these three people that no one beside themselves could make and act on. They were the effects of causes that were peculiar to themselves, to their individual histories, to their perceptions of their lives and circumstances, to their values and ideals, and to their views of the very different conditions under which they lived.

Hempel would say that their decisions and actions fit his schema of rational actions:

A was in situation of type C
A was a rational agent
In a situation type C any rational agent will do x
Therefore A did x.

According to Hempel, this schema yields "a descriptive generalization telling us how a rational agent will act in situations of that kind: but this restores the covering-law form of the explanation" (which is another name for nomological explanation).[20] But it does not, as becomes obvious if we recognize that the specifications of their situations are unique to David, Montaigne, and my friend. No one else could be in those situations and no descriptive generalization could follow from them. Who else, we might ask, could be the King of Israel robbing Uriah of his life and wife and being admonished by Nathan who was believed to be the messenger of God? Who else could be a minor aristocrat living in 16th-century France, who grew tired of public service and composed essays that became a glory of the Western tradition? And who else in the history of the world escaped from the rain into a museum in a city he happened to visit and was struck by a

19th-century painting so forcefully as to lift his depression and revive his hopes for a better future? Hempel's schema hides the flesh and blood of human beliefs, emotions, values, joys, and miseries behind the abstract symbolism of a contrived semi-logical notation.

It cries out for an explanation of how defenders of scientism, who are highly intelligent people, live in the world with other human beings, have at least some moral, political, and personal commitments, and have probably read some history and literature, how could such people end up with the view that actions are rational only if they fit the covering-law model of explanation? How could they think that given the specification of a situation that calls for a decision and an action, all rational agents will make the same decision and perform the same action? Do they not know that there are many rational interpretations of the same historical situation, that people have rational moral and political disagreements, and that they may think rationally but differently about the existence and the nature of a providential order, and that, most glaringly of all, they have a variety of rational personal commitments which lead them to act very differently in very similar situations?

I think that the explanation is that defenders of scientism start with the true assumption that the key to the enormous success of science is the scientific method that yields nomological explanations and reliable predictions. But then they go on to assume falsely that science is the paradigm of rationality and that non-scientific modes of understanding are rational to the extent to which they follow the scientific method. Science is undoubtedly a rational mode of understanding, but there are also rational non-scientific modes of understanding. There are rational modes of understanding the history of science, its moral and political importance, its conflicts with religion, and the personal significance of lives engaged in scientific research. These non-scientific understandings, often provided by scientists themselves, do not follow the scientific method, do not aim at nomological explanations, and are no less rational for that.

Why do defenders of scientism find it tempting to go on from the true assumption that science is rational to the false one that it is the paradigm of rationality? My conjecture is that they are convinced that rationality is like truth: if something is true, then it is true impersonally for everyone, and those who think otherwise are mistaken. If rationality were always like that, then indeed all rational agents in the same situation would have to make the same decisions and opt for the same actions. But rationality is like that only in the scientific mode of understanding, and only when disagreements have been laid to rest and scientists have arrived at impersonal nomological explanations that hold for everyone, always. When rational agents seek scientific understanding, they try as best as they can to abstract from their personal concerns and look at their subject-matter *sub specie aeternitatis.* But when rational agents seek historical, moral, political, personal, and to some extent religious understanding, then they look at their subject-matter *sub specie humanitatis.*

The differences between these points of view is further complicated by there being no single *sub specie humanitatis* understanding. Human understanding is always modal: historical, moral, political, religious, personal, or perhaps of some other kind. Each is a personal understanding, but each is a different kind of personal understanding. Each differs from impersonal scientific understanding but each differs from it in a different way. And the difference is not only in the mode of understanding sought, but also in what I will call the spirit in which it is sought. It may be serious or playful, realistic or romantic, aesthetic or prudential, rule-following or innovative, and so forth.

As these differences make obvious, non-scientific modes of understanding are concerned with human beings who are the products, not only of evolutionary but also of social and cultural influences that vary with societies, families, times, places, and contexts. Human beings and their actions can be understood only by understanding what kind of persons they have become as a result of these influences and how they differ from others. Historical, moral, political, religious, and personal understandings are to a large extent personal: by persons of persons. The understandings they arrive at may be good or bad, more or less rational, or even irrational, but to insist that they should be impersonal is to doom them to abject failure. Defenders of scientism insist on just that, and they insist on it because they think that since the scientific mode of understanding is impersonal and rational, so should be the non-scientific modes of understanding. And then they rank non-scientific modes of understanding by asking how closely they approximate impersonal nomological explanations, with the absurd results I have been inveighing against. (I will discuss the requirements of reason further in the Chapter 9.)

The Human World

The human world is not a world apart from all the rest of the vastness that exists. It is as much a part of the scheme of things as subatomic particles, galaxies, middle-sized material objects, animals, and all organic matter. The human world is the effect of non-human causes, could not exist without those causes, and how non-human causes lead to human effects may be explained, now or in the future, nomologically by science. I accept that all this is true, and nothing I have said against scientism is meant to deny it. What I mean to do is to stress that the human world has a special significance from our human point of view. This is not some kind of universal significance, since from the point of view of the universe nothing has significance. My complaint about scientism—not about science—is that its defenders fail to see that it would destroy the significance the human world has for us if non-scientific modes of understanding were made to conform to the impersonal requirements of scientific understanding. For the human world is our world of persons, and we derive from it the evaluative dimension of human lives. It is a world of personally felt experiences, meanings, and values; successes and failures; triumphs and tragedies; discoveries and disasters; all the good and bad things in individual human lives as they were in the past, are now, and perhaps will continue to be in the future. That there is such a human world chocked full of significance is a fact, just like millions of other facts. But it is a fact of the greatest importance for us, because we derive from it whatever meaning and value we think human life and our own life has. Without it nothing would matter, not even that nothing would then matter.

This human world of ours can be viewed from the outside, as science, and to a lesser extent, religion, enables us to view it. Some reasonable and reflective people recommend that we adopt the outside view. Nagel, for instance, writes that:

the wish to live so far as possible in full recognition that one's position in the universe is not central has an element of the religious impulse about it, or at least an acknowledgment of the question to which religion purports to supply an answer. A religious solution gives us borrowed centrality through the concern of a supreme being. Perhaps the religious question without a religious answer amounts to antihumanism, since we cannot compensate for the lack of cosmic meaning with a meaning derived from our own perspective.[21]

Nagel gives no reason why we should strive to abandon, or perhaps only to subordinate, our inside view of the human world from which we derive all that has meaning and value for us and adopt an antihumanistic view in which nothing has meaning and value. Nor does he give any reason why the meaning and value we derive from the human world could not compensate for the lack of cosmic meaning. That compensation is precisely one of the great benefits we derive from the human world. It creates for us a haven in the vast indifferent cosmos surrounding us. And such admittedly limited understanding of history, morality, politics, religion, and personal values as the human world contains provides us with more meanings and values than any one of us could possibly appreciate fully.

Science turns into scientism when the inside view is reduced to the outside one. The reduction proceeds by pointing out, truly, that the human world with its meanings and values is the effect of causes, and then concluding, falsely, that this somehow casts doubt on what we find meaningful and valuable. It is probably true that scientific theories of evolution, the brain, cognitive psychology, and artificial intelligence can now or in the future provide nomological explanations of how we come to hold the meanings and values that make human life worth living as the effects of causes. But meanings and values do not become less meaningful and valuable because they have causes. Effects are not mere appearance, and causes are not alone real.[22] Causes and effects are both real, even if the effects would not exist if it were not for the causes. If doubtful, bear in mind that all causes were once effects.

Science without Scientism

In order to avoid a possible misunderstanding I want to emphasize that this chapter is not intended as a salvo in the two cultures debate. In my opinion that debate is fraught with confusion and special pleading. It began in the early 1960s when science was expanding and the humanities were contracting. That trend has speeded up in recent years for several reasons: the successes of the sciences and the immediate practical benefits they are yielding; the attack on the humanities by cynics who deliberately or otherwise are undermining the values that make our life worth living; the shortsightedness of politicians who hold the purse-strings; and the opportunism of university administrators who list as the wind blows. It is an exceptionally silly response to this state of affairs to recommend, as Snow has done, that people in the arts and humanities should learn more about science. And it is no less silly to insist, as Leavis has so vociferously done, that science is not part of culture.[23] If by culture is meant the arts and the humanities, then science is obviously not part of it. If by culture is meant our world-view, then science is obviously part of it. My concern has not been to enter into this ill-advised debate, but to deny that science should be the overriding mode of understanding.

Our world-view has been greatly enriched by science, and our lives have been made in countless ways better by it. But the same is true of history, morality, politics, religion, and the personal mode of understanding. It is no less true that science can be and has been misused, as have been the others. The values of science—objectivity, impersonality, openness to criticism, dedication to the truth—are important, and we cannot do without them. But they are not our only values, nor the most important ones—not because other values are more important, but because there are no most important values. What is most important is to try to live and act so as to enjoy the benefits we can derive from as many of our values as possible and violate as few as we can. The key to the improvement of our condition is to balance our values. This is immensely difficult because our values are many and of various kinds, they change and conflict, the conditions in which we have to balance them continually shift, and the price we must pay for such balance as we may temporarily reach is that it is in the nature of their balance that we must put up with having less of each than we would like, in order to have some of the others.

Historicism, moralism, ideology, and scientism are all forces of imbalance. They all inflate the importance of the values they favor at the expense of other no less important values. What we need is history without historicism, morality without moralism, politics without ideology, religion without dogma, science without scientism, and personal commitments without self-centeredness. The pursuit of the values rightly favored by defenders of a mode of understanding must be limited by the no less rightly favored values of the other modes of understanding. The force of the "must" is that our world-view depends on it. Our world-view—containing our modes of understanding, their conflicts and the resulting philosophical problems, our practical and reflective approaches, as well as what we find meaningful and valuable—is our contingent, time-bound interpretation of the values of the human world. We should guard against allowing any of our modes of understanding to achieve more than a short-term and context-dependent priority over the others, and we should do as well as we can to balance their conflicting claims. Philosophical problems are obstacles we encounter in trying to maintain that balance. In Part Three I propose what I think is a better approach to balancing them.

PART III

Toward a Pluralist Approach

9

Good Reasons

To see the world from the human point of view is not an absurd thing for human beings to do. It is sometimes said that such a view implies that we regard human beings as the most important or valuable creatures in the universe. This would be an absurd thing to do, but it is not implied. To suppose that it is, is to make the mistake of identifying the point of view of the universe and the human point of view. No one should make any claims about the importance of human beings to the universe: the point is about the importance of human beings to human beings.

Bernard Williams[1]

In this third part of the book, I aim to work out a pluralist approach to resolving conflicts between modes of understanding and coping with philosophical problems. This approach, I claim, is better than either the absolutist or the relativist ones. According to absolutists, good reasons require that one of the modes of understanding should universally and unconditionally override the other modes when they come into conflict. If this were true, conflicts between modes of understanding would not lead to philosophical problems, but merely indicate that additional reasons are needed to resolve the conflicts and cope with the problems. Relativists agree with absolutists that good reasons must be universal and unconditional, but deny that such reasons can be found. They think that all reasons unavoidably depend on commitments for which ultimately no universal and unconditional reasons can be given. Conflicts between modes of understanding have only arbitrary resolutions, and philosophical problems indicate that reasons for or against them are doomed to remain inconclusive.

Pluralists agree with absolutists that resolving conflicts among modes of understanding and coping with philosophical problems depends on good reasons, but disagree that good reasons must be universal and unconditional. Particular and conditional reasons can be good enough for this purpose. Pluralists thus reject the assumption that absolutists and relativists both hold, namely, that good reasons must be universal and unconditional. The dispute between absolutists and relativists on one side, and pluralists on the other, turns on what good reasons are in this context. I concentrate on the dispute between absolutists and pluralists, and treat relativism as what would follow if absolutists and pluralists were both mistaken.

This chapter is about the reasons we need and can have in the context of conflicting modes of understanding and philosophical problems. Reasons have many uses—and abuses—and I discuss only a few of them. What follows is not anything close to a full-fledged theory. Chapters 10 and 11 are about how the good reasons identified in this chapter can be used to resolve specific conflicts between modes of understanding and cope with specific philosophical problems, but only as they arise in particular contexts that will change with time and conditions.

The Absolutist Approach

Thomas Nagel's defense of absolutism is the most direct, explicit, and thoughtful I know of. He is

concerned with an issue that runs through practically every area of inquiry and that has even invaded the general culture—the issue of where understanding and justification come to an end. Do they come to an end with objective principles whose validity is independent of our point of view, or do they come to an end within our point of view—individual or shared—so that ultimately, even the apparently most objective and universal principles derive their validity or authority from the perspective and practice of those who follow them?

Nagel believes that they come to an end with universal and unconditional reasons:

reason, if there is such a thing, can serve as a court of appeal not only against the received opinions and habits of our community but also against the peculiarities of our personal perspective. It is something each individual can find within himself, but at the same time it has universal authority.... Whoever appeals to reason purports to discover a source of authority within himself that is not merely personal, or societal, but universal—and that should persuade others who are willing to listen to it.[2]

Nagel regards absolutism and relativism as exclusive alternatives: one or the other must be true. I deny that they exhaust the options. Both may be false, and pluralism may be true. Understanding and justification, contrary to relativism, may be brought to a reasonable end, but, contrary to absolutism, the end is not some universal and unconditional reason.

The core of Nagel's defense of absolutism is that reason is "a form or category of thought from which there is no appeal beyond itself—whose validity is unconditional because it is necessarily employed in every purported challenge to itself" (7). Perhaps the simplest and most forceful argument for this is that the claim "Everything is subjective" [or relative, I add] must be nonsense, for it would itself have to be either subjective or objective. But it can't be objective, since in that case it would be false if true. And it can't be subjective, because then it would not rule out any objective claim, including the claim that it is objectively false. (15)

All reasons given in any context may be challenged, of course, but

any challenge mounted against reasoning would have to involve reasoning of its own, and this can only be evaluated rationally—that is, by methods that aspire to general validity.... Those who challenge the rationalist position by arguing that what it appeals to at every stage are really contingent and perhaps local intuitions, practices, or conventions may attempt to apply this analysis all the way down the line.... But I do not see how they can terminate the process with a challenge that does not invite rational assessment. (25)

Nagel accepts that reasons for conclusions supported by logic, science, ethics, or any other mode of understanding can be challenged and may be shown to be mistaken. But such challenges deserve to be taken seriously only if they are supported by reasons. Reasons, therefore, are presupposed by all challenges to reason. Reason itself may be challenged, of course, by faith, hope, intuition, passion, or whatever. A challenge to reason, however, must assume that it, rather than reason, should be accepted. If that assumption is justified, it must rest on some reason; if it is unjustified, then it should not be accepted. In either case the challenge to reason fails, so Nagel's argument may be interpreted.

On this interpretation, the argument is obviously mistaken. Suppose I hold that all conclusions supported by any mode of understanding ultimately rest on faith. I accept that any conclusion based on faith may be challenged and shown to be mistaken. But if such challenges are to be taken seriously, then they must be supported by faith. Thus faith is presupposed by all challenges to faith itself. It follows that all challenges to faith fail. This is plainly unacceptable, since faith in miraculous cures, charms that bring luck, and the good will of a government is often mistaken. What has gone wrong with Nagel's argument, given the above interpretation of it, is that it starts with the assumption that the argument is meant to prove. This is an elementary mistake and Nagel is much too good a philosopher to make it.

Nagel avoids this mistake by adding a crucial qualification to the argument. "There are some types of thought," he claims, "that we cannot avoid simply *having*—that it is strictly impossible to consider merely from the outside, because they enter inevitably and directly into any process of considering ourselves from the outside" (20). In order to avoid the objection that the same can be said by defenders of faith, Nagel has to specify what the types of thought are that we cannot avoid simply having, and why faith—or hope, intuition, passion, and so forth—is not such a type of thought. And he does specify that the types of thought are the cogito, logic, and mathematics (20), and "I believe," he writes, that "something similar is true of practical reasoning, including moral reasoning" (20). Further, "challenges to the objectivity of science can be met only by further scientific reasoning, challenges to the objectivity of history by history, and so forth" (21).

Now this seems precisely what Nagel claims relativists are saying, which is that "understanding and justification come to an end... within our point of view—individual or shared—so that ultimately, even the apparently most objective and universal principles derive their validity or authority from the perspective and practice of those who follow them" (3). According to Nagel, challenges to the cogito, logic, mathematics, morality, science, history, and so forth can be met only within these types of thought. How, then, is Nagel's absolutism different from relativism?

It is different because Nagel denies and relativists insist that these modes of understanding can be challenged from the outside. Nagel thinks that there are categories of thought "that we cannot get outside of" and "the range of examples turns out to be quite wide" (21). The question of whether we should "withdraw a first-order judgment" made within these categories of thought "are questions *within*" them. For instance, "one cannot just *exit* from the domain of moral reflection: It is simply there.... It's the same everywhere," in science, history, and so forth (21). "If one tries to occupy a standpoint entirely outside of it, one will fail" (20). Relativists insist on challenging modes of understanding or categories of thought by claiming that they can be justified only by their own standards, because there are no "objective principles whose validity is independent of our point of view" (3). And this, relativists claim, makes them merely conventional, context-dependent, and ultimately arbitrary.

Nagel denies this on the ground that external challenges to the cogito, logic, mathematics, morality, science, history, and so forth are incoherent, because they can be stated only by appealing to what they challenge. Reasoning within these categories of thought or modes of understanding cannot be coherently challenged by faith, hope, intuition, or passion because the challenge relies on reason. But faith, intuition, and so forth can be coherently challenged because challenges to them need not rely on what is being challenged. Since reason is universal and unconditional, it is necessarily involved in any challenge to it. As Nagel puts it, reason is "not merely personal, or societal, but universal" (4); its "essential characteristic is... generality. If I have reasons to conclude or believe or want something, they cannot be just reasons for me—they would have to justify anyone else doing the same in my place" (5); and any "challenge to the universal claims of reason has to propose an alternative that can be the object of something like a belief, or anyway acceptance; and none is available" (99). It is also "a form or category of thought from which there is no appeal beyond itself—whose validity is unconditional because it is necessarily employed in every purported challenge to itself" (7).

The absolutist requirement that good reasons must be universal and unconditional rests on numerous assumptions. I will mention only three of them because they have direct bearing on modes of understanding, their conflicts, and the philosophical problems that result from their conflicts. One is that the only alternative to the absolutist requirement that understanding and justification must be based on universal and unconditional reasons is the relativist view that, since such reasons cannot be found, understanding and justification must ultimately be based on some commitment for which no universal and unconditional reasons can be given. I will argue against this assumption that the pluralist view is another alternative. In the context of conflicting modes of understanding and philosophical problems, understanding and justification may be non-arbitrarily based on particular and conditional reasons.

Another assumption on which the absolutist view rests is that good theoretical and the practical reasons must be universal and unconditional. "If I have reasons to conclude or to believe or to want to do something, they cannot be reasons just for me" (5); reason "applies in both theory and practice, in the formation not only of beliefs but of desires, intentions, and decisions as well" (6); "the serious attempt to identify what is subjective and particular, or relative and communal, in one's outlook leads inevitably to the objective and universal. That is so whether the object of our scrutiny is ethics, or science, or even logic" (16). In that case, there could not be good practical reasons for acting in a way that failed to be universal and unconditional. Conflicts between universal and unconditional reasons could only be apparent. There must always be something that reason requires anyone in a particular situation to do, just as there always is a belief that reason requires anyone in a particular situation to hold. Uncertainty and conflict merely indicate that the search for universal and unconditional reasons has not gone far enough. I think that many practical reasons are particular, conditional, and good. If so, then absolutists and relativists are both mistaken in holding that practical reasons must be like theoretical reasons in being universal and unconditional.

A further assumption on which the absolutist approach rests is that historical, moral, political, religious, scientific, and personal beliefs and actions could not be challenged from the outside of these modes of understanding because all reasonable challenges must be made and responded to within the challenged mode. Take any one of them, "if one tries to occupy a standpoint entirely outside of it, one will fail. Thought always leads us back to the employment of unconditional reason if we try to challenge it globally, because one can't criticize something with nothing" (20). "Challenges to the objectivity of science can be met only by further scientific reasoning, challenges to the objectivity of history by history, and so forth. This does not mean that the results are unrevisable, only that the revision must proceed by the continuation of the process itself" (21–2). If this were true, then problems caused by conflicts between modes of understanding would not be philosophi-cal because all genuine problems must occur, and at least in principle be solvable, within one or another mode of understanding. But it is not true. Modes of under-standing can be reasonably challenged from the outside, and the challenge may succeed or fail on the basis of practical reasons that may be given for or against one or both of the conflicting modes of understanding.

These assumptions and my disagreements with them turn on the question of what good reasons are in this context. I will argue that while some good reasons are universal and unconditional, many others are not. Particular and conditional reasons may be perfectly good bases, in certain specifiable contexts, for holding some beliefs and performing some actions. Reliance on particular and conditional reasons need not be arbitrary, as relativists claim. Nor is reliance on them only a temporary and imperfect expedient that will do until they are sufficiently strength-ened by additional reasons and become universal and unconditional, as absolut-ists require. There are some good reasons that must be particular and conditional, and none the worse for that. And these are just the reasons that pluralists rely on in their approach to resolving conflicts between modes of understanding and coping with philosophical problems.

Theoretical and Practical Reasons

Theoretical reasons aim at true beliefs; practical reasons at successful actions. In some cases theoretical reasons guarantee the truth of a belief, as in numbers form-ing an infinite series, *modus ponens*, the cogito, and human mortality. There are also cases in which theoretical reasons favor a particular action and oppose any alternative to it, as in eating, breathing, and resting if one wants stay alive. In these cases, good reasons are universal and unconditional: they require everyone to hold these beliefs and perform these actions rather than any alternatives contrary to them. If all cases were like these, absolutists would be right: good theoretical and practical reasons would have to be universal and unconditional.

Many cases, however, are quite different. Suppose I believe that I should get a divorce. I weighed all the reasons for and against it, considered the interests of all directly affected parties, I am not deceiving myself, my belief is formed after long and careful reflection, I discussed it with my wife, and we agree that since our differences are basic and irreconcilable, we should divorce. All relevant theo-retical reasons support my belief, I conclude that my belief is true and acting on it reasonable. Let us suppose that I do not merely believe all this, but that my belief is true and that no one could point at any additional theoretical or practical reason that I have failed to take into account.

Are the theoretical reasons for this true belief and the practical reasons for subsequent action universal and unconditional, as absolutists say that they must be? It may be thought that they are because if all the reasons favor the belief, and if the belief is indeed true, then anyone in the same situation, after having weighed the reasons as seriously as I have, would either accept the belief as true and act on it, or fail as a result of having made some mistake in reasoning.

This thought, however, is mistaken because no one else could be in my situation. The essential features of my situation are my own and my wife's characters and expectations in life, our estimate of how our children would be affected by the divorce, the history of our marriage with its ups and downs, pleasures and pains, fights and reconciliations, and how both I and my wife want to live. The relevant theoretical and practical reasons are particular to me and to her. They are conditional on biographical facts that are facts only about me, about who I am and how I became who I am. Consequently no one else could have the theoretical and practical reasons I have for divorce.

Absolutists may acknowledge this and say that my reasons are particular and conditional only because there are presently insuperable practical obstacles to others having access to all the relevant reasons for and against my divorce. If they had access and my reasons for divorce were indeed good, then they would universally and unconditionally endorse them. The obstacle, in the way of access, absolutists would say, is not theoretical but practical. If it were surmounted, say by great advances in cognitive neuroscience, it would make my psychological states, history, and how I want to live accessible to others, and then it would become clear whether my reasons were indeed good. They would be good if they were universal and unconditional. Absolutists would say that this case of divorce does not show that good reasons need not be universal and unconditional. It shows only that the present limitations of scientific knowledge make it impossible for others to test the reasons that guarantee the truth of my beliefs and the success of my actions.

This absolutist rejoinder, however, is unconvincing, even if we accept the science fiction on which it rests. The trouble with it is not that my psychological states are necessarily private and that I alone have direct access to them. Let us accept that in one way or another it becomes possible to gain access to the psychological states of others. The access would make it possible to observe psychological states, much as it is now possible to observe physical states. Access to my psychological states could show others, however, only the reasons that led me to believe that I should get a divorce and made me prepared to act on it. It would not show that my belief

and action are reasonable. For whether they are reasonable depends on my evaluation of the relative importance of the considerations whose balance led me to hold
the belief and act on it. Access would enable others to know how I evaluate the relative importance of relevant considerations, but not whether my evaluation is right
or wrong. The evaluation is of how *I* evaluate their relative importance, not how
it would be reasonable universally and unconditionally to evaluate it. The facts
underdetermine their evaluation. My evaluations could perhaps be explained and
predicted by others, but they could not experience, feel, identify with my evaluations as I do, because my evaluation is a product of the totality of the experiences,
influences, education, successes, and failures that have formed my character, and
of how I want to live. This, of course, is true not just of me, but of countless others.
The totality of the conditions that have formed us—the relative importance we
attribute to these conditions, and how, given these differences, we want to live—
differs from person to person. That is why in many cases the reasons for our beliefs
and actions must be particular and conditional, cannot be universal and unconditional, and yet be good reasons.

Absolutists may say that I have just conceded that there is a universal and
unconditional standard of evaluation. It is the totality of conditions that have
formed each one of us. The universal and unconditional reason for a particular
evaluation is what follows from this standard. But this is not an acceptable reply.
For the totality of formative conditions varies with persons. It is true that there is
a totality of conditions that have formed each one of us, but it is a different totality
because the particular formative conditions differ. And since they differ, so will the
evaluations that follow from them. It does not follow from it being reasonable that
I should get a divorce that it would be reasonable for anyone else to get a divorce.
Whether others should get a divorce depends on the totality of conditions that
have formed them, and those conditions will be different from my own, and
indeed from anyone else's.

It is, of course, possible that our understanding of the totality of conditions that have formed us is mistaken or incomplete. We are all fallible, liable to
self-deception, wishful thinking, shying away from facing unpleasant facts, and so
forth. Of course we should be critical of our own understanding and suspicious of
our certainties. But when it is all said and done, the best we can do in the context
of deciding how we should live is to hold relevant beliefs and perform relevant
actions that after critical reflection we have reason to endorse and no reason to
suspect. Those reasons, however, will still be particular and conditional.

These particular and conditional reasons are no less objective than universal
and unconditional reasons. Truth does not become less objective if it holds only
of one person rather than of everyone. Perhaps it is a universal and unconditional

truth that what we believe and do depends on the totality of the conditions that have formed us. But this truth, if it is one, is like the truths that every event has a cause, or that what will be will be, or that the good is better than the bad. These truths are so general as to be useless if we want to know the cause of a particular event, try to predict what will happen, or decide whether something is good. If reasons are to help us to know how we should live, they must leave such vacuous generalities behind and be anchored in the particularities that make up the totality of the facts and our evaluations of them. And that makes the reasons for how we should live conditional on those particularities. Absolutists fail to see this. They rightly stress that some beliefs and actions are universally and unconditionally required by reason, but wrongly assume that all good reasons for beliefs and actions must be universally and unconditionally required.

The Disunity of Reasons[3]

Another mistaken assumption on which absolutism rests is the unity of theoretical and practical reason. The assumption is that the requirements of theoretical and practical reasons are the same. Since theoretical reasons must be universal and unconditional, so must be practical reasons. The source of this assumption is Kant, who requires "the unity of practical with speculative [i.e. theoretical] reason in a common principle, since there can, in the end, be only one and the same reason, which must be distinguished merely in its application."[4] This is clear enough, but what Kant says in "The Canon of Pure Reason" in the first *Critique* makes things far more complicated, and I might as well confess that after numerous readings I am still not sure what Kant is saying there.[5]

Be that as it may, Nagel does follow what Kant says in the quoted passage: "if there is such a thing as practical reason, it does not simply dictate particular actions but, rather, governs the *relations* among actions, desires, and beliefs—just as theoretical reason governs the relations among beliefs" (107). The underlying assumption is, then, that the logical structure of theoretical and practical reasons is the same. The difference between them is only that one aims at true beliefs, while the other aims at successful actions.

What leads absolutists to assume this, I conjecture, is the thought that if the requirements of theoretical and practical reason were different, they could conflict. Theoretical reasons may prompt us to act in one way and practical reason in another, and then we could not rely on reason to guide what we should believe or do. Absolutists find this unacceptable. Pluralists regard it as a fact of life. It is a routine experience in virtually all of our lives that we have theoretical reasons for not taking a risk, telling the truth, or selling our house, and contrary practical reasons for taking that risk to alleviate boredom, prudently keeping our mouth shut, or waiting until the economy improves. Absolutists accept, of course, that this often happens, but they think that when it does, it is because we have not carried reasoning as far as we should have. It shows that we have failed to be sufficiently reasonable, not that theoretical and practical reason may conflict.

Absolutists, however, owe an answer to the question of why theoretical and practical reasons could not conflict, why additional reasons would eliminate conflicts between what we should believe and do. It is not an acceptable answer that if the reasons are strong enough, then they will eliminate conflicts. Perhaps the truth is that having as many additional reasons as possible may still lead to contrary conclusions about what we should believe and do. Absolutists need to explain why conflicts are not plain facts of life, rather than symptoms of a failure to be sufficiently reasonable. Why should we not accept that we have to live with conflicts, much as we live with scarcity, ill health, and mortality? These are unfortunate facts and obstacles to the improvement of our lives, but that is not an adequate reason for blaming us for them, rather than accepting them as part of the scheme of things.

Absolutists, however, have a better answer than this kind of hand-wringing about the human condition. Their answer is to point at the truth-directedness of theoretical reason. Theoretical reason is the best way we have of arriving at true beliefs and eliminating false ones, as the history of logic, mathematics, and science show. If a belief is true, it cannot conflict with another true belief. If beliefs conflict, it is because one or both are false. Furthermore, if a belief is shown to be logically, mathematically, or scientifically true, then it is true universally and unconditionally. The failure to accept it as true is a sign of ignorance, inattention, or a failure of reason. And reason requires that if we can, we should act on true beliefs supported by theoretical reason, rather than on unexamined or false beliefs. In this absolutists are right, and pluralists agree with them.

What this line of thought misses is that the true beliefs we seek are about what we should do given who we are and what we have to do in a particular context. Theoretical reason can lead to true beliefs about the nature of the risk we may or may not take, the likely consequences of telling or not telling the truth, and of how the prospects of the economy may affect our real estate transactions, but that is not enough for us to make a reasonable decision about what we should do. What we should do also depends on what our aims are and on how we evaluate our context. It depends on how bored we actually are and how willing to live with uncertainty; on how strongly we and our society are committed to truth-telling and how important we think telling the truth is in that particular context; or on how much we like or dislike the house we have and what our financial needs and circumstances actually are. In trying to make a reasonable decision about what we should do, we pursue certain aims and depend on our evaluation of the context in which we have to make the decision. These aims and evaluations are our own and typically not generalizable to other people.

In defending absolutism, Nagel writes that

the first step on the path of ethics is the admission of *generality* in practical judgments. That is actually equivalent to the admission of the existence of reasons, for a reason is something one person can have only if others would also have it if they were in the same circumstances (internal as well as external). (119)

I have been arguing that this cannot be right. If it were, we could not form an ethical judgment about what we should do in pursuing our particular aims in our particular contexts, when both are essentially formed by our individual character, history, and how we want to live, none of which is usually generalizable to other people. It is a desperate expedient to try save this implausible ethical requirement to insist that my judgment can be reasonable only if anyone in that situation would make the same judgment, when no one else could be in my situation. On countless occasions, reasonable ethical judgments are made in the contexts of intimate relationships, like marriage, friendship, or parenthood, which are formed by individuals whose characters and interlocking histories make reasonable generalizations to others impossible.

True beliefs about our aims and contexts must certainly be part of any reasonable decision we may arrive at. And the beliefs, if true, are true universally and unconditionally no matter who has to make the decision. But our aims and the evaluations of our context are particular and conditional. They are aims we have partly because of who we are and how we want to live. They are conditional on our character, history, and often also on our relationships with others; and the same is true of our evaluations. The relevance of the true beliefs we seek by means of theoretical reasons partly depends on the aims we try to achieve and on the evaluations of our contexts that we form by means of practical reason. Practical reasons certainly depend on true beliefs based on theoretical reasons, but, no less certainly, theoretical reasons in turn depend on the aims and evaluations of contexts based on practical reasons.

Theoretical and practical reasons, therefore, are interdependent in contexts in which we have to decide what to do. Of course, there are other contexts, such as logic, mathematics, and science, in which we have to decide what to believe. And in those contexts theoretical reasons are likely to be far more important than practical reasons. The relative importance of universal and unconditional theoretical reasons and particular and conditional practical reasons depends on the aims we are trying to achieve and the contexts in which we are trying to achieve them. If our aim is to form true beliefs about some segment of the world *sub specie aeternitatis*, then theoretical reasons will be far more important than practical reasons. If our aim is to make reasonable decisions about how we, the individuals that we are, should live *sub specie humanitatis*, say in ethical, political, or personal contexts, then practical reasons will be more important than theoretical reasons. The relative importance of theoretical and practical reasons, therefore, is context-dependent.

This has damaging consequences for both absolutism and relativism. The plausibility of the absolutist claim that reasons must be universal and unconditional depends on supposing that our primary aim in relying on reason is to form a view of the world *sub specie aeternitatis*. As we have seen, however, that is only one of our aims. We also aim to make reasonable decisions about how we should live *sub specie humanitatis*, and when we aim at that, then many of our reasons will be particular and conditional. There is no good reason to suppose, as absolutists do, either that the first of these aims should always take precedence over the second, or that universal and unconditional reasons set the standard of which particular and conditional reasons are imperfect approximations.

These reasons for rejecting the excessive claims of absolutists, however, are not reasons for accepting the claim of relativists that ultimately all reasons rest on arbitrary decisions. Reasonable decisions about how we should live *sub specie humanitatis* may be as objective and non-arbitrary as true beliefs are about the world *sub specie aeternitatis*. It is true that the beliefs we form and the actions we take depend on our aims and contexts, but given the aim of trying to understand the world and trying to decide how to live, the beliefs we form and the actions we take may be perfectly reasonable and the best means to achieving our aims. Of course, our aims may be misguided and our evaluations of the contexts in which we have to act may be faulty. Relativists, however, must recognize that we have aims and that makes it unreasonable for us not to rely on reason, which is the best means of achieving our aims. If relativists think that our biases always lead to wrong evaluations of the contexts in which we have to pursue our aims, then they owe an explanation of how specifically we go wrong. If we form beliefs about the world that all reasons available to us support and none causes us to doubt, and if we make decisions about how we should act that actually help us live as we want, then the claim that our beliefs and actions are ultimately arbitrary and lead us to the wrong evaluation of our aims and contexts becomes indefensible.

These considerations lend support to the pluralist approach that accepts that reasons may be theoretical or practical, universal and unconditional, or particular and conditional, and that both our beliefs and actions based on such reasons may be as objective as it is possible for fallible human beings to hold and to do.

The Universal and the Human Points of View

The human point of view is anthropocentric. It is the world viewed *sub specie humanitatis*, and concerned with how we should live, given the world as we find it. The universal point of view is non-anthropocentric. It is the world viewed *sub specie aeternitatis*, from a perspective that is indifferent to how the world affects us. These two points of view are of course connected, since how it is reasonable for us to live depends on how the world is and our view of the world is formed by us—we are unavoidably affected by the possibilities and limits set by our nature. The two perspectives are different and have different aims, but we have good reasons to seek understanding both of the world in which we have to try to improve our lives and of what specifically we can do to improve them given our individuality and context.

It may seem, however, that these two points of view are not only different, but conflicting. This is how it appears to Nagel, who thinks that the conflict between them is real, fundamental, and unavoidable. He writes about this conflict:[6] "think of how an ordinary individual sweats over his appearance, his health, his sex life, his emotional honesty, his social utility, his self-knowledge," but when these worries are considered

sub specie aeternitatis—the view is at once sobering and comical.... Yet when we take this view and recognize what we do as arbitrary, it does not disengage us from life, and there lies our absurdity: not in the fact that such an external view can be taken of us, but in the fact that we ourselves take it, without ceasing to be the persons whose ultimate concerns are so coolly regarded. (15)

He concludes that this "sense of the absurd is a way of perceiving our true situation," which is that *sub specie humanitatis* our concerns matter, but "*sub specie aeternitatis* there is no reason to believe that anything matters" (23), and we hold both points of view.

He refers to the universal or *sub specie aeternitatis* point of view sometimes as outer and sometimes as objective, and to the human point of view, by contrast, as inner and subjective. He writes:[7]

the uneasy relation between inner and outer perspectives, neither of which we can escape, makes it hard to maintain a coherent attitude toward the fact that we exist at all, toward our deaths, and toward the meaning and point of our lives, because a detached view of our own existence, once achieved, is not easily made part of the standpoint from which life is lived. From far enough my birth seems accidental, my life pointless, and my death insignificant, but from inside my never having been born seems nearly unimaginable, my life monstrously important, and my death catastrophic. Though the two viewpoints clearly belong to one person—these problems wouldn't arise if they didn't—they function independently enough so that each can come as something of a surprise to the other. (209)

And he goes on: their conflict is "impossible to eliminate.... Some may dismiss these existential worries as bogus or artificial," but he finds that response "unacceptable, because the objective standpoint, even at its limits is too essential a part of us to be suppressed without dishonesty... even if complete integration inevitably eludes us" (210). The problem is real because "we cannot compensate for the lack of cosmic meaning with a meaning we derive from our own perspective" (210).

Nagel does not say why the meaning we derive from the human point of view could not compensate for the lack of meaning from the universal point of view. The pluralist approach is precisely that the meaning we derive from the human point of view and our values is a reasonable alternative to the futile search for universal meaning. Nagel is certainly right in this: from the universal point of view our position in the universe is not central and has no more value than anything else, since from that point of view nothing has value. But from the human point of view our lives and their improvement are valuable, because we care about them, even though we live in a universe that does not care about anything. It would be, then, the height of folly for us to seek to understand our lives from the universal rather than from the human point of view. Yet Nagel thinks that we should strive to do that, and he acknowledges that his position "amounts to a strong form of anti-humanism: the world is not our world" (108).

I think that the conflict Nagel regards as real, fundamental, and unavoidable is in fact bogus or artificial. The source of Nagel's mistake is twofold. Part of it is that he regards the universal point of view as objective and the human point of view as subjective. He supposes that the latter is subjective, because that is how he thinks it appears from the universal point of view. But why should we take an external, *sub specie aeternitatis*, view, from which our lives and how we should make them better appear to have no value? Why is it absurd to suppose that things matter to us, even if we acknowledge that we live in an indifferent universe from whose point of view nothing matters? Why should we think that the values of the human point of view are subjective?

They are certainly subjective in the sense that they are held by subjects, namely us. In that sense, however, the universal point of view is also subjective because it too is held by us, since the universe has no point of view. But neither the universal nor the human point of view is subjective in the sense that obviously matters, namely that understanding and acting according to one or the other may or may not improve our lives. It is an objective fact whether acting according to a particular value aids, hinders, or has no effect on the improvement of our lives. And it is as objective as any historical, moral, political, religious, scientific, or personal fact, regardless of whether it is viewed from the universal or the human point of view.

If we ask, as we should, why Nagel thinks otherwise, we come to another source of the mistake that leads him to regard a bogus and artificial conflict as real, fundamental, and unavoidable. The mistake, by now familiar, is to think that what is objective must be universal and unconditional, and then conclude that since many values on which the improvement of our lives depends are context-dependent and thus particular and conditional, they are subjective. He thinks that reason requires that what we believe or do must be based on universal and unconditional reasons. Beliefs and actions based on particular and conditional reasons fail to be objective and reasonable. They are subjective and, at best, insufficiently reasonable, because they fail to meet the requirements set by theoretical reason. Led by these thoughts, Nagel finds our condition absurd, because when our efforts are guided by practical reason they are ultimately unreasonable and arbitrary, just as relativists believe, unless additional reasons make them universal, unconditional, and thus sufficient. The conflict that he supposes is real, fundamental, and unavoidable is in fact a by-product of the mistaken claim that practical reason is an incomplete form of theoretical reason.

Absolutism, Pluralism, and Relativism

By way of an interim summary, it may be helpful to have a visual representation of the agreements and disagreements among these three approaches to the requirements that must be met by good reasons.

Of the three approaches, the relativist is the simplest to explain: the requirements of good reasons are that they must be universal and unconditional, but the requirements cannot be met. Universal and unconditional reasons are impossible because all reasons are ultimately derived from particular and conditional social or individual commitments which are context-dependent and cannot be derived from further reasons. Particular and conditional reasons are possible, but unavoidably insufficient. They could be made sufficient only by additional reasons

The requirements of good reasons

	Absolutism	Pluralism	Relativism
Theoretical Universal Unconditional	Necessary	Possible	Impossible
Practical Particular Conditional	Insufficient	Often Sufficient	Insufficient

that transform them into universal and unconditional reasons, but this cannot be done because additional reasons will also be context-dependent.

According to the absolutist approach, good reasons must and can be universal and unconditional. Many theoretical reasons, especially logical, mathematical, and scientific ones, meet these requirements because challenges to them presuppose the reasons that are challenged. Practical reasons may also meet them, provided additional reasons make them universal and unconditional, and thus immune to coherent challenge. Moral and political reasons, among others, are insufficient unless they meet this requirement by relying on a principle like the categorical imperative.

Defenders of the pluralist approach hold that both theoretical and practical reasons may be good even if they are particular and conditional, rather than universal and unconditional. Many theoretical reasons, especially logical, mathematical, and scientific ones, are universal and unconditional. There are also some good theoretical reasons, for instance historical and prudential ones, that are not universal and unconditional, because they are context-dependent. In their own context, however, they are as good reasons as they are required to be, even if they are not generalizable to other contexts. Many practical reasons, especially ethical, political, and personal ones, are particular and conditional. They hold only in particular contexts, and are based on considerations that vary with social or individual conditions. Such reasons are good if the relevant considerations favor them and no contrary reasons cast doubt on them. Being dependent on a context, they cannot become universal and unconditional, but they may nevertheless be as good and sufficient reasons as necessary in that context.

I have treated relativism as the approach that follows if both the absolutist and the pluralist approaches turn out to be mistaken. My view is that the absolutist approach is mistaken, but pluralist one is not, so relativism does not follow. The dispute between the pluralist and the absolutist approaches, as we can now see, turns on the question of whether particular and conditional reasons fail to be good because they are unavoidably insufficient. I have argued that the absolutist requirement that good reasons must be universal and unconditional is based on the mistake of thinking that theoretical reasons set the standard and practical reasons can be sufficient only if they conform to that standard. According to pluralists, good practical reasons are particular and conditional on the requirement of improving our lives in ways that vary with social and individual contexts.

Absolutists may argue against the pluralist approach that such variety is only apparent, and that practical reasons could be made universal and unconditional if they took into account all relevant considerations. It is the failure of pluralists to take all relevant considerations into account that makes particular and conditional practical reasons insufficient and fall short of being good reasons. I now turn to this absolutist argument.

Relevance

Nagel's defense of absolutism assumes that the relevant considerations that must be taken into account are the facts of the context at hand. "Challenges to the objectivity of science can be met only by further scientific reasoning, challenges to the objectivity of history by history, and so forth" (21). "Definite conclusions on these matters depend on more substantive investigation of whether . . . our actual uncertain efforts in that direction are a reflection of something that might be further perfected" (80). And:

> moral considerations occupy a position in the system of human thought that makes it illegitimate to subordinate them completely to anything else. Particular moral claims are constantly being discredited for all kinds of reasons, but moral considerations per se keep arising again to challenge in their own rights any blanket attempt to displace, defuse or subjectivize them (105).

The particular facts on which reasons are based, for instance in science, history, and morality, may be rightly challenged. But the reasons for both the challenges and the efforts to meet them depend on further facts within science, history, or morality. It is always further facts of the same kind that strengthen or weaken the challenge, and the challenges can be reasonably directed only against particular facts, not the domain itself. "One cannot just *exit* from the domain of moral reflection: It is simply there" (21), and the same is true of the domain of history, science, and, presumably, of all the other modes of understanding.

If the only considerations relevant to such challenges were facts, then this absolutist assumption would be plausible. If reasons are particular and conditional because they are based on insufficient facts, then they are indeed not good enough. Making them better would depend on seeking further and further facts until they are no longer vulnerable to challenge by further facts because all relevant facts are in. This is an ideal, of course, but it is one, according to absolutists, that reason requires aiming at. Reasons are good, on this view, to the extent to which they approximate this ideal. The closer they come to it, the more they approximate being universal and unconditional, and the more unreasonable it becomes to fail to accept the facts vouchsafed for by such reasons.

The absolutist assumption, however, is mistaken, because the relevant considerations include not just facts but also the evaluation of the significance of the facts. Even if reasons are based on the consideration of all the relevant facts, they may still fail to be universal and unconditional if the evaluations of the significance of the facts are particular and conditional. And the pluralist view is that when the significance of the relevant facts is evaluated from the human point of view, from the point of view of making our lives better, then the evaluations are typically particular and conditional, because they are made from the point of view of different modes of understanding. The significance of the facts relevant to improving our lives may be evaluated from a historical, moral, political, religious, scientific, or personal point of view. Any of these evaluations will be unavoidably particular and conditional because it is made from the point of view of one of several possible modes of understanding. I have been arguing that these evaluations often conflict and give rise to philosophical problems. And these conflicts and problems make it impossible to form a universal and unconditional point of view that combines all the particular points of view that follow from the various modes of understanding.

These conflicts and philosophical problems are left untouched by the absolutist requirement that reason requires the consideration of all the relevant facts. Reason also requires the consideration of all relevant evaluations of the significance of the facts, and since they proceed from different points of view, they will be particular and conditional. The remarkable feature of Nagel's argument is that he acknowledges this and yet fails to see how damaging the acknowledgment is for the absolutist approach. He writes:

The normative cannot be transcended by the descriptive. The question "What should I do?" like the question "What should I believe?" is always in order. It is always possible to think about the question in normative terms, and the process is not rendered pointless by any fact of a different kind—any desire or emotion or feeling, any habit or practice or convention, any contingent cultural or social background. Such things may in fact guide our actions, but it is always possible to take their relation to action as an object of further normative reflection and ask "How should I act, given that these things are true of me or of my situation?". The type of thought that generates answers to this question is practical reason. (105–6)

But the answers to normative questions are routinely given from the conflicting points of view of different modes of understanding, and this will make all the answers particular, conditional, and thus, according to absolutists, insufficiently reasonable.

Nagel denies this on the ground that both factual and normative questions that arise within a mode of understanding must be answered within that mode. Questions external to them are incoherent because they presuppose the answers they aim to challenge. Giving as examples "first-order arithmetic or ethical reasoning" he writes: "we must ask whether the proposed 'external' explanations make it reasonable to withdraw our assent from any of these propositions or to qualify it in some way," and the answer he gives is that "these are questions *within* arithmetic or ethics" (21).

Now this is an extraordinary view. It implies that it is contrary to reason to question the legitimacy of any mode of understanding, and that all normative questions about a whole mode of understanding are contrary to reason. It is contrary to reason to ask whether history should not become a science based on laws that govern human behavior; whether morality might not just be a facade for personal interests; whether politics is anything more than morality by other means; whether religion might not be merely sublimated fear; whether scientific research should not be guided by moral, political, or religious values; or whether personal values are anything more than failures to remember one's indoctrination. According to Nagel, the mere asking of these questions—questions that seemed deep and important to countless thoughtful people—are contrary to reason. The questions skeptics ask about reason, Vico about science, Rousseau about civilization, Hume and Freud about religion, Hegel about classical logic, Marx about politics and the law, Nietzsche about morality, Hempel about history, anthropologists and sociologists about all absolute values, and so on and on, are all misplaced. All those whose deep immersion in a mode of understanding led them to wonder about its overall legitimacy have been asking questions to which the uniformly conclusive answer, according to Nagel, is to do more of what they have been doing and stop the misguided questioning of the legitimacy of doing it.

What is the source of this doctrinaire absolutist opposition to the reflective questioning of our own theoretical and practical commitments? It is the supposition that answers to them must rely on particular and conditional reasons, and thus lead to relativism. If the just-criticized strategy of denying the legitimacy of such questions fails, and if absolutists are right to claim that particular and conditional reasons are not good enough, does it then not follow that relativists are right? I can think of two ways in which absolutists may try to avoid this.

The first is to claim that one of the conflicting modes of understanding is overriding because it is presupposed by all the other modes. I have argued against this in Part Two—that defenders of each mode of understanding can make this claim for the mode they favor and give reasons in support of it. Each one of the historical, moral, political, religious, scientific, and personal modes of understanding depends on some evaluations that follow from other modes. And defenders of these other modes regard the evaluations as having overriding significance. The absolutist claim that the evaluations that follow from one of these modes of understanding should always be overriding begs the question at issue.

The second way in which absolutists may try to avoid relativism is to rely, as Nagel does, on what I will call, using his phrase, the it-is-just-there strategy. Given our world-view, history, morality, politics, religion, science, and personal concerns are just there. We derive our evaluations of what we should believe and do from them. But this is not nearly enough to show which of the conflicting evaluations we derive from them we have good reasons to accept in preference to the others. From the it-is-just-there strategy it perhaps follows what the relevant considerations are, but it does not follow from them which of the relevant but conflicting considerations reason requires us to regard as overriding the others.

It seems, therefore, that absolutists do not have a satisfactory reason for rejecting the relativists' claim that ultimately all reasons are particular, conditional, and rest on context-dependent commitments. According to relativists, particular and conditional reasons cannot be made universal and unconditional by providing additional reasons for them because the additional reasons will also be particular and conditional, and the same will be true of all reasons. I conclude that the absolutist approach is mistaken. Can pluralists give good reasons for rejecting the relativist approach if they accept that the evaluations of the significance of relevant considerations are particular, conditional, and routinely conflict?

Yes they can, by rejecting the assumption absolutists and relativists accept that good reasons must be universal and unconditional. Pluralists need to show that there can be good particular and conditional reasons in particular contexts for resolving conflicts between the evaluations that follow from different modes of understanding and for coping with philosophical problems caused by their conflicts. Showing this can and must be done by considering actual contexts, conflicts, and problems, and that is the topic of the Chapters 10 and 11.

10

The Pluralist Approach to Good Lives, Providential Order, and the Ideal State

One who properly recognises the plurality of values is one who understands the deep creative role that these various values can play in human life.... It is to try to build a life round the recognition that these different values do each have a real and intelligible human significance, and are not just errors, misdirections or poor expressions of human nature. To try to build a life in another way would now be an evasion, of something which by now we understand to be true. What we understand is a truth about human nature.

Bernard Williams[1]

Introduction

The aim of this and Chapter 11 is to provide good reasons for accepting the pluralist approach to each of the philosophical problems I have been considering throughout the book. The discussion is divided into two chapters, but only to avoid having one inordinately long chapter. The reasons for the pluralist approach are strengthened by the critical arguments of earlier chapters directed against the absolutist and the relativist approaches. I have argued that both approaches rest on an arbitrary assumption. The absolutist assumption is that one of the modes of understanding is always overriding and that the reasons derived from it are always better than those derived from conflicting modes. The relativist assumption is that resolving conflicts between modes of understanding and coping with philosophical problems ultimately depend on commitments for which no reasons can be given.

The pluralist approach takes the form of context-dependent, particular, and practical proposals. The approach rests on the conclusions reached in the preceding chapters that we have a plurality of irreducibly different modes of understanding, conflicts among them unavoidably recur, the conditions in which we have to cope with them are forever changing, and the improvement of our lives depends on finding new ways of coping with their conflicts in changing conditions. Given these assumptions, the pluralist approach to the six philosophical problems I have been discussing must be context-dependent, particular, and practical. We have good reasons for it if it enables us to cope with these philosophical problems and thus improve our lives in our present circumstances.

If the critical and constructive arguments in the preceding nine chapters have been successful, then the approach to coping with particular philosophical problems proposed in this chapter and the next will appear obvious and anti-climactic. These arguments were intended to show that philosophical problems appear to be formidably difficult because they have been misunderstood as theoretical problems in need of theoretical solutions. The pluralist view is that if we avoid this misunderstanding, give up the idea that any mode of understanding could always be overriding, and do not assume that good reasons must be universal and unconditional, then it becomes clear how we should go about coping with philosophical problems.

We need to balance personal satisfactions and moral responsibilities, without allowing either to overwhelm the other; make our society less unjust, without despairing about the contingencies of life or nurturing illusions about a benevolent cosmic order; ameliorate dissatisfactions with our political arrangements, without illusions about human goodness and rationality; increase our control over how we live, without inflating either our possibilities or our limits; hope for a better future, without the taint of despair or sentimentalism; and recognize the importance of moral values, without absolutist dogmas or relativist arbitrary commitments.

These pluralistic proposals of what we need to do are commonsensical because we have long been endeavoring to do anyway what pluralists propose we should be doing. Our efforts, however, have been obstructed by absolutists who directed us to look for an overriding mode of understanding, and relativists who urged us to abandon the search for ultimate reasons and be content in the end with arbitrary commitments. If these obstructions are removed, we can continue making the commonsensical efforts. I hope that even if it will seem obvious and anti-climactic that we should be making these efforts, making them still remains as difficult as it has always been, because it involves doing different things in different contexts by different individuals. That is why I have been insisting throughout that we can only cope with but not solve philosophical problems.

I must stress, however, that the approach that follows is not of fully worked ways of coping with philosophical problems, but only indications of what such ways may be. They are tentative first steps toward resolving conflicts between modes of understanding and coping with the resulting problems here and now, given our context, our world-view, and the present state of our modes of understanding. I acknowledge that much work needs to be done beyond these first steps. And even after the needed work has been done, the resulting proposals will not be once-and-for-all solutions but only reasonable ways of coping with these particular philosophical problems in our particular context. These modest proposals are nevertheless better than the absolutist and relativist alternatives. The references to "we" and its cognates in the proposals are further indications of their context-dependence and particularity. "We" are those who are immersed in our world-view and are concerned with giving good reasons for what we believe and do in the conditions that prevail now in our time-bound and changing part of the world.

What Makes Lives Good?

Lives are made good by meeting personal and moral conditions. The personal condition is trenchantly expressed thus: "every person has a life of his own, his one and only life, and that life he leads. But some more so than others." Good lives partly depend on:

the varying degrees to which people, persons, manage to give to their lives a pattern, an overallness, or the different degrees of success that they have in making their lives of a piece.... Such integration of life [is] something that, in many ages, for many cultures, has been in the nature of an ideal—a grace to be cultivated or a triumph to be won.[2]

This is a fine ideal, but nothing in it excludes lives whose grace is cultivated and triumph achieved at great cost to others. We believe, however, that good lives must be lived within moral limits and they must meet not just personal but also moral conditions: they must be personally satisfying—interpreting satisfaction in a broad sense—but they must also be morally responsible.

Many excellent books and articles have been written about what precisely these conditions are and should be. I will nevertheless leave them aside, and focus instead on our common experience that these two conditions, whatever they precisely are, routinely conflict. Meeting moral responsibilities may curtail our personal satisfactions and seeking personal satisfactions may be contrary to our moral responsibilities. Most of us, except perhaps saints and monsters, experience such conflicts. The question is how we might cope with them reasonably. It is no answer at all that coping depends on deciding which of the conflicting satisfaction and responsibility is more important. Part of the problem is that we are uncertain about how to make that decision. It is just such conflicts in everyday life that lead us to reflect and turn for help to modes of understanding. What we get, however, are modal problems within the personal and moral modes of understanding, and the philosophical problem that morality seems to require us to forgo satisfactions that make our life worth living and satisfying lives may be morally unacceptable. How, then, should we cope with such familiar conflicts?

Absolutists and relativists agree that we should be guided by good reasons, but they think that reasons come to an end. They disagree only about whether the end is an overriding mode of understanding or whether it is set by the conventions of the context which we have been brought up to accept. If pluralists are to do better than either, then they must avoid the arbitrariness of saying, as absolutists and relativists both do, that "if I have exhausted the justifications I have reached bedrock, and my spade is turned. Then I am inclined to say: 'This is simply what I do.'"[3] This simply will not do, since what we do may be ignorant, unreasonable, vicious, or just plain stupid. There are good reasons for looking further for good reasons.

I turn to two suggestions of Montaigne about where we find further good reasons, and then develop them in ways that I am unsure whether Montaigne would accept.[4] Montaigne's first suggestion is that "there is no one who, if he listens to himself, does not discover in himself a pattern all his own, a ruling pattern" (615). If we have such a personal "pattern established," we can "test our actions." The pattern allows us to say to ourselves that I "have my own laws and court to judge me" (613). Montaigne recognizes that the personal pattern is established by drawing on the values of our context. In that context, values

have their own weights and measures and qualities, but once inside, within us, she [the soul] allots them their qualities as she sees fit.... Health, conscience, authority, knowledge, riches, beauty, and their opposites—all are stripped on entry and receive from the soul new clothing, and coloring... which each individual chooses.... Let us no longer make the external qualities of things our excuse, it is up to us to reckon them as we will. (220)

We take our moral and non-moral values from our context, but the relative importance we attribute to them depends on the pattern we give to our lives.

Having such a pattern, of course, does not exempt us from living in the social world:

He who walks in the crowd must step aside, keep his elbow in, step back or advance, even leave the straight way, according to what he encounters. He must live not so much according to himself as according to others, not according to what he proposes to himself but according to what others propose to him, according to the time, according to the men, according to the business. (758)

"We must live in the world and make the most of it as we find it" (774). We unavoidably find, therefore, that our personal pattern prompts us to act in one way and the exigencies of the context in which we live often prompt us to act in a conflicting way. Montaigne understood this clearly, and his second suggestion is about how to cope with the resulting conflicts.

In our lives, he writes, "*the whole world plays a part*. We must play our part duly, but as part of a borrowed character. Of the mask and the appearance we must not make a real essence, nor what is foreign what is our very own.... It is enough to make up our face, without making up our hearts" (773). This is as realistic now as it was in Montaigne's own 16th century, but we may suspect that its realism is nothing but expediency that leads us to be untrue to our personal pattern when it conflicts with the customs of our context. Montaigne faced that conflict as well and he proposed a way of resolving it.

We must recognize that between the personal and the social there is "a very clear separation," and we should say to ourselves that "I do not involve myself so deeply and entirely" (774). "Not all things are permissible for an honorable man in the service of... the common cause or of the laws.... We commit a fallacy in thinking that everyone is obliged to perform... an action merely because it is useful" (609–10). What is and is not permissible should ultimately be determined by the integrity of our personal pattern. We can prudently compromise with the demands of our context, but only within the limits set by our personal pattern. To fail to do so is "the worst condition of man (245), it is "spiritual leprosy" (776), for then we lend ourselves to "the inconstant and variable movements of Fortune" (163). We cannot, of course, control fortune, but we can control our attitude to it. And the attitude Montaigne recommends is that "not being able to rule events, I rule myself, and adapt myself to them" (488), but only within the limits set "by my own laws and court to judge me" (613).

The laws and the court set by the personal pattern we have made for ourselves, however, are formed of values we have taken over from our context. But we have made the values our own by assigning to them their own weights and measures on the basis of their importance to living in the way we want. Some of these values will be moral, some personal, and some both at once. If they conflict, as they will, we should do what we can to cope with the conflicts between personal satisfactions and moral responsibilities by evaluating their relative importance on the basis of our personal pattern. Without such a pattern, we flounder; with it, we have a guide to how we should live. Good reasons do not come to an end with what we do. If we are reasonable, the reasons are derived from the personal pattern according to which we want to live.

This much, I think, is faithful to Montaigne's approach to coping with conflicts between the personal and the moral modes of understanding. There is, however, an obvious difficulty that Montaigne has not addressed, and I will now discuss. We are fallible, and the moral and non-moral values we take over from our context and the personal pattern we form of them may be mistaken. Following their promptings may make our lives worse, not better. Or they may lead us to ignore available values and other patterns acting on which would be more likely to make our lives better than those we have embedded in the pattern we have given our lives. The reasons we derive from our personal pattern may not be good reasons. If pluralists are to do better than absolutists and relativists, they must explain how we can tell whether our reasons are good.

What has daunted absolutists and relativists is the infinite regress involved in seeking reasons for reasons. For whatever reasons we have, we can ask whether they are good reasons, and if they are good only if we have good reasons for them as well, then we can never have good reasons. There is, however, something else we can reasonably do, and this is the key practical, context-dependent, and particular proposal that makes the pluralist approach to good lives better than the absolutist and relativist approaches. Instead of looking for reasons that would guarantee that the reasons we have are good, we should ask whether we have reasons to doubt that the reasons we have are good. What might such reasons be in the context of coping with the conflict between personal satisfactions and moral responsibilities?

They would be reasons for doubting that acting on the values that form part of the personal pattern according to which we want to live would be more likely to make our lives better than acting on other values available to us. If we have no reasons to doubt that, then we have as good reasons as we can have to act on them. But the question of whether we do or do not have reasons to doubt the values that form part of our pattern can be answered reasonably only by examining both the particular values and the reasons we have or might have for doubting them. What such reasons might be depends on the particular values in question and the context in which we live.

The simplest values we need to have and the reasons why we might doubt them have to do with the satisfaction of basic needs all human beings normally have for nutrition, rest, oxygen, and so forth. The satisfaction of such needs is a universal value that must form part of any reasonable pattern in accordance with which we might want to live, and it sets limits that any reasonable pattern must acknowledge. One reason for doubting the supposedly universal values of our pattern is that they are in fact not universal, and acting on them might be detrimental or irrelevant to the satisfaction of our basic needs. If, however, acting on them does lead to their satisfaction, then we have no reason to doubt them and reasons to accept them. Of course, a life we might reasonably want to live involves not just universal but also social and personal values, and doubts about them cannot be so easily handled.

There is a bewildering plurality of social values in the context of all societies. These values are not universal because they vary with different societies and with times within the same society. They are, however, general because those who live in a society are expected to conform, if not to all, then at least to very many of them. Social values are conventional. Following Hume, we might call them artificial, provided it is understood that they need not be, although they might be, arbitrary or optional. They may be thought of as forming some of the possibilities that we and others living together in a society might incorporate in the pattern in accordance with which we want to live.

These possibilities are embedded in conventions that guide relations with family members, friends, neighbors, colleagues, and strangers; recognized ways of making a living; attitudes toward sex, illness, death, the law, competition, property, leisure, education, travel, and so on and on for the many dimensions of ways of life that are recognized possibilities in the context of our society. Social values, taken jointly, form a loose, more or less coherent, and forever changing system. It informs our expectations, and we share them with others who live in our society. Holding such values and having shared expectations form our common social identity. We draw from it many of the values we make our own and incorporate in the pattern we aim to give to our lives by assigning to them their relative importance, their weights and measures as Montaigne says. And this pattern, together with our education, experiences, and preferences, largely constitutes our personal identity, the evaluative dimension of our lives formed of the particular universal, social, and personal values recognized in our social context.

The importance of personal identity understood in this way is that we derive from it what we believe are good reasons for living and acting as we think we should. What we take to be good reasons, however, may not be, because our pattern may be faulty. The particular universal, social, and personal values that form it may unreasonably exclude possibilities that would make our life better or include possibilities that would make it worse. What these faulty exclusions and inclusions may be depends on the particular values and the context in which we hold them.

Universal values may be faulty if they fail to recognize the importance of satisfying basic needs that all human beings normally have, or if they regard needs as basic that are in fact dictated by optional and perhaps arbitrary moral, political, or religious commitments. Social values may be faulty if they fail to recognize possibilities that would enrich our lives, or if they insist on the importance of possibilities that reflect only the personal values held by various authorities. And personal values may be faulty if they prompt us to pursue possibilities that are unsuitable given our character, personality, temperament, talents, and weaknesses, or if they prevent us from pursuing suitable possibilities.

The pluralist approach is better than the absolutist and relativist ones, because it does not lead to an infinite regress of seeking reasons for reasons. Its practical proposal is to ask whether we have reason to doubt that the values we hold and in accordance with which we live may be faulty. They are faulty if acting on them makes our life worse rather than better. This proposal is practical because it tells us what we should do to determine whether our reasons for living in a particular way are good. What we should do is to examine our reasons critically by asking whether they follow from the values of our pattern and whether we have reason to doubt that acting according to them will actually improve our lives.

If we approach the conflict between personal satisfactions and moral responsibilities by following this pluralist proposal, we will cope with their conflict by considering whether or not we have reason to doubt the values that prompt us to seek the particular satisfactions and discharge the particular responsibilities. If our personal satisfactions and moral responsibilities conflict, as they often do, then we have a reason to doubt the conflicting values. But it need not be a reason for abandoning either of them. We can continue to hold both, provided we find a way of balancing them. And that, in turn, depends on judging the relative importance of the conflicting particular values to the overall pattern in accordance with which we want to live in our context. The result of such judgment may be to increase or decrease the relative importance of the particular personal satisfaction we seek and the particular moral responsibility we think we ought to meet. Such judgments can be reasonable, but even reasonable judgments can be mistaken. If they are mistaken, they lead us to act contrary to the pattern in accordance with which we want to live and will make our life worse than it might be. And that is the ultimate test of whether the judgment has been reasonable.

This pluralist approach does not resolve any particular conflict between any one of our personal satisfactions and moral responsibilities, but it is a particular, context-dependent, and practical proposal of what each of us can do to resolve it reasonably, given the particular values of ours that conflict, the particular social and personal contexts in which we live, and the particular context from which the conflicting values are derived. It is this particularity, context-dependence, and practicality of the pluralist proposal for coping with this philosophical problem that excludes once-and-for-all solutions and yet provides a reasonable way of coping with it.

Is There a Providential Order?

To this question, defenders of the religious and the scientific modes of understanding give conflicting answers. They accept that there is a cosmic order, but the first asserts and the second denies that it is good. According to the religious mode of understanding, it follows from the goodness of the cosmic order that ultimately all is for the best and that human lives go well to the extent to which they conform to it. According to the scientific mode of understanding—interpreted as the unified view formed of the current state of knowledge provided by the various sciences— the cosmic order is an impersonal nomological system. All that exists is subject to it. The cosmic order, however, is neither good nor bad, but entirely insensate, incapable of having concerns about the effect it has on us or anything else. It has no evaluative dimension. Both modes of understanding, as well as their conflict, are metaphysical, for they concern the ultimate nature of the scheme of things.[5] Their conflict leads to the philosophical problem that is popularly and much too crudely conceived, at least in our world-view, as caused by contrary views about the existence of God.

The majority of reflective and unreflective people in the past and present have accepted some form of religious understanding. Although they disagree both about the nature of God or gods and the details of the cosmic order, they agree that the order is good and that we understand it imperfectly. They also agree that how life goes for us depends on conforming to it.[6] Defenders of religious understanding acknowledge that there is much misery in human existence, but they attribute it to our failure to live according to the good cosmic order.

There has also been a minority view, deplored as early as in the *Psalms* 53: 1, "The fool hath said in his heart, *There is* no God. Corrupt are they, and have done abominable iniquity: *there is* none that doeth good." It has also been celebrated more recently as "The greatest recent event—that 'God is dead,' that the belief in the Christian god has become unbelievable." "For the few at least…this ancient and profound trust has been turned into doubt."[7] Between biblical times and ours, there have been religious thinkers who recognized that the wretchedness of much of human existence is a serious problem for believing in the goodness of the cosmic order. "If it be asked, Why does God permit so much sin in his creation? I confess, I cannot answer the question, but must lay my hand upon my mouth. He giveth no account of his conduct to the children of men. It is our part to obey his commands."[8]

The religious and scientific approaches to the philosophical problem caused by their conflict are both absolutist and metaphysical. The pluralist approach is neither. It begins with the everyday problem created by the contingencies of life: we are vulnerable to forces, events, laws, and conditions we cannot control. The result is that we often do not get what we deserve and get what we do not deserve. It offends our sense of justice, especially when we and those we care about suffer from its consequences. This remains a serious problem even for those who accept either the religious or the scientific view that the contingencies are only apparent. Perhaps if our knowledge of the cosmic order were less imperfect, we would see apparent contingencies as parts of a divine or nomological cosmic order. But since our knowledge is imperfect, it makes no practical difference to us whether there actually is a cosmic order. The fact is that whatever may happen in the long run, in this world or the next, here and now we often do not get what we deserve and get what we do not deserve. Reasonable defenders of both the religious and the scientific modes of understanding will not deny this lamentable fact and will agree with pluralists that this is a problem. Whatever the correct metaphysical view turns out to be, the practical problem is to make us less vulnerable to what seem to be the contingencies of life.

The pluralist approach to coping with this problem is the practical proposal to endeavor to do better what we have been doing anyway from biblical times to our own. We have a system of conventions intended to guide us in deciding who deserves what. The conventions are many and various, but perhaps the most important ones concern the recognition of individual merit and demerit, the obligations that follow from formal and tacit agreements, the rights of the ownership and transfer of property, and the appropriate conduct in personal and impersonal relationships. These conventions, taken jointly, form a large part of the system on which we are expected to rely in order to decide who deserves what, how to remedy deviations from it, and how to settle disputes about what is deserved. The conventions of the system, then, can be said to guide our efforts to distribute what is deserved, correct faulty distributions, and resolve conflicts about distribution and correction. Maintaining this system has traditionally been thought of as one of the chief aims of justice.[9] The system, however, remains imperfect, because the conventions that form it are often defective and fail to lead to the just distribution of what we deserve, and because even the right conventions are frequently not followed by those who, for good, bad, or no reason, pursue aims contrary to them.

Societies ruled by tyrants and terror may endure for a while without just conventions, but no regime will be stable, secure, and supported by those who are subject to it, unless it maintains a system most of whose conventions can be relied on to guide the process whereby we get what we deserve and not what we do not deserve. As Hobbes rightly argued, without such a system a society will be anarchic, insecure, unstable, and those living in it will be constantly at odds. This is a familiar argument, and the pluralist approach rests on it.

It is perhaps less widely recognized that the system of justice will be unavoidably imperfect even if most of the prevailing conventions are just and largely followed. The contingencies of life may still prevent us from getting what we deserve. The scarcity of resources—including raw materials, money, skills, talents, and the capacity to adjust to rapid changes—may make it impossible to distribute resources so that all and only those who deserve them will actually get them. The consequences of bad luck, mortality, illness, natural disasters, changing conditions, and the unintended and unforeseeable consequences of both reasonable and unreasonable policies may be so harmful as to make proportional compensation for undeserved harms physically, morally, politically, or practically impossible. And conflicts about what is and what is not deserved may have deep sources in contrary but reasonably held moral, political, religious, or personal values that prevent the resolution of such conflicts in a way that would be acceptable to all the disputants.

These contingencies lead pluralists to recognize that the system of justice has always been and is likely to remain imperfect. We should not aim at the unattainable ideal of all of us getting no more and no less than we deserve, but at making justice here and now less imperfect. The pluralist practical proposal is to endeavor to approximate this realistic aim by doing what we reasonably can to maintain particular just conventions and correct particular unjust ones, so that we come closer to a society in which we get what we deserve. This raises two large questions: what are the reasons for accepting the pluralists' claim that these conventions are particular and context-dependent, rather than universal requirements of justice, as absolutists suppose? And how can we reasonably distinguish between reasonable conventions that help and unreasonable ones that hinder the approximation of the distributive, corrective, and conflict-resolving aims of justice?

In attempting to answer the first question, we may begin with the many conventions to which we appeal in deciding who deserves what. It is pointless to try to reduce their plurality by imposing on them a rigid typology, but, as I have suggested earlier, it is reasonable to suppose that there ought to be conventions in all civilized societies that guide the recognition of merit, the obligations created by agreements, the rights of the ownership of property, and the appropriate ways of treating others. I do not know whether all civilized societies have conventions regarding such matters, but it is not far-fetched to suppose that they do, because it is hard to imagine an acceptable and feasible form of life that lacks them. I assume that maintaining just conventions, correcting unjust ones, and resolving conflicts about whether they are just or unjust, then, are necessary conditions of coping with contingencies that prevent us from getting what we deserve and not what we do not deserve.

This may appear to be a universal claim about the requirements of justice that hold in all contexts, and contrary to the pluralist view that just conventions must be particular and context-dependent. The appearance, however, is misleading. The claim appears to be universal only if left abstract, formal, and thus lacking in content. The universal claim would tell us as little about what the actual conventions of justice are or ought to be as the similarly contentless claim that all events have a cause tells us about the actual cause of an actual event.

We can answer the question of whether any particular convention is just only if we understand the role it plays in the context of a society. We will recognize then that it is particular and context-dependent. It will depend on the virtues and vices, achievements and failures, excellences and deficiencies that are regarded as having merit or demerit in the context of a particular society; on the prevailing social arrangements that depend on formal or informal agreements, rather than on some form of coercion; on whether resources are freely available and thus non-competitive, as elementary education has become, or whether they are scarce, like high-paying jobs, competition for which needs to be regulated; on what particular properties are owned by the state, by individuals singly or jointly, or by various quite different kinds of organizations, such as businesses, clubs, political parties, or publishers; and on what are the expectations about how married or unmarried couples, parents and children, teachers and students, professionals and their clients, friends, neighbors, or colleagues should treat each other.

We cannot make reasonable judgments about what people deserve on the basis of their merits, agreements, properties, or relationships, unless we understand the prevailing conventions and conditions of the society that guide these areas of life. And these conventions, of course, are plural, and vary with societies, times, and changing conditions. That is why pluralists are right to insist on their particularity and context-dependence, why absolutists are wrong to seek universal principles of justice, and why relativists are also wrong in supposing that unless universal principles of justice are found, justice will ultimately rest on commitments for which reasons cannot be given. It is perhaps a universal truth that all societies ought to be just, but actual societies must have particular and context-dependent conventions about what counts as just.

Understanding this, however, is only necessary but not sufficient for making reasonable judgments about whether our prevailing conventions are in fact just. Even if they are mostly followed, they may not be just, because they may fail to lead to appropriate arrangements that would make it more likely that we get what we deserve and not what we do not deserve. This brings us to the second question pluralists must answer: how can we reasonably distinguish between conventions that help and those that hinder the approximation of the distributive, corrective, and conflict-resolving aims of justice?

Pluralists are not committed to a mindless conservatism that defends conventions simply because they are held in a particular society at a particular time. Any convention may be mistaken. Pluralists defend only conventions that can be supported by the following reasons: they have endured for a considerable length of time, measured in decades or more rather than in months; they have endured, because people in that context by and large accept them voluntarily, without being coerced, indoctrinated, or otherwise manipulated; and because the conventions provide the secure and stable conditions which will make it more likely that they and others get what they deserve. It is reasonable to accept and follow conventions that meet these conditions, and unreasonable to accept those that fail to meet one or more of them.

It hardly needs saying that there are likely to be conflicting views about whether or not particular conventions meet these conditions. Such conflicts lead to many of the moral and political controversies that abound in civilized societies. But they are conflicts about whether the disputed conventions meet the relevant conditions, not whether the conditions should be met. The aim is that people should get what they deserve and not what they do not deserve. The conflicts are about what they deserve on the basis of their merits, agreements, properties, and relationships. One chief source of such conflicts is that the prevailing views about these bases on which we rely for deciding who deserves what are always changing in response to changing conditions. If in doubt, think about the radical changes we are undergoing in respect to sexual attitudes, medical advances, secularization, globalization, population explosion, communication, information processing, migrations across traditional borders, and so on. We have sharply conflicting views about who deserves what and for what reason, but not about the justice of us all having whatever it is we deserve.

The improvement of our lives depends, among many other things, on struggling with and trying to resolve such conflicts. Doing so is in our common interest. We all have good reasons to try to become less vulnerable to contingencies and make it more likely that we get what we deserve and not what we do not deserve. That aim will be shared by all reasonable people, and we can appeal to it to evaluate the relative weight of the reasons for the conflicting practical proposals about how this aim is best pursued in a particular context. Of course, there will be conflicts also about the relative weight of reasons, but they will not be deep conflicts about our shared aim, but far more tractable conflicts about how to go about approximating it.

In sum, the pluralist approach to coping with the philosophical problem caused by conflicting answers to the question of whether there is a providential order is as follows. The question can be interpreted either as metaphysical or practical. On the practical interpretation, the question is whether we can improve our lives by making us less vulnerable to contingencies we cannot control. This question remains regardless of whether or not the cosmic order is good, since it is agreed by everyone that our understanding of the cosmic order, if there is one, is imperfect.

What we must do, then, from the practical point of view is to concentrate on making us less vulnerable to contingencies by doing what we can to come closer to all of us getting what we deserve and not what we do not deserve. The pursuit of this aim depends on having a system of justice whose conventions guide the distribution of what we deserve, correct unjust distribution, and resolve conflicts about distribution and correction. These conventions are unavoidably particular and context-dependent, and so will be the answers to the question of who deserves what. The practical proposal of the pluralist approach is to continue to improve our system of conventions so that we will come closer to all of us having what we deserve rather than what we do not deserve, and thereby reduce our vulnerability to the contingencies of life.

This practical proposal is no more than the recommendation to do better what we have been doing anyway. But this unexciting proposal has the great virtue of being better than the available alternatives to it, be they absolutist or relativist. Coping with the contingencies of life always depends on particular and context-dependent conventions, so there cannot be an ideal system of conventions that absolutists claim that reason requires everyone to aim at always and in all contexts. The failure to find such an ideal does not mean, as relativists suppose, that instead of good reasons we must rely on commitments for which ultimately no reasons can be given. The pluralist approach shows that we can have good reasons for or against particular conventions, even though the reasons and the conventions are particular and context-dependent.

Can There Be an Ideal State?

By "state" I mean the political system of a society, usually of a nation. The components of this system are many, various, and I doubt that they can be defined or enumerated. They are likely, however, to include the legislative, executive, and judiciary branches of the government; state organs whose task is to conduct foreign affairs, enforce the laws, and maintain the armed forces; they include as well formal laws and informal practices according to which these branches and organs are expected to function. All these components are conventional and have a history. They emerged gradually, and were then maintained and adjusted to cope with changing circumstances and to correct malfunctions. They form the expectations and a large part of the social identity of those who are subject to them.

An ideal state would be the best possible political system any society could have, whatever differences there may be in the conditions of different societies, because it would safeguard the political conditions of the well-being of those who are subject to it. What these conditions are depends in part on human nature, which is thought to be the same everywhere, always, for everyone, since they are the conditions that make us human. As Hume observed: "It is universally acknowledged, that there is a great uniformity among the actions of men, in all nations and ages, and that human nature remains the same, in its principles and operations."[10]

A great variety of political thinkers assume, although Hume did not, that it follows from the uniformity of human nature that there must be an ideal state. It may be Plato's Republic, Augustine's city of God, Hobbes' Leviathan, Rousseau's state of nature, Kant's kingdom of ends, the apotheosis of Hegelian dialectic, Marx's classless society, the utilitarians' greatest happiness, and so on. They may disagree whether some particular trait is among the uniform ones, but they all agree that human well-being and the ideal state depend on whatever the uniformities of human nature are. They also agree that aiming at the ideal state is a requirement of reason, because our well-being depends on it, and that failing to aim at it is contrary to reason, because it is to fail to make our lives better when we could.

These political thinkers acknowledge that as a result of different conditions that exist at different times and places, there are differences among human beings. They claim, however, that these differences are merely different ways in which the uniformity of human nature manifests itself. Seeking pleasure and avoiding pain, preferring satisfaction to frustration, needing virtues and avoiding vices, are among the uniformities of human nature and conditions of human well-being. Particular forms that pleasures and pains, satisfactions and frustrations, virtues and vices may take depend on the prevailing conditions, but human well-being in all contexts depends on having as much of the first and as little of the second member of each of these pairs as possible. From the point of view of human well-being, the uniformities are far more important than the differences. And the ideal state is one that provides the best possible protection of the uniform conditions in the midst of unavoidable changes. It is an absolute and context-independent requirement of reason to do what we can to transform our society, and indeed all others, so as to approximate the ideal state as closely as possible. It may be that this requirement can never be fully met because human shortcomings, adverse conditions, or the contingencies of life prevent it—nevertheless, human well-being depends on aiming at it. This line of thought leads to the conclusion that the political mode of understanding is overriding because it provides the conditions on which the pursuit of all else depends.

A contrary line of thought is that there can be no ideal state because human nature and the requirements of human well-being vary with the conditions of societies. As Berlin puts it:

The conviction, common to Aristotelians and a good many Christian scholastics and atheistical materialists alike, that there exists...a single discoverable goal, or pattern of goals, the same for all mankind—is mistaken; and so, too, is the notion bound up with it, of a single true doctrine carrying salvation to all men everywhere, contained in natural law, or the revelation of a sacred book, or the insight of a man of genius, or the natural wisdom of ordinary men, or the calculations made by an elite of utilitarian scientists set up to govern mankind.[11]

How human beings conceive of their well-being depends on the particular moral, political, religious, and personal values they hold in particular contexts. What these values are and how they could be pursued depends on the prevailing climatic, demographic, economic, international, social, and technological conditions, and on the ceaseless changes of these conditions. These changing values and conditions make it impossible to specify what an ideal state would be. A state could be better than an existing one, but only relative to and dependent on how the prevailing conditions of a society shape the nature of those living in it, on the values they have been brought up to hold, and on the conceptions of well-being they have. From the point of view of human well-being, therefore, differences among human beings are far more important than uniformities. Understanding these differences depends on understanding the historical processes that have led to them. In this context, the historical mode of understanding is thought to be overriding, because it is the key to understanding why the conditions and the reasons for them on which human nature, values, and conceptions of well-being depends are what they are, and how they became it. Since these conditions vary with societies, there could not be an ideal state that reason requires every society in all conditions to aim at.

The two lines of thought I have just described are radical versions of the political and historical modes of understanding. They give conflicting answers to the question of whether there can be an ideal state, and their answers form the background against which the philosophical problem about its possibility arises. The first answer is absolutist, the second is relativist. Both modes of understanding also have a moderate version. They reject both the absolutist view that human nature is context-independent, uniform, and unchanging, and the relativist view that human nature is context-dependent, variable, and changing in response to changing conditions.

The moderate versions thus defuse the conflict to which the radical versions lead, and thereby remove the cause whose effect is the philosophical problem about whether there can be an ideal state. Defenders of the moderate versions accept instead the far more reasonable view that some aspects of human nature are uniform regardless of changing contexts, and some other aspects are variable and responsive to changing conditions. But they still disagree whether, from the point of view of human well-being, the uniformities or the differences are more important, whether the political system of a society should focus more on uniformities or differences.

Those who advocate focusing on uniformities stress the primacy of universal human rights and basic political values, while those who think that differences matter more stress the historically conditioned ways in which particular political values are interpreted in a particular society. The first are closer to absolutism because they accept the prima facie claim that some political values are universal, even though they allow that the prevailing conditions may justify overriding them. The second are closer to relativism because they think that even basic political values must be interpreted in the light of the historical conditions of the society in which they are held. The first stress the importance of the political mode of understanding; the second the importance of the historical mode.

The pluralist approach to coping with the philosophical problem caused by the conflict between the radical versions of the political and historical modes of reflection rejects both versions, but without accepting the moderate ones. The latter are certainly preferable to the former, yet they remain problematic because both moderate versions continue to seek a theory in order to answer the question of whether there can be an ideal state. They differ about the extent to which the theory would have to be historical, but they agree that whatever the right theory is, it depends on one or another mode of understanding.

Pluralists disagree: they think that the question is practical, and so is the answer to it. They think that

in political activity...men sail a boundless and bottomless sea; there is neither harbour for shelter nor floor for anchorage, neither starting-place nor appointed destination. The enterprise is to keep afloat on an even keel....A depressing doctrine, it will be said....But in the main the depression springs from the exclusion of hopes that were false and the discovery that guides reputed to be of superhuman wisdom and skill, are, in fact, of a somewhat different character. If the model deprives us of a model laid up in heaven, at least it does not lead us into a morass where every choice is equally good or equally to be deplored.[12]

According to pluralists, there is a reasonable approach that leads to a particular, context-dependent, practical proposal about how we can improve our political conditions without embracing either an absolutist or a relativist theory, or indeed any theory at all. The pluralist approach is practical, not theoretical. Its aim in this context is to cope with the particular political problems that stand in the way of improving our political conditions.

The reasons for the pluralist proposal become apparent if we understand the problems that eventually lead to the conflict between the radical versions of these modes of understanding. These problems are familiar features of everyday life. They stem from our dissatisfactions with our political system, because we find that its policies are contrary to one or more of the basic political values we hold. It will perhaps be agreed that these values include democracy, education, equality, individual rights, justice, liberty, order, peace, private property, prosperity, public health, rule of law, and security. I do not claim that this is a complete list, and I acknowledge, indeed insist, that we disagree about the interpretation and relative importance of these values. But I do think that we generally agree that the political system of our society should maintain and protect these values. Yet we find that it often fails to do so, and that is why we are dissatisfied with it. This is one of our most acute political problems, and the pluralist proposal depends, in the first instance, on understanding how it arises.

Among the causes of these problems are the cognitive, ethical, or prudential failings of those who wield political power. The problems may be caused by their inexperience, stupidity, immorality, ignorance, abuse of political power by placing private over public interests, or some combination of these and other causes. But these causes are personal, not structural. They are the failings of politicians, not of the political system. The latter causes are far more serious than the former, because they will occur even if the politicians are as intelligent, well-informed, and as ethical as humanly possible. They will occur because the basic political values we hold conflict. They are often so related that the more we have of one, the less we can have of the other. Such conflicts are between liberty and justice, equality and private property, democracy and the rule of law, public health and individual rights, and so on.

These and similar conflicts among the basic political values to which we are committed are part of our daily experience, and a large part of day-to-day politics is concerned with coping with them. But that cannot take the form of abandoning one or another of the conflicting values, because they are basic to our political system and we are committed to them, as well as to the system that upholds them. Coping with these problems must consist in giving greater weight to one of the conflicting basic values and correspondingly lesser weight to the others. And that means that maintaining our political system requires compromising the basic values of the very system we are committed to maintaining. Dissatisfaction with our political system is a natural and unavoidable consequence of such conflicts.

The fact that unavoidable conflicts permeate our political system has to be accepted and coped with. To do so we need to change our attitude toward the ubiquitous conflicts among our basic political values. The change is from believing that we have only two alternatives and we must choose between them: between persisting in the futile absolutist search for an ideal state as a way of avoiding conflicts, and resigning ourselves to the relativist view that we have nothing better to fall back on in order to cope with our political conflicts than commitments for which ultimately no good reasons can be given. There is a third alternative: to change our attitude by accepting that political conflicts are facts of life with which we have to live, realizing that the resulting dissatisfactions with our political system are unavoidable, and nevertheless seeking a reasonable approach to coping with conflicts between basic political values. The practical proposal of the pluralist approach is of a way of living with the conflicts, having a reason to put up with our particular dissatisfactions, and coping with context-dependent conflicts reasonably.

The key to the pluralist approach is the reminder that we have a very good reason for protecting our political system—our basic political values depend on it—and that this reason is much stronger than the reason we have for any one of our particular political values. This recognition provides a standard on which we can rely for a reasonable way of coping with conflicts between our particular basic political values. The standard is the protection of our political system on which all of our basic political values depend. The pluralist proposal is that if two particular basic political values conflict, as they often do, then the most reasonable way of resolving their conflict is in favor of the value which, in that context, is more important for the protection of the political system.

Given this standard, any basic political values may, in some contexts, override or be overridden by any of the others. It is always a matter of judgment which one should override which, but such judgments need not be arbitrary. Reasonable ones depend on familiarity with the relevant facts and alternative judgments, weighing their likely consequences, bearing in mind how other political values may be affected by the proposed conflict-resolutions, and giving reasons for one judgment and against the others. Making such judgments is difficult, and requires political experience and prudence. Some politicians are good at it, others not, and most are middling. But we know that reasonable judgments can be made because they have been made on numerous occasions in the past. Labor laws have been enacted, Nazism and Communism have been defeated, racial, sexual, and religious discrimination has been outlawed, higher education has been made more widely available, homosexuality has been decriminalized, and so on.

Consider in the light of this pluralist approach to conflict-resolution some of the current conflicts, for example, about abortion, assisted suicide, capital punishment, gay marriage, illegal immigration, legalizing drugs, pornography, the rising cost of health care, or the protection of privacy. Reasoned cases have been and are being made on both sides in these conflicts, but neither side has succeeded in convincing the other. It does not seem that any practical proposal can lead to resolving these conflicts in a way that all the parties to it would find acceptable. There is something, however, that can be done by those who manage, at least temporarily, to see the conflicts not as partisan participants, but as observers who are willing to take a larger view of the political context of which the conflicts are merely small parts. No matter how divided the partisans are, they can be reminded that they have a common interest in maintaining the political system that protects the conditions in which conflicts like theirs can be debated in a peaceful and orderly manner. If the partisans recognize this, and see their conflict in this light, they will see also that they have a very good reason to protect the political system that makes their conflict possible. They will continue, then, to make the case in favor of their own side and against the other side, but only within the limits set by the political system they both accept.

The pluralist approach to conflict-resolution is the practical proposal to remind those involved in a particular conflict that they should not allow the conflict to get out of hand, no matter how strongly they believe that their side is right and the other wrong. The reason is to protect the political system on which the improvement of their lives depends. This reason also constitutes a standard that can be appealed to if it becomes necessary to make a decision that favors one of the sides. The standard is to make the decision that is less likely to damage the political system on which both sides depend. What that decision will be is, of course, a matter of judgment. All such judgments are complex, difficult, and fallible, but the reasonable ones will be context-dependent because they will focus on the nature of the particular conflict about which the decision has to be made, on the condition of the political system that forms the background against which the judgment must be made, and on how the decision will affect the rest of the political system.

The pluralist proposal does not promise a way of resolving any conflict and solving any problem. But it does point at a possible way of coping with them, and it has a number of advantages. It is an alternative to the untenable absolutist assumption that there is a political value that should always and in all contexts override any other value that conflicts with it. It is an alternative also to the relativist view that resolving conflicts and coping with problems ultimately depends on commitments for which no good reason can be given. It recognizes that dissatisfactions with our political system are unavoidable because our political values are plural and often conflict. Its approach is practical, not theoretical. Its aim is to cope with our particular dissatisfactions in our particular context. It denies that coping with them depends on immersion in the historical mode of understanding the influences that have formed our political values, or appealing to the political mode of understanding that advocates commitment to an ideal political state that privileges some political values at the expense of others. And by being practical rather than theoretical, it prevents existing conflicts from turning into philosophical problems.

Interim Conclusion

Philosophical problems arise out of the everyday problems we routinely face. We have to turn to modes of understanding to help us cope with them because the resources of everyday life are insufficient. But modes of understanding are beset by both internal modal problems and external philosophical problems that arise because modes of understanding conflict. The pluralist approach avoids philosophical problems by using practical, context-dependent proposals for coping with particular everyday problems.

One of our everyday problems is that our lives are made good by having personal satisfactions and meeting moral responsibilities, but they often conflict. Our problem is that we do not know how to resolve their conflicts. The personal and moral modes of understanding help us understand the force of the reasons we have for resolving their conflicts, but these reasons also conflict, and we are left as uncertain as we were before. The pluralist practical proposal is to resolve their conflicts by judging their relative importance to the personal pattern we have formed of the universal, social, and personal values by which we want to live. Our pattern, values, and judgments may be mistaken, may hinder rather than aid us in improving our lives, and we need to do what we can to correct their mistakes, given the particularity and context-dependence of our pattern, values, and judgments.

Other everyday problems we encounter are the contingencies of life that prevent us from having what we deserve. The religious and the scientific modes of understanding lead to different ways of understanding contingencies, but neither tells us what we should do to make us less vulnerable to them. The pluralist practical proposal is to cope with contingencies by appealing to our society's historically conditioned system of conventions for deciding who deserves what on the basis of particular merits, agreements, rights, and relationships. The conventions may be mistaken, but we can correct their mistakes by ascertaining whether they have endured because most of us in our society voluntarily adhere to them, and because they actually make us less vulnerable to contingencies.

A further everyday problem is that the basic political values of our society often conflict. We rely on them for the improvement of our lives, but the more we have of one of the conflicting values, the less we can have of the other, and, since we need both, their conflict is an obstacle to improving our lives. The historical and political modes of understanding provide conflicting reasons for resolving such conflicts. Both derive reasons from their understanding of human nature, but one stresses its uniformities and the resulting universality of basic political values, while the other stresses the different forms it takes in different circumstances. The pluralist practical proposal is to cope with the conflicts by deciding which of the conflicting values is more important for maintaining the whole system of basic political values in our present conditions.

Each of these pluralist proposals aims to find good reasons that are practical, not theoretical; particular and context-dependent, not universal and the same in all contexts; and are reasons for correcting mistakes we have made, not reasons for new solutions. The pluralist approach thus avoids both the absolutist arbitrariness of claiming that a reason that follows from one of the modes of understanding is always overriding, and the relativist claim that ultimately we have no good reasons for anything.

11

The Pluralist Approach to Control, Reasonable Hope, and Moral Absolutes

[Faust opening the New Testament on John 1:1]
It says: "In the beginning was the *Word*."
Already I am stuck! And who will help afford?
Mere word I cannot possibly so prize,
I must translate it otherwise.
Now if the Spirit lends me proper light,
"In the beginning was the *Mind*" would be more nearly right.
... Can it be the mind that makes and shapes all things?
But even as I write down this word too,
Something warns me that it will not do.
Now suddenly the Spirit prompts me in my need,
I confidently write: "In the beginning was the *Deed*!"

Johann Wolfgang von Goethe[1]

Can We Be in Control of Our Lives?

In considering this question, I once again begin with a problem we encounter in everyday life. We find that the control we have over how we live is severely limited by our genetic inheritance, health, upbringing, political conditions, the necessity of earning a living, the prevailing conventions, and the need to get along with others with whom we must and sometimes want to live. We can try to overcome some of these limits, but the attempt is often beyond our power. If we are reflective about how we live, it will occur to us that our control is limited not only by what we can do but also by the beliefs, emotions, and wants that motivate us to live as we do. We may wonder then whether we would have these motives if our experiences and social conditions had been different. And we may realize that we are all saddled with the burden of our history, that it informs our psychological condition, and consequently our actions. We may wonder also whether we have sufficient control over our psychological condition to change it if we are dissatisfied with it. If such reflections lead us to accept that our beliefs, emotions, and wants have been formed by social conditions over which we have little or no control, we will be likely to conclude that we have even less control over how we live than we have supposed before we became more reflective. Contrary to the widely held belief, reflection on how we live may not lead to greater control, but to the realization of how little control, if any, we have.

There are three familiar theoretical approaches to coping with this problem: determinist, libertarian, and compatibilist. Determinists approach the problem by drawing on the resources of the scientific mode of understanding, the unified view that emerges from the various sciences. They hold that the physical, physiological, social, and psychological conditions of our lives are equally the effects of causes over which we have no control. We are links in a vast chain of causes and effects that has no beginning and no end. It is an illusion to suppose that we are islands of control in this vast ocean of necessity.[2]

The libertarian approach is to rely on the personal mode of understanding. According to it, we all know from personal experience that sometimes in some respects we can go against our causal antecedents, make genuine choices about how we live, and thereby exert some control. Physical, physiological, and social conditions certainly limit the control we have, but within the limits they set we can control our internal psychological conditions, including our beliefs, emotions, wants, and motives.[3]

Compatibilists deny that there is a genuine conflict between the libertarian and determinist approaches. They agree with determinists that all the conditions of our lives are the effects of causes, but, in agreement with libertarians, they claim that we have the capacity to alter our psychological condition that includes our beliefs, emotions, and wants, and the motives that lead us to act on them. The extent to which we can control our lives depends on the extent to which we exercise that capacity.[4]

The conflicts among these three approaches are wellknown.[5] It would be tedious to go over their details. I merely note that the conflicts lead to the philosophical problem, usually phrased as the problem of whether our will is free or whether we can make free choices. Determinists say no; libertarians and compatibilists, for different reasons, say yes. They all assume that we need a theory to solve the problem, although they differ about what the right theory is. They also assume that if we have found the right theory, it will be general, hold in all contexts, and be equally applicable to all individuals.

The pluralist approach differs from all three, although it is so close to the compatibilist one as to be regarded as an amended version of it. According to it, the possibility of control is a practical, not a theoretical problem. It is a problem about what we—the individuals we are, situated in our ambient social conditions—can do, not a problem about what theory we should hold about what we can do. The problem is whether we can exercise whatever capacity for control we have, not what the causes of the capacity are. It is also a particular problem that we as individuals have, given our particular psychological condition and particular context, not a problem that could have a general and context-independent solution that holds for all human beings. And it is also the problem of whether we can overcome the particular obstacles that prevent us from controlling how we live, not the theoretical problem of the freedom of the will or of our choices. Pluralists agree with determinists that how we live is the effect of causes, but in disagreement with them hold that we can sometimes control some of the causes that affect us. They agree with libertarians that within certain limits we can control how we live, but disagree that control depends on freeing ourselves from all causal necessities. And they agree with compatibilists as well that we can sometimes exercise our capacity to control the psychological condition that leads us to live as we do, but disagree with them about this being a universal human capacity.

These differences between the pluralist and the three other approaches can be expressed by saying that although they are all interested in the possibility of control, libertarians, determinists, and compatibilists have traditionally asked and attempted to answer the theoretical question of whether control is at all possible and, if it is, how is it possible. Pluralists ask and attempt to answer the practical question of whether we can increase whatever control we happen to have. Pluralists have four reasons for reformulating the question.

First, the attempts to answer the theoretical question have been unsuccessful, as shown by centuries of inconclusive disputes.[6] Second, the everyday problem that matters to us now is to increase our control, not the problem of deciding the relative merits of the determinist, libertarian, and compatibilist theories. If pluralists are right, we can sometimes increase the control we have regardless which of the three theories is correct. Third, determinists, libertarians, and compatibilists rely on modes of understanding in formulating and attempting to find the right theory. As we know from the long history of their disputes, their attempts have been frustrated by the modal problems within the mode of understanding on which they rely, and by philosophical problems caused by conflicts between their own and other modes of understanding. The pluralist approach attempts to avoid getting bogged down in these theoretical disputes. Pluralists accept that the personal and scientific modes of understanding give us a much deeper understanding of the causal and psychological aspects of our lives than what we would have if we relied only on the resources of everyday life, but neither one mode, nor the other, nor their combination helps us cope with the problem of increasing our control over how we live. Fourth, by reformulating the problem from a theoretical one that leads to the familiar disputes to a practical one, pluralists propose a way of coping. It depends on understanding the problem as the particular one regarding whether we—the individuals we are, living in our context, having the particular beliefs, emotions, and wants we have—can overcome some of the context-dependent obstacles that prevent us from increasing whatever control we happen to have.

What, then, can we do, according to pluralists, to increase our control over how we live? We are part of the world, and subject to its laws. We have no control over these laws, and it is futile to try to seek exemption from them. We cannot increase our control that way. But we can have some control over the conditions in which particular laws hold. These conditions are either external or internal to us. According to the pluralist approach, the possibility of increasing our control depends on our efforts to change some of the internal conditions, in particular, some of the psychological ones. I refer collectively to the internal conditions that we might attempt to change as attitudes.

Attitudes are complex, their main components are beliefs, emotions, wants, and motives to act on them. We are alike in having attitudes, understood in this way, but we differ in their particular components. We have different beliefs, emotions, wants, and motives, and even if we happen to have the same ones, we differ about their relative strengths, and consequently about how likely it is that we will act on them. Changing the internal conditions depends on changing some of our beliefs, emotions, wants, and motives. Because we differ in these ways about the particular components of our attitudes, we will differ also about what we can do to increase our control. That is why there can be no theoretical answer to the question of what we can do to increase our control. But there is a practical answer we can find, if we look for it reasonably and in favorable conditions.

The practical answer is to reflect on the beliefs, emotions, and wants that motivate us to live in a particular way and strengthen or weaken their motivating force on the basis of our reflection. It is psychologically far more plausible to think of the possibility of changing these components of our attitudes in terms of strengthening or weakening them than in terms of replacing them with new ones. It is a rare occurrence if we can simply abandon a belief, emotion, want, or motive about the centrally important matter of how we want to live. Sudden conversions sometimes do occur, but few of us have had life-changing experiences. What usually happens is that we meet a charismatic person, fall in love, have a serious setback, find ourselves surprised by injustice, grief, humiliation, beauty, or a book, and it makes us question the way in which we have been living. We ask whether we should continue to be motivated by our familiar beliefs about what is and what is not important; by what we habitually like or dislike, are proud or ashamed of, envy or scorn, fear or hope; by wanting to pursue the pleasures, prizes, comforts, victories, and status we have been accustomed to pursue so assiduously. And as we ask these questions, we may come to doubt the answers we have been giving, especially if our new experience acquaints us with hitherto undreamt of possibilities. Or, it may happen that after questioning our beliefs, emotions, wants, and motives, we conclude that we can reasonably continue to live and act according to them, or, perhaps less reasonably, that it would be far too risky and difficult to make serious changes to how we live, and then we allow the impact of the new experience to fade as we continue to live as we did before.

The result of reflection, therefore, may be either to strengthen or to weaken the motivating force of our beliefs, emotions, and wants. But whichever happens, we will have increased our control over how we live. What used to be our habitual, unquestioned way of life has ceased to be that. We have realized that different, perhaps better ways are possible, or that the way we have is preferable to ways we might have. We have acquired the possibility of changing how we live by changing the beliefs, emotions, wants, and motives that prompt us to live as we have been doing. The significant fact that reflection has brought about is that the possibilities of how we might live have been enlarged. And that increases our control over how we live, regardless of whether we make use of the enlarged range of possibilities of which we have become aware.

The temptation to idealize reflection, however, should be resisted.[7] It is just as liable to be mistaken as anything else we do. What we take to be new possibilities, may not be, or may not be better or worse than the possibilities we have recognized without reflection. Our satisfactions or dissatisfactions with our present way of life may be the results of self-deception, or merely reactions to nugatory successes or failures whose importance we have exaggerated. Reflection can be as superficial as our existing beliefs, emotions, wants, or motives. Nor is it the key to our well-being, since it may make us more dissatisfied with our lives than we were before we began to reflect on it. And it should also be recognized that many people are content with living conventional lives, filled with domestic matters, family ties, work, routine social interactions, and leisure activities, without being assailed by wrenching crises, existential anxieties, tragic conflicts, religious doubts, or philosophical problems. They are not seriously bothered by the limits that constrain how they live, and they are not provoked into reflection, not even when they face adversities which all of us are likely to encounter at some time or another. It is not true that the unexamined life is not worth living. There are those who for one reason or another prefer an examined life, but that need not make their lives more worth living. It may just make them more examined and more aware of the limits that constrain them.

Determinists may accept all this and point out against libertarians, compatibilists, and pluralists as well that whether we have the capacity to reflect, whether we exercise the capacity if we have it, and whether we do or do not change how we live as a result of reflection are also the effects of causes over which we have ultimately no control. The further back we go in tracing the causes to which we are all unavoidably subject the more we find that the external causes of our psychological condition overwhelm the internal ones. The beliefs, emotions, wants, and motives we start out with in life are barely conscious responses to physical and physiological stimuli, and as we mature and begin to change them, we do so in response to new causes that are likely to be far more complex social ones. But the internal conditions that gradually emerge and over which we may have some control, as well as the capacity for control itself, are also the effects of causes and of the earlier beliefs, emotions, wants, and motives that we are in the process of changing. Nothing that goes on within us can alter the fact that what is within us is the effect of causes outside of us, and that ultimately none of them can be controlled by us.

Pluralists cannot reasonably deny that the facts are as the determinists claim, but the significance of the facts is a different matter. Their significance is not merely that when we look from the present toward the past conditions that have formed us and others, we find that psychological causes are more and more outweighed first by physical and physiological, and later by social ones. The significance of the facts is also that when we look from the past toward the present condition of individuals we find that, in favorable conditions, the physical, physiological, and social causes are more and more overladen by psychological ones. We cannot undo or free ourselves from the influence of any of these causes, but their influence on how we live may be more and more informed by psychological causes, which include our beliefs, emotions, wants, and motives. This is the process that pluralists mean by increasing our control, and it is this respect in which they agree with compatibilists.

It is certainly not an inevitable process. Physical, physiological, and social causes may be irresistible and unalterable by psychological causes; or, for good or bad reasons, we may not exercise our capacity to control them, or we temporarily or forever lack the capacity as a result of some trauma, genetic defect, or illness. But many of us normally, in civilized circumstances, have the capacity to shape our responses to physical, physiological, and social causes by our beliefs, emotions, wants, and motives, and thus we normally have the capacity for control, even if we do not exercise it. Reflection may or may not lead us to exercise it more. We may prefer to put up with a narrower range of possibilities than to risk the unpredictable consequences of seriously changing our lives. But even if we do not exercise it, we have it, and could increase, for better or worse, the control we have over how we live.

This is the practical significance of the pluralist approach to answering the question of whether we can control how we live. This answer does not in any way depend on which, if any, of the theoretical approaches of determinists, libertarians, and compatibilists is correct. If the possibility of increasing control is understood as pluralists understand it, it makes no difference to it whether determinists are right, and how we live is the effect of causes; or whether libertarians are right, and we can somehow free ourselves from the chain of causation; or whether compatibilists are right, and internal causes can dominate external ones. In all these cases, the pluralist approach, concentrating on the everyday problem of the possibility of increasing our control, enables us to avoid the philosophical problem that arises from the conflict between the personal and the scientific modes of understanding. It follows from the pluralist approach that no theoretical approach to increasing our control can succeed. Increasing our control depends on our individual psychological conditions, on the particular beliefs, emotions, wants, and motives we have, on their relative strengths, on our particular physical, physiological, and social conditions, and on whether our dissatisfactions are strong enough to prompt us to change how we live.

What Can We Reasonably Hope?

Kant wrote that "all the interests of my reason, speculative as well as practical combine in the three following questions: 1. What can I know? 2. What ought I to do? 3. What may I hope?"[8]

His answer to the third question is that "all *hoping* is directed toward happiness" (A806) and when "happiness stands in exact relation with morality, that is, with worthiness to be happy—I entitle the *ideal of the supreme good*" (A810). Kant was firmly committed to the religious mode of understanding, and he thought that hoping for the ideal of the supreme good requires making that commitment. Secular thinkers committed to the political mode of understanding, however, may reject the religious mode, and still accept the ideal as an inspiring one to aim at, even if human fallibility and the contingencies of life make it unattainable. They say that approximating the ideal depends on constructing a political system that provides the conditions in which we can all pursue happiness.

Defenders of the religious mode point out that millennia of efforts to construct such a political system have not diminished man's inhumanity to man, but led, at best, to new ways in which it manifests itself. Our best hope of happiness, therefore, remains to rely on divine inspiration and help. Secular defenders of the political mode respond by pointing out that man's inhumanity to man often took the form of persecuting those who hold contrary religious ideals of the supreme good.

And those with religious commitments say that the abuses of religion are as bad reasons for rejecting the religious ideal as the ideological abuses of politics are reasons for rejecting the political ideal. And so the recurring conflict between these two modes of understanding leads to the philosophical problem of whether and how the City of Man may come to approximate the City of God. The fact remains, however, that these religious and political thinkers share the optimistic hope that a theory about an ideal will be found for the betterment of human lives. They differ about whether the theory and the ideal should be religious or political.

Pluralists think that both theoretical approaches to an ideal are based on unrealistic illusions that ignore the undeniable and ubiquitous problems of everyday life. The fact is that contingencies, conflicts, scarcity, stupidity, imprudence, prejudice, ignorance, and ill will routinely disappoint even the noblest ideologies and the most devoutly held religious faiths. We certainly have much to hope for, but the historical record strongly implies that our hopes are not reasonable. Those who nurture such illusions should bear in mind Williams's fine words:

There are areas of philosophy which might be supposed to have a special commitment to not forgetting or lying about the[world's] horrors, among them moral philosophy. No one with sense asks it to think about them all the time, but, in addressing what it claims to be our most serious concerns, it would do better if it did not make them disappear. Yet this is what in almost all its modern forms moral philosophy effectively does. This is above all because it tries to withdraw our ethical interest from both chance and necessity. . . . Everything that an agent most cares about typically comes from, and can be ruined by, uncontrollable necessity and chance. . . . Necessity and chance and the bad news they bring with them are deliberately excluded [from moral philosophy].[9]

If pluralists are right about that, then they owe an answer to the question of whether hoping for the betterment of our lives could be reasonable. The answer is yes, but giving it depends on a more realistic understanding of the human condition than these defenders of religiously and politically based hope have shown. Of course, the pluralist approach can be accepted by both religious and political thinkers, but only if they abandon the illusion that a theory (any theory) about an ideal (any ideal) could be the key to improving our lives. A reasonable hope for improvement depends on deepening our practical understanding of the human condition, not on adding yet another theory to the dozens that have already been proposed about the supposedly right religious or political ideal.

The first step toward a deeper understanding is to recognize that we are beset by contingencies, natural and self-imposed constraints, misguided certainties, and the familiar vices of aggression, cruelty, fanaticism, greed, injustice, irrationality, prejudice, self-deception, and so on. The significance of these undeniable adversities is not just cognitive, but also affective. They provoke in us emotional reactions, such as pessimism, resignation, resentment, cynicism, rebelliousness, and despair. And these reactions will motivate us to seek or to lament the absence of a reliable authority that would tell us how to respond to the adversities; or to design a blueprint for the improvement of human nature; or to flee to aestheticism as an escape from the sordidness of life; or to rely on the supposed laws of history, sociology, or psychology to explain, predict, and control the tendency of even our best laid plans to get out of hand and redound to our detriment.

Going deeper yet, we may realize that such reactions are the effects of the misguided optimism that by making the right effort we can overcome the adversities that are unavoidable features of the human condition. Part of a deeper understanding is the recognition that such optimism is not just untenable but also a dangerous obstacle to forming a realistic view of the adversities with which we must cope. There are two very strong reasons why the persistent efforts throughout history to formulate a religious or political ideal of how life ought to be cannot possibly be a way of coping with the adversities we face.

First, if defenders of the religious or political ideal of how life ought to be recognized that the adversities we face are part of the human condition, then they would have to recognize that an ideal of life that is free of such adversities is impossible. And if they did not recognize it, then their ideal would not be one for human beings who have always faced such adversities, but for creatures invented so that the theory would have some application beyond keeping the theorists occupied. In either case, the ideal would be utterly unrealistic.

Second, many of the adversities we face are not contingencies, epidemics, natural disasters, scarcity, and the like that threaten us from the outside, but internal ones that are part of human nature, such as our fallibility, vices, weaknesses, limited intelligence, and so forth. Suppose, contrary to the historical record, that we or most of us come to agree that a particular ideal is the one we should aim to realize. If defenders of the ideal recognized that these adversities are part of our nature, then they would have to recognize that our attempts to overcome them will be frustrated by the very same adversities we are attempting to overcome. Such attempts involve trying to raise ourselves by frayed bootstraps, and that cannot succeed. If, however, defenders of the ideal did not recognize that some of the adversities we face our part of our nature, then their ideal would not be one for human beings. Once again, the ideal would be unrealizable on either alternative.

A deeper understanding of the human condition must acknowledge that we are inherently ambivalent. It is true that reason and good will are part of our nature, but it is no less true that unreason and ill will are also part of it. The persistent efforts to improve our condition by deducing from a theory and the ideal it postulates of how life ought to be, rest on the familiar illusion of concentrating on facts that support a theory its defenders want to be true and ignoring facts that are contrary to it. The illusion is the comforting one that both the human condition and we ourselves are better than we are. By giving up the illusion, we may come to the deeper but much less comforting realization that

the world was not made for us, or we for the world...our history tells us no purposive story, and...there is no position outside the world or outside history from which we might hope to authenticate our activities.... There is no Hegelian history or universal cost–benefit analysis to show that it will come out well in the end.

We can rely only on ourselves as we ambivalently are "dealing sensibly, foolishly, sometimes catastrophically, sometimes nobly, with a world that is only partially intelligible to human agency and in itself not necessarily well adjusted to ethical aspirations."[10] Or, more briefly but no less pungently, "there is no pre-established harmony between the furtherance of truth and the well-being of mankind."[11] The truth is that sometimes one, sometimes another part of our nature becomes dominant. But whichever has the upper hand, it will have it only temporarily, depending on the nature of our forever changing external conditions and the internal conditions some of which we cannot alter. But there are others that we can change, and that allows us to have some reasonable hope.

This reasonable hope is to improve our lives by trying to remedy our dissatisfactions with those of our internal conditions that are within our power to alter. Some of these conditions are psychological within ourselves, others are social within the society in which we live. These conditions are always particular and context-dependent. The psychological ones depend on our education, experiences, intimate relationships, the work we do, and the successes and failures we have had. The social ones depend on the contemporary state of the prevailing world-view, on the present state of the modes of understanding and of the conflicts among them, and on the climatic, demographic, economic, and technological factors that influence how we live. The impetus for trying to alter these conditions are our dissatisfactions with them. And the hope we can reasonably have is that by altering them we may become less dissatisfied. Such alterations, if they succeed, will always be, I repeat, particular and context-dependent, because so are the dissatisfactions we are trying to alter. That is why pluralists deny that the source of modest hope can be a theory, any theory, that has universal and context-independent application. We can, and of course constantly do, nurture hopes beyond these realistic ones, but it is hard to see how they could be reasonable. They may console us, they may unite us with others with whom we can hope together, but such hopes cannot be reasonable and realistic, if the pluralist approach is right.

Are There Moral Absolutes?

In Part Two I argued against forms of absolutism, including the moral one, which I called moralism. I interpreted absolutism as the claim that one of the modes of understanding is always overriding, that reason requires considerations that follow from it to override conflicting considerations that follow from any of the other modes. If moralism is indeed mistaken, then it follows that there are no moral absolutes, no moral principle or value such that reason requires that it should always override whatever non-moral consideration may conflict with it. This is indeed a central assumption on which the pluralist approach rests. Its succinct statement is Stuart Hampshire's aphorism that "there is no consideration of any kind that overrides all other considerations in all conceivable circumstances."[12] It is crucial to understanding the pluralist approach to be clear about what this statement does and does not exclude.

It does not exclude the claim that some considerations are sometimes overriding. It allows that there may be contexts in which it would be reasonable to override a non-moral with a moral consideration. According to the pluralist approach, this may be true not just of moral but also of non-moral considerations that follow from any of the modes of understanding. This is consistent with the pluralist denial that there is any consideration so strong as to make it a requirement of reason that it should always override any consideration that conflicts with it.

The pluralist approach certainly excludes absolutist claims about the requirements of reason, but it excludes also relativist claims that reason cannot require any consideration to be even sometimes overriding because the requirements of reason are ultimately groundless. According to relativists, reason could have requirements only if it were possible always to support reasons with other reasons, but infinite regress rules out this possibility. Strictly speaking, therefore, reason can have no requirements. It can predispose us to accept some considerations on the basis of some reasons we happened to have, but for those reasons ultimately no further reason can be given.

The pluralist approach, by contrast, is committed to the view that some considerations in some contexts are required by reasons. This happens when the balance of available reasons overwhelmingly supports the requirement. The acknowledged logical possibilities that the balance may shift and any or all the available reasons may eventually turn out to be mistaken, are not sufficient grounds for doubting that the balance in a particular context holds and that reason requires coping with the problem accordingly. The pluralist approach, therefore, is an intermediate between the indefensibly strong absolutist and the indefensibly weak relativist interpretation of the requirements of reason.

Let us now consider in the light of this general understanding the particular question of whether there are moral absolutes. Moral absolutists say yes; relativists say no, and pluralists agree with relativists that moral values and principles regarded as absolute and overriding in some context may not be so regarded in another context. Pluralists deny that reason requires that some particular moral value or principle should always override whatever non-moral consideration conflicts with it. It is not hard to think of contexts in which circumstances make it reasonable to override a supposedly absolute moral value or principle. It may be reasonable to commit murder (say of a vicious tyrant), torture someone (say a terrorist to prevent a massacre), enslave a person (say by sentencing a mass murderer to a life of forced labor), and so on. But such exercises in casuistry carry no conviction if the moral requirement holds in a normal, unexceptional context whose details are clear. In such contexts, it is an absolute moral requirement to save rather than take the life of an innocent person, to refrain from causing unnecessary suffering, and so on. No one can reasonably deny that some moral requirements are sometimes overriding, and pluralists certainly do not deny it. If relativists deny it on the ground that the requirement holds only in some contexts and may not hold in others, then they owe an explanation of why if the ordinarily overriding and absolute moral requirement is violated in a particular and in no way exceptional context, then that shows that the requirement does not hold, rather than that its violation is immoral.

If pluralists accept that reason requires that some moral requirement should override non-moral requirements that conflict with it, then how do they differ from moral absolutists? They differ in two ways. The importance of these ways is not merely that they mark differences, but also that they point at general considerations crucial to understanding the pluralist approach.

The first difference is that the fact that there are contexts in which reason requires that moral requirements should be overriding is not a reason for absolutism and against pluralism. Both accept that moral requirements may sometimes be overriding. The question is whether there is any moral requirement that is always overriding. And it is to that question that the absolutist answer is yes and the pluralist answer is no. Pluralists accept that reason requires that some contexts should be seen as having a predominantly moral significance, and failing to see them in that light is not merely a moral failure but also a failure of reason. These are contexts in which the balance of reasons clearly implies that the improvement of affected lives depends on meeting moral requirements. What pluralists reject is the absolutist view that whenever moral considerations are relevant in a context, then reason requires that they should be overriding. This is what turns a reasonable commitment to morality into an unreasonable commitment to moralism.

Furthermore, pluralists hold this not just about the moral mode of understanding, but about all the modes. According to pluralists, it is unreasonable to regard any of the modes of understanding as always overriding. This is perfectly consistent with holding that reason requires some historical, moral, political, religious, scientific, or personal consideration to be sometimes, in some contexts, overriding. Whether a consideration is indeed overriding in a context depends on whether the balance of reasons clearly favors it, rather than some other consideration being overriding. It is not enough for showing this to claim that the overriding consideration follows from a particular mode of understanding. For that is true of all the considerations: they all follow from some mode of understanding. What needs to be shown is that the nature of the context and the balance of reasons demand that it be understood predominantly from the point of view of a particular mode. That can certainly be sometimes shown, but only by adducing particular reasons that hold in that context. And that is why pluralists insist that deciding how a context should be understood depends on particular, context-dependent, and practical considerations, rather than on universal and context-independent ones that assume that all contexts must be understood predominantly from the theoretical point of view of the historical, moral, political, religious, scientific, or personal mode of understanding.

This leads to the second difference between moral absolutism and the pluralist approach. According to absolutists, if basic moral requirements are involved, then reason requires that they should be overriding regardless of what the context is. If we understand human rights as protecting the most basic conditions on which the improvement of human lives depend, then, moral absolutists claim, their protection is a requirement of both reason and morality, and it overrides whatever non-moral requirement may conflict with it. Pluralists disagree. They acknowledge, of course, that there are reasons for protecting human rights because they are basic requirements of improving human lives, but they deny that the moral reasons for it are unique or overriding. This is not because the moral reason based on human rights are weak or mistaken, but because the moral mode of understanding is not alone in its concern for improving human lives. There follow requirements from each mode of understanding that have basic importance for improving human lives.

The historical mode makes us beneficiaries of accumulated human experience and the knowledge gained from them. How else could we learn about the successes and failures of past policies and institutions, religious practices, scientific projects, and possible personal ways of life?[13] The political mode enables us to understand the laws, institutions, and conventions that create the framework within which we and others in our society can peacefully live together even though we have different moral, political, religious, and personal preferences.[14] The religious mode asks and attempts to answer fundamental questions about the meaning of life, the foundation of values, the nature of evil, the place of humanity in the scheme of things, and the role faith, hope, prayer, repentance, sin, and worship have or should have in our lives.[15] The scientific mode is the key to understanding what is perhaps the most successful of all human enterprises. It informs our lives in countless ways, and it has made a major contribution to the improvement of our condition.[16] We learn from the personal mode how to conduct our own experiment in living, take control of our life, develop our individuality, and become as much as possible our own master.[17]

These claims about the importance of each mode of understanding sometimes conflict, and that is what gives rise to the philosophical problems I have been discussing. Coping with philosophical problems cannot reasonably be based on appealing to the overriding importance of any of the modes of understanding, because defenders of each of the modes claim that for their own. This brings us to a summary account of how the pluralist approach proposes to cope with philosophical problems.

Conclusion

The previous two paragraphs repeat what I have been saying at much greater length and in more detail throughout the book about the importance of our modes of understanding. The reason for repeating it once more is to stress the point that each mode is concerned with fundamental conditions of the improvement of human lives, and that the moral mode is merely one of them. The considerations that follow from it are neither more nor less important than those that follow from the other modes. Moral absolutists are right to stress the importance of moral considerations, and wrong to think that when moral considerations conflict with historical, political, religious, scientific, or personal considerations, then reason requires that moral considerations should always override any non-moral consideration that conflicts with them. Reason may sometimes require this, but it may sometimes require the contrary. The pluralist approach is centrally committed to recognizing this, and that is one reason why it is reasonable to accept it in preference to moral, or indeed any other form of, absolutism.

If this much is accepted, the serious problem of course remains that the considerations that follow from different modes of understanding often conflict, and the improvement of our lives depends on finding some reasonable way of coping with such conflicts. I have been arguing that we cannot hope to rely on some theory to find a reasonable way of coping, for two reasons. One is that all theories presuppose one or another mode of understanding, and if we are committed to avoiding all forms of absolutism, then we cannot reasonably assume that any one mode of understanding is the key to resolving conflicts between it and the other modes. The other reason is that we have no other source of theories than the modes of understanding we have. The remaining alternative is that a reasonable way of coping with philosophical problems caused by conflicts between modes of understanding must be practical, not theoretical. And if it is practical, then it must take into account the particular features of the particular context in which the conflict occurs. It cannot be universal and context-independent. What might such a practical, particular, context-dependent way of coping be, if it is to be reasonable rather than arbitrary?

According to pluralists, a way can be found by remembering that the conflicts occur because, given only the resources available in everyday life, we do not know how to deal with some problem of everyday life. That is why we turn to modes of understanding for help. We sometimes find that from different modes of understanding conflicting ways of coping follow, and then we encounter the philosophical problems I have been discussing. Many of our problems, of course, are not philosophical, because we can cope with them without going beyond everyday life. Or they may be modal problems within a particular mode of understanding, and we can cope with them by using the resources of that mode. But if the resources of everyday life and modes of understanding are insufficient, then we end up with philosophical problems. And the question is what we might do to cope with them?

The pluralist answer is to rely on the way that follows from the mode of understanding that is more likely to help us cope with the everyday problem with which we began than any of the other modes. What that way is depends on what the everyday problem is and on the context in which it occurs. This answer is general and vague, and it would be unhelpful if it were meant as a proposal for coping with any particular problem. But that is not what it was meant to be. It is meant to indicate what a possible and reasonable way of coping would be.

It would have to be practical, because its aim is to cope with problems of everyday life beyond the resources of both everyday life and any particular mode of understanding. It could not be theoretical, because the only source of theories are modes of understanding and their resources have been found insufficient. It would have to be context-dependent and particular, because the everyday problem occurs and can be coped with only in a context that has specific physical and social features and resources, and one in which coping depends on the prevailing historical, moral, political, religious, scientific, and personal assumptions, all of which vary from context to context. A reasonable way of coping could not be either absolutist or relativist. It could not be absolutist, because even if the balance of available reasons justifies regarding the way of coping that follows from a particular mode of understanding overriding, both the reasons and their balance will shift as the context changes, and what was overriding will not remain so. And a reasonable way of coping could not be relativist either, because relativists, like absolutists, deny that the mere balance of available reasons is sufficient for making a particular way of coping reasonable. Absolutists and relativists both claim that reasonable ways of coping could not be merely practical, context-dependent, and particular, but must be theoretical, context-independent, and universal. The difference between them is that absolutists think that such ways can be found, while relativists deny it.

The pluralist response to both of them is that they are mistaken about what reasons would be sufficient for coping with philosophical problems. Philosophical problems are ultimately caused by everyday problems. And everyday problems occur because we become dissatisfied with some aspect of everyday life. Reasonable ways of coping with everyday problems are those that make us less dissatisfied. The cause of some of our dissatisfactions are conditions we cannot change, but other dissatisfactions are caused by conditions we can change. And changing them as best as we can, given the prevailing conditions, the available resources, and our historical, moral, political, religious, scientific, and personal assumptions, is the most reasonable way of coping we have and can have. To look for more is a dangerous illusion, and to respond by cynicism, despair, resentment, resignation, or wishful thinking that we can find an ideological or religious salvation if we look hard enough is just as dangerous.

Notes

Preface

1. Ludwig Wittgenstein, "Letter to Norman Malcolm, November 1944" in Norman Malcolm, *Ludwig Wittgenstein: A Memoir*, (London: Oxford University Press, 1958), 39.

Introduction

1. W.B. Gallie, *Philosophy and the Historical Understanding*, 2nd ed. (New York: Schocken Books, 1968), 7.
2. See R.G. Collingwood, *Speculum Mentis*, (Oxford: Clarendon Press, 1924) for "scale of forms"; Michael Oakeshott, *Experience and Its Modes*, (Cambridge: Cambridge University Press, 1933) for "modes of experience"; Alfred North Whitehead, *Modes of Thought*, (Cambridge: Cambridge University Press, 1938) for "modes of thought"; Ernst Cassirer, *Philosophy of Symbolic Forms*, trans. Ralph Mannheim, (New Haven: Yale University Press, 1923–29/1953–57) for "symbolic forms"; Rudolf Carnap, "Empiricism, Semantics, and Ontology" in *Meaning and Necessity*, (Chicago: University of Chicago Press, 1947/1950) for "linguistic frameworks"; Ludwig Wittgenstein, *Philosophical Investigations*, trans. G.E.M. Anscombe, (Oxford: Blackwell, 1953/1958) for "language games"; Nelson Goodman, *Ways of Worldmaking*, (Indianapolis: Hackett, 1978/1985) for "ways of worldmaking"; Clifford Geertz, *Local Knowledge*, (New York: Basic Books, 1983) for "cultural forms"; Donald Davidson, "On the Very Idea of a Conceptual Scheme" in *Inquiries into Truth and Interpretation*, (Oxford: Clarendon Press, 1974/1984) for "conceptual schemes".
3. David Hume, *A Treatise of Human Nature*, 2nd ed., rev. P.H. Nidditch, (Oxford: Oxford University Press, 1739–40/1978), xiii–xiv.
4. Rene Descartes, *Discourse on the Method of rightly conducting one's reason and seeking the truth in the sciences* in *The Philosophical Writings of Descartes*, vol. 1, trans. John Cottingham, et. al. (Cambridge: Cambridge University Press, 1637/1985), 114–15.
5. Immanuel Kant, *Prolegomena To Any Future Metaphysics*, trans. Lewis White Beck, (New York: Liberal Arts, 1783/1950), 4.
6. John Stuart Mill, *Utilitarianism*, (Indianapolis: Hackett, 1861/1979), 1.
7. Bertrand Russell, *The Problems of Philosophy*, (Oxford: Oxford University Press, 1912/1967), 90.
8. Ludwig Wittgenstein, *Tractatus Logico-Philosophicus*, trans. D.F. Pears and B.F. McGuinness, (London: Routledge, 1921/1960), 5.
9. Wittgenstein, *Philosophical Investigations*, x.

Chapter 1

1. Isaiah Berlin, "Philosophy and Government Repression" in *The Sense of Reality*, ed. Henry Hardy, (London: Chatto & Windus, 1953/1996), 68–9.

2. "Every person who is actually absorbed in any given form of experience is by this very absorption committed to the opinion that no other form is valid, that his form is the only one adequate to the comprehension of reality. Hence arise discords; for when artists and scientists, who after all do inhabit a common world of fact, meet and discuss their aims, each is apt to accuse the other of wasting his life on a world of illusions. The 'ancient quarrel between poetry and philosophy' is only one of a whole series of such quarrels in a ceaseless international war in which every country on our map is eternally embroiled with every other." R.G. Collingwood, *Speculum Mentis*, (Oxford: Clarendon Press, 1924), 307.

3. "Every culture seems, as it advances toward maturity, to produce its own determining debate over the ideas that preoccupy it: salvation, the order of nature, money, power, sex, the machine, and the like. The debate, indeed, may be said to *be* the culture, at least on its loftiest levels; for a culture achieves identity not so much through the ascendancy of one particular set of convictions as through the emergence of its particular and distinctive dialogue." R.W.B. Lewis, *The American Adam*, (Chicago: University of Chicago Press, 1955), 1–2.

4. Writing about "the general principles of what has been called Teleology, or the Doctrine of Ends; which borrowing the language of the German metaphysicians, may also be termed, not improperly, the principles of Practical Reason" we find "Necessity of an ultimate standard, or first principle of Teleology" which is that "There is, then, a Philosophia Prima peculiar to Art, as there is one which belongs to Science. There are not only first principles of Knowledge, but first principles of Conduct. There must be some standard by which to determine the goodness or badness, absolute and comparative, of ends, or objects of desire. And whatever that standard is, there can be but one: for if there were several ultimate principles of conduct, the same conduct may be approved by one those principles and condemned by another; and there would needed some more general principle, as umpire between them." John Stuart Mill, *A System of Logic*, Book VI, Sections 6–7, *Collected Works of John Stuart Mill*, vol. 8, ed. J.M. Robson, (Indianapolis: Liberty Fund, 1843/2006), 949–51.

5. "What has to be accepted, the given, is—so one could say—*forms of life.*" And "if I have exhausted the justifications I have reached bedrock, and my spade is turned. Then I am inclined to say: 'This is simply what I do.'" Ludwig Wittgenstein, *Philosophical Investigations*, trans. G.E.M. Anscombe, (Oxford: Blackwell, 1953/1968), I. 217, II. 226.

6. "It is enough, I think, to live by experience and without opinions, in accordance with the common observations and preconceptions, and to suspend judgment about what is said with dogmatic superfluity and far beyond the needs of ordinary life." Sextus Empiricus, *Outlines of Scepticism*, trans. Julia Annas and Jonathan Barnes, (Cambridge: Cambridge University Press, c. 2nd Century AD/1994), II. 246.

Chapter 2

1. Gilbert Ryle, *Dilemmas*, (Cambridge: Cambridge University Press, 1956), 1.
2. An eminent historian of politics writes of his own point of view that it "is one which can realistically hope to find an intellectually authoritative welcome within one of the most powerful currents of modern philosophical thinking—the holistic or, in some versions, the anti-realist strand which has roots in the American pragmatist tradition and especially in the thought of Quine." John Dunn, "What is living and What is Dead in the Political Theory of John Locke?" in *Interpreting Political Responsibility*, (Princeton: Princeton University Press, 1986/1990), 10. Dunn is one of a group of like-minded historically oriented political thinkers, such as Quentin Skinner, J.G.A. Pocock, and Raymond Geuss.
3. Thucydides, *The Peloponnesian War*, trans. Rex Warner, (Harmondsworth: Penguin, c. 5th Century BC/1954), Book II, Chapter 4.
4. Carl L. Becker, *The Heavenly City of the Eighteenth-Century Philosophers*, (New Haven: Yale University Press, 1932), 6–7.
5. Bertrand Russell, "A Free Man's Worship" in *Mysticism and Logic*, (Harmondsworth: Penguin, 1902/1953), 51.
6. See John Kekes, *Enjoyment*, (Oxford: Clarendon Press, 2008), Chapter 6 and *The Human Condition,* (Oxford: Clarendon Press, 2010), Chapters 5–9.
7. "Equal concern is the sovereign virtue of political community," Ronald Dworkin, *Sovereign Virtue*, (Cambridge, MA: Harvard University Press, 2000), 1. "Justice is the first virtue of social institutions," John Rawls, *A Theory of Justice*, (Cambridge, MA: Harvard University Press, 1971), 3. "The argument of this book will demonstrate how far-reaching are the implications of political liberty, how they affect our conceptions of justice, equality, prosperity and other political ideals," Joseph Raz, *The Morality of Freedom*, (Oxford: Clarendon Press, 1986), 2. "Individuals have rights, and there are things no person or group may do to them (without violating their rights). So strong and far-reaching are these rights that they raise the question of what, if anything, the state and its officials may do," Robert Nozick, *Anarchy, State, and Utopia*, (New York: Basic Books, 1974), ix.
8. "[Political] ends may clash irreconcilably. When this happens questions of choice and preference inevitably arise. Should democracy in a given situation be promoted at the expense of individual freedom? or equality at the expense of artistic achievement; or mercy at the expense of justice; or spontaneity at the expense of efficiency; or happiness, loyalty, innocence at the expense of knowledge and truth. The simple point I am concerned to make is that where ultimate values are irreconcilable, clear-cut solutions cannot, in principle, be found. To decide rationally in such situations is to decide in the light of . . . the over-all pattern of life pursued by a man or a group or a society. . . . When such dilemmas arise it is one thing to say that every effort must be made to resolve them, and another that it is certain *a priori* that a correct, conclusive solution must always in principle be discoverable." Isaiah Berlin, *Four Essays on Liberty*, (Oxford: Oxford University Press, 1958/1969), xlix–l
9. "Pressing and urgent matters . . . are the things that we are faced with in everyday life. The reason for beginning with ideal theory is that it provides, I believe, the only basis

for the systematic grasp of these more pressing problems.... A deeper understanding can be gained in no other way, and that the nature and aims of a perfectly just society is the fundamental part of the theory of justice." Rawls, *Theory of Justice*, 9.

10. "Politics is the activity of attending to the general arrangements of a collection of people who, in respect of their common recognition of a manner of attending to its arrangements, compose a single community.... This activity, then, springs neither from instant desires, nor from general principles, but from the existing traditions of behaviour themselves. And the form it takes, because it can take no other, is the amendment of existing arrangements by exploring and pursuing what is intimated in them." Michael Oakeshott, "Political Education" in *Rationalism in Politics and Other Essays*, new and expanded edition, ed. Timothy Fuller, (Indianapolis: Liberty Press, 1962/1991), 56.

11. "The religious dimensions adds...a framework within which nature is revealed as more than just a set of characteristics that a certain species happens intermittently to possess, but instead as pointing to the condition that a Being of the utmost benevolence and care that we can conceive of desires us to achieve. Focusing on this dimension, moreover, encourages us with the hope that the pursuit of virtue...contributes however minutely to the establishment of a moral order." John Cottingham, *The Meaning of Life*, (London: Routledge, 2003), 72.

12. "[Religion]is not a magical overcoming of impossible odds, but a certain mindset which will not judge the value of sticking to the side of goodness by reference to its success or failure measured in terms of outcome, but which generates courage to endure, irradiated by hope.... Such a mindset is hard to describe in purely cognitive terms; for it is not primarily characterisable in terms of propositions assented to, but is a matter of a certain orientation in which emotions and beliefs and practices of worship and moral convictions merge together in...a passionate commitment to a certain form of life. The hope involved here is closer to an emotional allegiance to the idea of the power of goodness than to a cognitive attitude of expectation that outcomes will be...favourable.... [It is] a matter of something in the human spirit which can respond to the deepest stress and weakness in ways which are transforming." Cottingham, *Meaning of Life*, 74–5.

13. Religious belief does this by "providing a powerful *normative framework* or *focus* for the life of virtue...encourages us with the hope that the pursuit of virtue...contributes however minutely to the establishment of a moral order," Cottingham, *Meaning of Life*, 72.

14. "[The]objective of science is to arrive at general laws and theories that yield predictions concerning future events and retrodictions concerning unexamined past ones.... [to] explain why a given event came about by showing that it occurred in certain particular circumstances...in accordance with certain general laws of nature or well-established theoretical principles.... Thus, the phenomenon is explained by showing that, under given particular conditions, it 'had to' occur according to the specified laws." Carl G. Hempel, *The Philosophy of Carl G. Hempel*, ed. James H. Fetzer, (New York: Oxford University Press, 1973/2001), 331, 333–4.

15. "Surely, one who is seriously concerned to enhance the welfare and happiness of mankind would still have to proceed by the standards of *scientific* rationality in search for knowledge about suitable means to achieve those ends," Hempel, *Philosophy of Carl*.

G. Hempel, 364. "Scientific behavior, taken as a whole, is the best example we have of rationality...and if history or any other empirical discipline leads us to believe that the development of science depends essentially on behavior that we have previously thought to be irrational, then we should conclude not that science is irrational, but that our notion of rationality needs adjustment," T.S. Kuhn, "Notes on Lakatos" in *Boston Studies in the Philosophy of Science*, 8(1971): 144.

16. Karl R. Popper, "Truth, Rationality, and the Growth of Knowledge" in *Conjectures and Refutations*, (New York: Harper & Row, 1963), 216–17.

17. Ludwig Wittgenstein, *Tractatus Logico-Philosophicus*, trans. D.F. Pears & B.F. McGuinness, (London: Routledge, 1921/1961), 6.52–6.521.

18. "Valuations are...important motivational factors that affect the conduct of inquiry. Such factors must therefore be taken into account in efforts, such as those made in the psychology, the sociology, and the history of science, to *explain* scientific research behavior." Hempel, *Philosophy of Carl G, Hempel*, 373.

19. Karl Joachim Weintraub, *The Value of the Individual: Self and Circumstance in Autobiography*, (Chicago: University of Chicago Press, 1978), 379.

20. Jerome B. Schneewind, *The Invention of Autonomy*, (New York: Cambridge University Press, 1998), 4–5.

21. For a fine description of this process of discovery and articulation, see Charles Taylor, *Sources of the Self*, (Cambridge, MA: Harvard University Press, 1989).

22. "Things in themselves may have their own weights and measures and qualities; but...health, conscience, authority, knowledge, riches, beauty, and their opposites—all are stripped on entry and receive from the soul new clothing, and coloring that she chooses....Let us no longer make the external qualities of things our excuse; it is up to us to reckon them as we will." Michel Montaigne, *Essays* in *The Complete Works of Montaigne,* trans. Donald M. Frame, (Stanford: Stanford University Press, 1588/1943), 220.

23. Isaiah Berlin, "Two Concepts of Liberty" in *Four Essays on Liberty*, (Oxford: Oxford University Press, 1958/1969), 131.

Chapter 3

1. Stuart Hampshire, *Justice is Conflict*, (Princeton: Princeton University Press, 2000), 33–4.

Chapter 4

1. R.W.B. Lewis, *The American Adam*, (Chicago: University Chicago Press, 1955), 1–2.

2. George Berkeley, *Three Dialogues between Hylas and Philonous*, (Indianapolis: Hackett, 1713/1979), Preface.

3. "There exists at present a living human body, which is *my* body. This body was born at a certain time in the past, and has existed continuously ever since, though not without undergoing changes; it was, for instance, much smaller when it was born, and for some time afterwards, than it is now....There have also existed many other things, having shape and size in three dimensions....The earth had existed also for many years before

my body was born; and for many of these years, also, large numbers of human bodies had, at every moment, been alive upon it; and many of these bodies have died. . . . I am a human being, and I have, at different times since my body was born, had many different experiences" and so on. G.E. Moore, "A Defence of Common Sense" in *Philosophical Papers*, (London: Allen & Unwin, 1925/1959), 32–3.

4. "English law has evolved and regularly uses a standard which does not depend on counting heads. It is that of the reasonable man. . . . He is not expected to reason about anything and his judgement may be largely a matter of feeling. It is the viewpoint of the man on the street. . . . He might also be called the right-minded man." Patrick Devlin, "Morals and the Criminal Law" in *The Enforcement of Morals*, (London: Oxford University Press, 1959/1965), 14–15.

5. G.E. Moore, "Proof of an External World" in *Philosophical Papers*, 1925/1959, 145–6.

6. See S.A. Grave, *The Scottish Philosophy of Common Sense*, (Oxford: Clarendon Press, 1960).

7. See Sextus Empiricus, *Sextus Empiricus: Outlines of Scepticism*, trans. Julia Annas and Jonathan Barnes, (Cambridge: Cambridge University Press, c. 2nd Century AD/1994); Tad Brennan, *Ethics and Epistemology in Sextus Empiricus*, (New York: Garland, 1999); Myles Burnyeat, ed. *The Skeptical Tradition*, (Berkeley: University of California Press, 1983).

8. David Hume, *An Enquiry Concerning Human Understanding*, ed. Tom L. Beauchamp, (Oxford: Oxford University Press, 1772/1999), Section 12, Part 3: 208–9.

9. David Hume, *An Enquiry Concerning Human Understanding*, 208–9.

10. Sextus, *Outlines*, I.22, II. 46. See also "the aim of the Sceptic is tranquillity in matters of opinion and moderation of feeling in matters forced upon us" (I. 25). "Men of talent, troubled by the anomaly in things and puzzled as to which of them they should rather assent to, came to investigate what in things is true and what false, thinking that by deciding these issues they could become tranquil" (I. 12). But skeptics proceed differently because they find that "opposed to every account there is an equal account . . . purporting to establish something in dogmatic fashion, equal to it in convincingness or lack of convincingness" (I. 202). For this reason, skeptics say, "we come to hold no beliefs" (I. 12), and explain that as "when we say that Sceptics do not hold beliefs, we do not take 'belief' in the sense . . . [of] acquiescing in something; for Sceptics assent to the feelings forced on them by appearances. . . . Rather, we say that they do not hold beliefs in the sense in which some say that belief is assent to some unclear object of investigation in the sciences; for Pyrrhonists do not assent to anything unclear" (I. 13).

11. W.B. Gallie, *Philosophy and the Historical Understanding*, 2nd ed. (New York: Schocken Books, 1968).

12. John Stuart Mill, *On Liberty*, (Indianapolis: Hackett, 1859/1978), Chapter II, 19.

Chapter 5

1. Isaiah Berlin, "Historical Inevitability" in *Four Essays on Liberty*, (Oxford: Clarendon Press, 1958/1969), 42–3.

2. See Maurice Mandelbaum, "Historicism" in *The Encyclopedia of Philosophy*, vol. 4, ed. Paul Edwards, (New York: Macmillan, 1967); Georg G. Iggers,

"Historicism" in *Dictionary of the History of Ideas*, vol. II, ed. Philip P. Wiener, (New York: Scribner's, 1973).

3. Bernard Williams, *Truth and Truthfulness: An Essay in Genealogy*, (Princeton: Princeton University Press, 2002), 20. See also "The crux of the theory is recognition of genealogy as an expression of radical historicism, rejecting both appeals to transcendental truths and principles of unity or progress in history, and embracing nominalism, contingency, and contestability.... Genealogies operate as denaturalizing critiques of ideas and practices that hide the contingency of human life behind formal ahistorical or developmental perspectives," Mark Bevir, "What is Genealogy?" *Journal of the Philosophy of History* 2(2008): 263–75. And "Genealogy takes as its objects precisely those institutions and practices which, like morality, are usually thought to be totally exempt from change and development. It tries to show the way in which they too undergo changes as a result of historical developments. And it also tries to show how such changes escape our notice and how it is often in the interest of these practices to mask their specific historical origins and character." Alexander Nehamas, *Nietzsche: Life as Literature*, (Cambridge, MA: Harvard University Press, 1985), 112.

4. Isaiah Berlin, "Two Concepts of Liberty" in *Four Essays on Liberty*, (Oxford: Oxford University Press, 1958/1969), 172.

5. Bevir, "What is Genealogy?" and *The Logic of the History of Ideas*, (Cambridge: Cambridge University Press, 1999); Craig, "Genealogies" and *Knowledge and the State of Nature*, (Cambridge: Cambridge University Press, 1990); Raymond Geuss, "Nietzsche and Genealogy" in his *Morality, Culture and History*, (Cambridge: Cambridge University Press, 1999) and "Genealogy as Critique" *European Journal of Philosophy* 10(2002): 209–15; Nehamas, *Nietzsche*; Williams, *Truth and Truthfulness*.

   Perhaps it is appropriate to explain here two omissions from the list of genealogists. One is Michel Foucault whose work on genealogy I do not discuss because I found his historical references unreliable and his arguments, if that is what they are meant to be, below the level of serious philosophy. The other is Richard Rorty, who calls himself a historicist and a pragmatist, but to the best of my knowledge never claims to be a genealogist. His historicism and pragmatism, however, are different labels for an extreme form of relativism that is most succinctly explained in his three Northcliffe Lectures and reprinted as the first three essays in his *Contingency, Irony, and Solidarity*, (Cambridge: Cambridge University Press, 1989).

6. See e.g. Hans Reichenbach, *Experience and Prediction*, (Chicago: University of Chicago Press, 1938), Chapter 1; Ernest Nagel, "Malicious Philosophies of Science" in *Sovereign Reason*, (Glencoe, IL: Free Press, 1954); Carl G. Hempel. "Valuation and Objectivity in Science" in *The Philosophy of Carl G. Hempel*, ed. James H. Fetzer, ((New York: Oxford University Press, 1973/2001).

7. Thomas Hobbes, "Of the Naturall Condition of Mankind" in *Leviathan*, ed. Richard Tuck, (Cambridge: Cambridge University Press, 1651/1996), Book I, Chapter 13, 89.

8. Jean-Jacques Rousseau, *Discourse on the Origin of Inequality*, trans. Donald A. Cress, (Indianapolis: Hackett, 1754/1987), 38.

9. Nehamas, *Nietzsche*, 112.

10. Williams, *Truth and Truthfulness*, 32.
11. The account in this paragraph is my understanding of the accounts of Craig and Williams in the works cited in Note 5 above.
12. Immanuel Kant, "Speculative Beginning of Human History" in *Perpetual Peace and Other Essays*, trans. Ted Humphreys, (Indianapolis: Hackett, 1786/1983), 53, 57–8, 59.
13. John Stuart Mill, *On Liberty*, (Indianapolis: Hackett, 1859/1978), Chapter II, 28.
14. Williams, *Truth and Truthfulness*, 268.
15. Friedrich Nietzsche, *Human, All Too Human*, trans. R.J. Hollingdale, (Cambridge: Cambridge University Press, 1880/1996), I. #517.
16. Friedrich Nietzsche, *Human, All Too Human*, I. #2.
17. Rorty, *Contingency, irony, and solidarity*, 8.
18. Nietzsche, *Human, All Too Human*, I. #2.
19. Richard Rorty, "Is Natural Science and Natural Kind?" in *Objectivity, Relativism, and Truth*, (Cambridge: Cambridge University Press, 1991), 61.
20. Bevir, "What is Genealogy?", 270.
21. Oscar Wilde, *The Picture of Dorian Gray*, (Harmondsworth: Penguin, 1891/1949), 29.
22. Karl Marx and Friedrich Engels, "Theses on Feuerbach" in *The German Ideology*, (Moscow: Foreign Languages Publishing House, 1846/1968), Thesis XI.
23. Bevir thinks that "genealogy opens novel spaces for personal and social transformation precisely because it loosens the hold on us of entrenched ideas and institutions," "What is Genealogy", 272. According to Nehamas, "genealogy has direct practical consequences because, by demonstrating the contingent character of the institutions that traditional history exhibits as unchanging, it creates the possibility of changing them," *Nietzsche*. 112. Williams says that when genealogies provide a subversive explanation of people's beliefs, values, or practices, then "if they come to accept the explanation, their outlook will have to change," *Truth and Truthfulness*, 37.
24. T.S. Eliot, "Four Quartets" in *The Complete Poems and Plays*, (New York: Harcourt, 1971), 145.
25. Ludwig Wittgenstein, *Philosophical Investigations*, trans G.E.M. Anscombe, (Oxford: Blackwell, 1953/1968), II. 226.

Chapter 6

1. Iris Murdoch, "Metaphysics and Ethics" in *Existentialists and Mystics*, (London: Allen Lane, 1957/1998), 74–5.
2. Immanuel Kant, *The Metaphysics of Morals*, trans. Mary Gregor, (Cambridge: Cambridge University Press, 1797/1996), 182.
3. John Stuart Mill, *Utilitarianism* in *Collected Works of John Stuart Mill*, ed. J.M. Robson, (Indianapolis: Liberty Fund, 1861/2006), vol. 10, 218, 232.
4. Peter Singer, *Practical Ethics*, 2nd ed. (Cambridge: Cambridge University Press, 1993), 222.
5. Ronald Dworkin, *Sovereign Virtue*, (Cambridge, MA: Harvard University Press, 2000), 1.
6. For illuminating discussion, see C.A.J. Coady, *What's Wrong with Moralism?* (Oxford: Blackwell, 2006) and *Messy Morality*, (Oxford: Clarendon Press, 2008);

Raymond Geuss, *Philosophy and Real Politics,* (Princeton: Princeton University Press, 2008).

7. E.g. Kurt Baier, *The Moral Point of View,* (Ithaca: Cornell University Press, 1958) and *The Rational and the Moral Order,* (Chicago: Open Court, 1995); Lawrence C. Becker, *Reciprocity,* (London: Routledge, 1986); Richard B. Brandt, *A Theory of the Good and the Right,* (Oxford: Clarendon Press, 1979); Alan Donagan, *The Theory of Morality,* (Chicago: University of Chicago Press, 1977); Philippa Foot, *Natural Goodness,* (Oxford: Clarendon Press, 2001); Alan Gewirth, *Reason and Morality,* (Chicago: University of Chicago Press, 1978); R.M. Hare, *The Language of Morals,* (Oxford: Clarendon Press, 1952), *Freedom and Reason,* (Oxford: Clarendon Press, 1963), and *Moral Thinking,* (Oxford: Clarendon Press, 1981); Christine M. Korsgaard, *Creating the Kingdom of Ends,* (Cambridge: Cambridge University Press, 1996), *The Sources of Normativity,* (Cambridge: Cambridge University Press, 1996), and *Self-Constitution,* (Oxford: Clarendon Press, 2009); Thomas Nagel, *The Last Word,* (New York: Oxford University Press, 1997); W.D. Ross, *The Right and the Good,* (Oxford: Clarendon Press, 1930) and *Foundations of Ethics,* (Oxford: Clarendon Press, 1939); T.M. Scanlon, *What We Owe to Each Other,* (Cambridge, MA: Harvard University Press, 1998); Samuel Scheffler, *Human Morality,* (New York: Oxford University Press, 1992). A full list would be very long, especially if it included the plethora of articles.

8. Bernard Williams, "Persons, character and morality" in *Moral Luck,* (Cambridge: Cambridge University Press, 1981), 14.

9. Ross, *The Right and the Good.*

10. E.g. David Copp, "The Ring of Gyges: Overridingness and the Unity of Reason" *Social Philosophy and Policy* 14(1997): 86–106; Roger Crisp, *Reasons and the Good,* (Oxford: Clarendon Press, 2006); W.D. Falk, "Morality, Self and Others" in *Morality and the Language of Conduct,* eds. Hector-Neri Castaneda and George Nakhnikian, (Detroit: Wayne Street University Press, 1963); Philippa Foot, "Morality as a System of Hypothetical Imperatives" and "Are Moral Considerations Overriding?" *Virtues and Vices,* (Berkeley: University of California Press, 1978); J.L. Mackie, *Ethics: Inventing Right and Wrong,* (Harmondsworth: Penguin, 1978); Bernard Williams, "Persons, character and morality" and *Ethics and the Limits of Philosophy,* (London: Fontana, 1985); Susan Wolf, "Moral Saints" *Journal of Philosophy* 79(1982): 419–39 and "Morality and the View from Here" *Journal of Ethics* 3(1999): 203–23.

11. Niccolo Machiavelli, *The Prince,* trans. Harvey C. Mansfield, Jr. (Chicago: University of Chicago Press, 1513/1985); Bernard Mandeville, *The Fable of the Bees,* (Indianapolis: Liberty Classics, 1714/1988); Friedrich Nietzsche, *The Genealogy of Morals,* trans. Walter Kaufmann, (New York: Random House, 1887/1966); and more recently Richard Garner, *Beyond Morality,* (Philadelphia: Temple University Press, 1994); Richard Joyce, *The Myth of Morality,* (Cambridge: Cambridge University Press, 2001); and Hans-Georg Moeller, *The Moral Fool,* (New York: Columbia University Press, 2009).

12. Immanuel Kant, *Groundwork of the Metaphysics of Morals* in *Practical Philosophy,* trans. and ed. Mary J. Gregor, (Cambridge: Cambridge University Press, 1785/1996), 47.

13. John Stuart Mill, *A System of Logic* in *Collected Works of John Stuart Mill,* ed. J.M. Robson, (Indianapolis: Liberty Fund, 1861/2006), vol. 8, 951.

14. Kant, *Groundwork*, 47.
15. Henry Sidgwick, *The Methods of Ethics*, 7th ed. (Indianapolis: Hackett, 1907/1981), 508 and 386.
16. Quoted in J.M. Schneewind, *Sidgwick's Ethics and Victorian Moral Philosophy*, (Oxford: Clarendon Press, 1977), 352.
17. Falk, "Morality, Self and Others", 50–1.
18. Falk, "Morality, Self and Others", 50–1.
19. Copp, "The Ring of Gyges" and Owen McCleod, "Just Plain 'Ought' " *The Journal of Ethics* 5(2001): 269–91.
20. Foot, "Morality as a System of Hypothetical Imperatives", 169.
21. "When we deliberate about what to do, we may try to take into account all relevant considerations and to make the best or the right decision. We may not want to make a decision that is merely right or best from one standpoint. We may want to make the decision that is best *period*. This would be the decision required by Reason-as-such....I believe that there is no such thing as Reason-as-such. First, I do not believe we have any clear conception of what such a thing would be. Consider any candidate for the standard of Reason. Call it 'S'. It is quite unclear what status S could have that would give it the kind of supremacy it would need in order to qualify as the standard of Reason....The claim that the candidate S has the property of supremacy is the claim that it is normatively more important than any other standpoint." Copp, "The Ring of Gyges," 100–1.
22. Fyodor Dostoyevsky, *The Brothers Karamazov*, trans. David Magarshack, Part Two, Book Five, Chapter Four, "Rebellion", (Harmondsworth: Penguin, 1880/1958), 287.
23. William James, "The Moral Philosopher and the Moral Life" in *William James: Writings 1878–1899*, (New York: Library of America, 1891/1992), 598.

Chapter 7

1. Adam Smith, *The Theory of Moral Sentiments*, (Indianapolis: Liberty Classics, 1759/1969), 380–1.
2. Michael Freeden, "Ideology, Political Theory and Political Philosophy" in *Handbook of Political Theory*, eds. Gerald F. Gaus and Chandran Kukathas, (London: Sage Publications, 2004), 6. For a more detailed account, see his *Ideologies and Political Theory: A Conceptual Approach*, (Oxford: Clarendon Press, 1996).
3. For a historical study of this mentality, see Norman Cohn, *The Pursuit of the Millennium*, (London: Secker & Warburg, 1957) and *Europe's Inner Demons*, rev. ed. (Chicago: University of Chicago Press, 1975/2000).
4. Clifford Geertz, "Ideology as a Cultural System" in *The Interpretation of Cultures*, (New York: Basic Books, 1973), 219–20.
5. John Rawls, *A Theory of Justice*, (Cambridge, MA: Harvard University Press, 1971).
6. Rawls, *A Theory of Justice*, 3.
7. Rawls, *A Theory of Justice*, 587.
8. Rawls, *Theory of Justice*, 9, 246.
9. This point has been made very clearly by Popper: "If we...create a new world on the basis of blue-prints, then we shall very soon have to alter the new world, making little changes and adjustments. But if we are to make these little changes and adjustments, which will be needed in any case, why not start them here and now in the social world

we have? It does not matter what you have and where you start. You must always make little adjustments. Since you will always have to make them, it is very much more sensible and reasonable to start with what happens to exist at the moment, because…we at least know where the shoe pinches. We at least know of certain things that they are bad and that we want them changed," Karl R. Popper, *Conjectures and Refutations*, (New York: Harper & Row, 1963), 131.

10. E.g. Rawls' view is that the ideology will be followed because it tells us what justice is and "men's propensity to injustice is not a permanent aspect of community life," "a well-ordered society tends to eliminate or at least control men's inclinations to injustice," "the sense of justice is continuous with the love of mankind," and "a moral person is a subject with ends he has chosen, and his fundamental preference is for conditions that enable him to frame a mode of life that expresses his nature as a free and equal rational being." *Theory of Justice*, 245, 476, 561.

11. Jean-Jacques Rousseau, *Discourses on the Origin and Foundation of Inequality Among Man*, trans. Donald A. Cress, (Indianapolis: Hackett, 1754/1988) and *Letter to Beaumont* in *Oeuvres completes*, 5 vols. (Paris: Gallimard, 1959–95), trans. and cited by Timothy O'Hagan, *Rousseau*, (London: Routledge, 1999), 15.

12. Immanuel Kant, *Religion within the Bounds of Reason Alone*, trans. Theodore M. Greene and Hoyt H. Hudson, (New York: Harper & Row, 1794/1960), 39, 31.

13. John Stuart Mill, *Utilitarianism* in *Collected Works of John Stuart Mill*, vol. 10, ed. J.M. Robson, (Indianapolis: Liberty Fund, 1861/2006), 231.

14. "It is…no argument against individual freedom that it is frequently abused. Freedom necessarily means that many things will be done which we do not like. Our faith in freedom does not rest on the foreseeable results in particular circumstances but on the belief that it will, on balance, release more forces for the good than for the bad," Friedrich Hayek, *The Constitution of Liberty*, (Chicago: Regnery, 1960/1972), 31. "Men's propensity to injustice is not a permanent aspect of community life; it is greater or less depending in large part on social institutions, and in particular on whether they are just or unjust." And "a moral person is a subject with ends he has chosen, and his fundamental preference is for conditions that enable him to frame a mode of life that expresses his nature as a free and equal rational being," John Rawls, *A Theory of Justice*, (Cambridge, MA: Harvard University Press, 1971), 245 and 561. "The essence of evil is that it should *repel* us. If something is evil, our actions should be guided, if they are guided by it at all, toward its elimination rather than toward its maintenance. That is what evil *means*. So when we aim at evil we are swimming head-on against the normative current.… From the point of view of the agent, this produces an acute sense of moral dislocation," Thomas Nagel, *The View from Nowhere*, (New York: Oxford University Press, 1986), 182. "Moral evil is 'a kind of natural defect'," "acting morally is part of practical rationality," and "no one can act with full practical rationality in pursuit of a bad end," Philippa Foot, *Natural Goodness*, (Oxford: Clarendon Press, 2001), 5, 9, 14. "It is human nature to be governed by morality, and from every point of view, including his own, morality earns its right to govern us. We have therefore no reason to reject our nature, and can allow it to be a law to us. Human nature, moral government included, is therefore normative, and has authority for us," Christine M. Korsgaard, *The Sources of Normativity*, (Cambridge: Cambridge University Press, 1996), 66.

15. Niccolo Machiavelli, *The Discourses*, trans. David Wootton, (Indianapolis: Hackett, 1531/1994), 92.
16. David Hume, "Of the Independency of Parliament" in *Essays Moral, Political, and Literary*, (Indianapolis: Liberty Classics, 1777/1985), 42–3.
17. Isaiah Berlin, "Two Concepts of Liberty" in *Four Essays in Liberty*, (Oxford: Oxford University Press, 1967/1979), 165; Ronald Dworkin, *Sovereign Virtue*, Cambridge, MA: Harvard University Press, 2000), 1; Friedrich Hayek, *The Constitution of Liberty*, (Chicago: Regnery, 1960/1972), 6; John Stuart Mill, *On Liberty*, (Indianapolis: Hackett, 1859/1956), 13; Robert Nozick, *Anarchy, State, and Utopia*, (New York: Basic Books, 1974), ix; and Rawls, *Theory of Justice*, 3.
18. Rawls, *Theory of Justice*, 126.
19. Rawls, *Theory of Justice*, 45–6.
20. John Dunn, *The Cunning of Unreason*, (New York: Basic Books, 2000), 363.

Chapter 8

1. Ludwig Wittgenstein, *The Blue and Brown Books*, 2nd ed. (Oxford: Blackwell, 1958/1969), 18.
2. Carl G. Hempel, "Science Unlimited?" in *The Philosophy of Carl G. Hempel*, ed. James H. Fetzer, (New York: Oxford University Press, 1973/2001), 329.
3. Ludwig Wittgenstein, *Tractatus-Logico-Philosophicus*, trans. D.F. Pears and B.F. McGuinness, (London: Routledge, 1921/1961), 6.52.
4. Hempel, "Science Unlimited?" 341, 329.
5. Its history and the reasons for its untenability have been well discussed in Tom Sorell, *Scientism: Philosophy and the Infatuation with Science*, (London: Routledge, 1971), Chapter 1.
6. "Scientific inquiry has come to be widely acknowledged as the exemplar of rationality in pursuit of reliable knowledge," Hempel, "Scientific Rationality" in *Philosophy of Carl G. Hempel*, 357; "Scientific behavior, taken as a whole, is the best example we have of rationality... and if history or any other empirical discipline leads us to believe that the development of science depends essentially on behavior that we have previously thought to be irrational, then we should conclude not that science is irrational, but that our notion of rationality needs adjustment," T.S. Kuhn, "Notes on Lakatos" in *Boston Studies in the Philosophy of Science* 8(1971): 144; "Science is one of the very few human activities—perhaps the only one—in which errors are systematically criticized and fairly often, in time, corrected. This is why we can say that, in science, we often learn from our mistakes, and why we can speak clearly and sensibly about making progress there. In most other fields of human endeavour there is change, but rarely progress...for almost every gain is balanced, or more than balanced, by some loss. And in most fields we do not even know how to evaluate change," Karl R. Popper, "Truth, Rationality, and the Growth of Knowledge" in *Conjectures and Refutations*, (New York: Harper & Row, 1963), pp. 216–17; "What reality is like is the business of scientists, in the broadest sense, painstakingly to surmise; and what there is, what is real, is part of that question. The question how we know what there is is simply part of the question...of the evidence for truth about the world. The last arbiter is

so-called scientific method, however amorphous," W.V.O. Quine, *World and Object*, (Cambridge, MA: MIT Press, 1960), 22–3.

7. Hempel, "Science Unlimited?" 333–4.
8. Hempel, "Science Unlimited?" 364.
9. Hempel, "Explanation in Science and History," 295.
10. Paul Churchland, *The Neurocomputational Perspective*, (Cambridge, MA: MIT Press, 1989), 132–4.
11. Churchland, *The Neurocomputational Perspective*, 134.
12. Hempel, "Rational Action" in *Philosophy of Carl G. Hempel*, 311–26. References in the text are to the pages of this essay.
13. David Hume, *A Treatise of Human Nature*, 2nd ed., rev. P.H. Nidditch, (Oxford: Oxford University Press, 1739–40/1978), Book II, Section III, 416.
14. W.V. Quine, "On the Nature of Moral Values" in *Theories and Things*, (Cambridge, MA: Harvard University Press, 1978/1981), 66.
15. See e.g. Pierre Duhem, *The Aim and Structure of Physical Theory*, trans. P.P. Wiener, (Princeton: Princeton University Press, 1906/1954) and W.V. Quine, "Two Dogmas of Empiricism" in *From a Logical Point of View*, (Cambridge, MA: Harvard University Press, 1953.
16. Quine, "Two Dogmas," 41, 46.
17. Quine, "On the Nature of Moral Values," 65.
18. I have used this story once before, but for a different purpose in John Kekes, *Enjoyment*, (Oxford: Clarendon Press, 2008), Chapter Five.
19. Michel de Montaigne, *Essays* in *The Complete Works of Montaigne*, trans. Donald M. Frame, (Stanford: Stanford University Press, 1588/1943).
20. Hempel, "Rational Action," 317.
21. Thomas Nagel, *The View from Nowhere*, (New York: Oxford University Press, 1986), 210.
22. "Seeing our *Lebenswelt* as the product of primary material process does not make what is revealed in our world false. It is open to us, even while accepting the scientific view as causally fundamental, to regard what is revealed in our experience as a legitimate disclosure of the world, one which is available only to us," Anthony O'Hear, "The real or the Real? Chardin or Rothko?" in *The Landscape of Humanity*, (Exeter: Imprint Academic, 2008), 75.
23. See the excellent retrospective discussion by Anthony O'Hear, " 'Two Cultures' Revisited" in *Landscape of Humanity*.

Chapter 9

1. Bernard Williams, *Ethics and the Limits of Philosophy*, (London: Fontana, 1985), 118.
2. Thomas Nagel, *The Last Word*, (New York: Oxford University Press, 1997), 3–4. Parenthetical references in the text are to the pages of this work. A very similar formulation of the problem is: "We are asked to choose between order, unity, and closure, on one side, and disorder, plurality, and unsettledness, on the other.... Under certain circumstances these radical choices can seem to force themselves on us. They can seem both important and unavoidable. This happens almost inevitably when we step back

from the affairs of daily life and engage in that peculiar human activity known as philosophizing." And he writes later, "those who think that the rationalist ideal can be satisfied swing one way; those who think it cannot, swing the opposite way. Under the rationalist ideal, no middle ground seems possible, and none is tolerated. Left to itself, reason polarizes itself into extreme positions, each untenable in its own way, gaining all its strength…from the amenability of its opposite." Robert Fogelin, *Walking the Tightrope of Reason*, (New York: Oxford University Press, 2003), 3, 11.

3. The thoughts that follow in this section are indebted to David Copp's "The Ring of Gyges: Overridingness and the Unity of Reasons" in *Social Philosophy and Policy* 14(1997): 86–106 and Owen McCleod's "Just Plain 'Ought'," *The Journal of Ethics* 5(2001): 269–91.

4. Immanuel Kant, *Groundwork of the Metaphysics of Morals in Practical Philosophy*, trans. and ed. Mary J. Gregory, (Cambridge: Cambridge University Press, 1785/1996), 47.

5. An admirable effort at exegesis is Susan Neiman's *The Unity of Reason*, (New York: Oxford University Press, 1994).

6. Thomas Nagel, *The View from Nowhere*, (New York: Oxford University Press, 1986). References that follow are to the pages of this work.

7. Thomas Nagel, "The Absurd" in *Mortal Questions*, (Cambridge: Cambridge University Press, 1979), 15, 23.

Chapter 10

1. Bernard Williams, "Introduction" to Isaiah Berlin, *Concepts and Categories*, (London: Hogarth Press, 1978), xviii.

2. Richard Wollheim, "On Persons and Their Lives" in *Explaining Emotions*, ed. Amelie Rorty, (Berkeley: University of California Press, 1980), 299.

3. Ludwig Wittgenstein, *Philosophical Investigations*, trans. G.E.M. Anscombe, (Oxford: Blackwell, 1953/1958), I. 217.

4. Michel de Montaigne, *Essays* in *The Complete Works of Montaigne*, trans. Donald F. Frame, (Stanford: Stanford University Press, 1588/1943). Parenthetical references are to the pages of this edition.

5. The best account of these two views that I know of is Isaiah Berlin's "Historical Inevitability" in *Four Essays on Liberty*, (Oxford: Oxford University Press, 1958/1969).

6. See the wonderful study of this idea by Genevieve Lloyd, *Providence Lost*, (Cambridge, MA: Harvard University Press, 2008).

7. Friedrich Nietzsche, *The Gay Science*, trans. Walter Kaufmann, (New York: Vintage, 1887/1974), #343.

8. Thomas Reid, *Essays on the Active Powers of the Human Mind*, (Cambridge, MA: MIT Press, 1788/1969), 358.

9. "Life for life, eye for eye, tooth for tooth, hand for hand, foot for foot, burn for burn, wound for wound, stripe for stripe," *Exodus* 21: 24. "I the LORD search the mind and try the heart, to give to every man according to his ways, according to the fruit of his doings," *Jeremiah* 17:10. "Awards should be according to merit; for all men agree that what is just in distribution most be according to merit in some sense," Aristotle, *Nicomachean Ethics*, trans. W.D. Ross, rev. J.O. Urmson, in *The Complete Works*

of Aristotle, ed. Jonathan Barnes, (Princeton: Princeton University Press, 1984), 1131b24–6. "Justice is a constant and unceasing determination to render everyone his due," Justinian, *Institutes*, trans. Peter Birks and Grant McCleod, (Ithaca, NY: Cornell University Press, 533 ad/1987), I.iii.1. "As every man doth, so it shall be done to him, and retaliation seems to be the great law which is dictated to us by nature. . . . The violator of the laws of justice ought to be made to feel himself that evil which he has done to another; and since no regard to the sufferings of his brethren is capable of restraining him, he ought to be overawed by the fear of his own," Adam Smith, *The Theory of Moral Sentiments*, (Indianapolis: Liberty Classics, 1759/1969), 160. "It is universally considered just that each person should obtain that (whether good or evil) which he *deserves*; and unjust that should obtain a good, or be made to undergo an evil, which he does not deserve. This is, perhaps, the clearest and most emphatic form in which the idea of justice is conceived by the general mind," John Stuart Mill, *Utilitarianism*, Chapter V, (1861/2006) in *Collected Works of John Stuart Mill*, ed. J.M. Robson, (Indianapolis: Liberty Fund, 1861/2006), 242.

10. David Hume, *An Enquiry Concerning Human Understanding*, ed. Tom L. Beauchamp, (Oxford: Oxford University Press, 1772/1999), 150.
11. Berlin, "John Stuart Mill and the Ends of Life" in *Four Essays on Liberty*, 188.
12. Michael Oakeshott, "Political Education" in *Rationalism in Politics and Other Essays*, new and expanded edition, ed. Timothy Fuller, (Indianapolis: Liberty Fund, 1962/1991), 60.

Chapter 11

1. Johann Wolfgang von Goethe, *Faust*, trans. Charles E. Passage, (Indianapolis: Bobbs-Merrill, 1790/1965), Part One, 1224–37.
2. For recent defenses of determinism, see Ted Honderich, *A Theory of Determinism*, (Oxford: Clarendon Press, 1988); Galen Strawson, *Freedom and Belief*, (Oxford: Oxford University Press, 1986). For a general survey and bibliography, see Carl Hoefer, "Determinism" *Stanford Encyclopedia of Philosophy*, <http:/plato.Stanford.edu/>
3. For a recent defense of libertarianism, see John Martin Fischer, *The Metaphysics of Free Will*, (Oxford: Blackwell, 1994); Robert Kane, *The Significance of Free Will*, (New York: Oxford University Press, 1998). For a general survey and bibliography, see Timothy O'Connor, "Free Will" *Stanford Encyclopedia of Philosophy*, <http:/plato. Stanford.edu/>
4. For recent defenses of compatibilism, see Daniel Dennett, *Elbow Room*, (Cambridge, MA: MIT Press, 1984); Harry Frankfurt, *The Importance of What We Care About*, (New York: Cambridge University Press, 1988); Stuart Hampshire, *Thought and Action*, (London: Chatto & Windus, 1960); Peter Strawson, "Freedom and Resentment" in *Freedom and Resentment*, (London: Methuen, 1974); and Charles Taylor, *Human Agency and Language*, (Cambridge: Cambridge University Press, 1985), essays 1, 2, and 4. For a general survey and bibliography, see Michael McKenna, "Compatibilism," *Stanford Encyclopedia of Philosophy*, <http:/plato.Stanford.edu/>
5. For an excellent introductory account of these disputes, see Robert Kane, *A Contemporary Introduction to Free Will*, (New York: Oxford University Press, 2005).

A more advanced account is Robert Kane, ed. *The Oxford Handbook of Free Will*, (New York: Oxford University Press, 2002). An anthology of some of the best defenses of the disputed views are Gary Watson, ed. *Free Will*, (Oxford: Oxford University Press, 1982), and its second much enlarged edition, (Oxford: Oxford University Press, 2003).

6. For some concurring opinions, see "My present opinion is that nothing that might be a solution [of the problem of free will] has yet been described. This is not a case where there are several possible candidate solutions and we don't know which is correct. It is a case where nothing believable has...been proposed by anyone in the extensive public discussion of the subject," Thomas Nagel, *The View from Nowhere*, (New York: Oxford University Press, 1986), 112. "The question, then, of whether determinism is true or of whether men have free will is no longer regarded as a simple or even a philosophically sophisticated question by many writers. Concealed in it is a vast array of more fundamental questions, the answers to which are largely unknown," Richard Taylor, "Determinism" in *Encyclopedia of Philosophy*, ed. Paul Edwards, (New York: Macmillan, 1967), vol. 2, 372. "Although the terms of the debate have been considerably sharpened, it is fair to say that the basic issue...still lives....It is hard to say where this argument will go, or even where it should go....Either free agency is ineffable, free agency...is illusory, or compatibilism is true. Take your pick (if you can)," Gary Watson, "Free Action and Free Will" *Mind* 96(1987): 145–172.

7. There is a widespread tendency in contemporary thought to vastly overestimate the importance of reflection on how we live. It is referred to as second-order volitions, e.g. Harry Frankfurt, *The Importance of What We Care About*, (New York: Cambridge University Press, 1988); or explicit knowledge and clearly formed intention, e.g. Stuart Hampshire, *Thought and Action*, (London: Chatto & Windus, 1960); or autonomy, e.g. Christine M. Korsgaard, *Self-Constitution*, (Oxford: Clarendon Press, 2009); or strong evaluation, e.g. Charles Taylor, *Human Agency and Language*, (Cambridge: Cambridge University Press, 1985). An excellent historical account of the emergence of this tendency is J.B. Schneewind, *The Invention of Autonomy*, (New York: Cambridge University Press, 1998).

8. Immanuel Kant, *Critique of Pure Reason*, trans. Norman Kemp Smith, (London: Macmillan, 1781/1933), A805.

9. Bernard Williams, "The Women of Trachis" in *The Sense of the Past*, (Princeton: Princeton University Press, 2006), 54.

10. Bernard Williams, *Shame and Necessity*, (Berkeley: University of California Press, 1993), 166, 163, 164. I have changed the order of the quoted lines.

11. Friedrich Nietzsche, *Human, All Too Human*, trans. R.J. Hollingdale, (Cambridge: Cambridge University Press, 1880/1966), I. 517.

12. Stuart Hampshire, *Innocence and Experience*, (London: Allen Lane, 1989), 32.

13. "At the time of our birth we join the onward march of history....It is a condition of our participation in the march that we cannot see the way in which we are marching. We can only look backwards, and observe when, how, in what direction our predecessors marched. That is all we have to go on as a help for our own footsteps. I cannot see how history can be viewed as a study without utility. It has the greatest utility of any study. It is our principal teacher, and although we may not heed its lessons and although we may ignore the content of its doctrines whether moral or practical, nevertheless it is

the experience of others which alone can guide us in coming to grips with what we ourselves are destined to experience." Geoffrey Woodhead, *Thucydides on the Nature of Power*, (Cambridge, MA: Harvard, 1970), 173.

14. "Political discourse is...used to diagnose situations alleged to call for redress in an official response, to identify the shapes of the features and characteristics of a state or alternative more desirable shapes, to express and recommend beliefs, doctrines, or dispositions alleged to be important in formulating political proposals....It purports to express the conflicts, the tensions, and the alignments of political belief and design which are characteristic of modern states." Michael Oakeshott, "Talking Politics" in *Rationalism in Politics and Other Essays*, new and expanded edition, ed. Timothy Fuller, (Indianapolis: Liberty Press, 1962/1991), 438.

15. "Religion is not a magical overcoming of impossible odds, but a certain mindset which will not judge the value of sticking to the side of goodness by reference to its success or failure measured in terms of outcome, but which generates courage to endure, irradiated by hope.... Such a mindset is hard to describe in purely cognitive terms; for it is not primarily characterisable in terms of propositions assented to, but is a matter of a certain orientation in which emotions and beliefs and practices of worship and moral convictions merge together in...a passionate commitment to a certain form of life. The hope involved here is closer to an emotional allegiance to the idea of the power of goodness than to a cognitive attitude of expectation that outcomes will be...favourable.... [It is] a matter of something in the human spirit which can respond to the deepest stress and weakness in ways which are transforming." John Cottingham, *The Meaning of Life*, (London: Routledge, 2003), 74–5.

16. "Science is one of the very few human activities—perhaps the only one—in which errors are systematically criticized and fairly often, in time, corrected. This is why we can say that, in science, we often learn from our mistakes, and why we can speak clearly and sensibly about making progress there. In most other fields of human endeavour there is change, but rarely progress...for almost every gain is balanced, or more than balanced, by some loss. And in most fields we do not even know how to evaluate change." Karl R. Popper, "Truth, Rationality, and the Growth of Knowledge" in *Conjectures and Refutations*, (New York: Harper & Row, 1963), 216–17.

17. "I wish my life and decisions to depend on myself, not on external forces....I wish to be the instrument of my own, not of other men's, acts of will. I wish to be a subject, not an object; to be moved by reasons, by conscious purposes, which are my own, not by causes which affect me, as it were, from outside. I wish to be...self-directed...conceiving goals and policies of my own and realizing them. This is at least part of what I mean when I say that I am rational....I wish, above all, to be conscious of myself as a thinking, active being, bearing responsibility for my choices and able to explain them by references to my own ideas and purposes." Isaiah Berlin, "Two Concepts of Liberty" in *Four Essays on Liberty*, (Oxford: Oxford University Press, 1958/1969), 131.

References

Aristotle, *Nicomachean Ethics*, trans. W.D. Ross, rev. J.O. Urmson, in *The Complete Works of Aristotle*, ed. Jonathan Barnes (Princeton: Princeton University Press, 1984).

Baier, Kurt, *The Moral Point of View* (Ithaca: Cornell University Press, 1958).

Baier, Kurt, *The Rational and the Moral Order* (Chicago: Open Court, 1995).

Becker, Carl L., *The Heavenly City of the Eighteenth-Century Philosophers* (New Haven: Yale University Press, 1932).

Becker, Lawrence C., *Reciprocity* (London: Routledge, 1986).

Berkeley, George, *Three Dialogues between Hylas and Philonous* (Indianapolis: Hackett, 1713/1979).

Berlin, Isaiah, "Philosophy and Government Repression" in *The Sense of Reality*, ed. Henry Hardy (London: Chatto & Windus, 1953/1996).

Berlin, Isaiah, *Four Essays on Liberty* (Oxford: Oxford University Press, 1958/1969).

Berlin, Isaiah, *Concepts and Categories* (London: Hogarth Press, 1978).

Bevir, Mark, *The Logic of the History of Ideas* (Cambridge: Cambridge University Press, 1999).

Bevir, Mark, "What is Genealogy?" *Journal of the Philosophy of History* 2(2008): 263–75.

Brandt, Richard B., *A Theory of the Good and the Right* (Oxford: Clarendon Press, 1979).

Brennan, Tad, *Ethics and Epistemology in Sextus Empiricus* (New York: Garland, 1999).

Burnyeat, Myles, ed. *The Skeptical Tradition* (Berkeley: University of California Press, 1983).

Carnap, Rudolf, *Meaning and Necessity* (Chicago: University of Chicago Press, 1947/1950).

Cassirer, Ernst, *Philosophy of Symbolic Forms*, trans. Ralph Mannheim (New Haven: Yale University Press, 1923–29/1953–57).

Churchland, Paul, *The Neurocomputational Perspective* (Cambridge, MA: MIT Press, 1989).

Coady, C.A.J., *What's Wrong with Moralism?* (Oxford: Blackwell, 2006).

Coady, C.A.J., *Messy Morality* (Oxford: Clarendon Press, 2008).

Cohn, Norman, *The Pursuit of the Millennium* (London: Secker & Warburg, 1957).

Cohn, Norman, *Europe's Inner Demons*, rev. ed. (Chicago: University of Chicago Press, 1975/2000).

Collingwood, R.G., *Speculum Mentis* (Oxford: Clarendon Press, 1924).

Copp, David, "The Ring of Gyges: Overridingness and the Unity of Reason" *Social Philosophy and Policy* 14(1997): 86–106.

Cottingham, John. *The Meaning of Life* (London: Routledge, 2003).

Craig, Edward, *Knowledge and the State of Nature* (Cambridge: Cambridge University Press, 1990).

Crisp, Roger, *Reasons and the Good* (Oxford: Clarendon Press, 2006).

Davidson, Donald, *Inquiries into Truth and Interpretation* (Oxford: Clarendon Press, 1974/1984).

Dennett, Daniel, *Elbow Room* (Cambridge, MA: MIT Press, 1984).

Descartes, Rene, *Discourse on the Method of rightly conducting one's reason and seeking the truth in the sciences* in *The Philosophical Writings of Descartes*, vol. 1, trans. John Cottingham, et. al. (Cambridge: Cambridge University Press, 1637/1985).

Devlin, Patrick, *The Enforcement of Morals* (London: Oxford University Press, 1959/1965).

Donagan, Alan, *The Theory of Morality* (Chicago: University of Chicago Press, 1977).

Dostoyevsky, Fyodor, *The Brothers Karamazov*, trans. David Magarshack (Harmondsworth: Penguin, 1880/1958).

Duhem, Pierre, *The Aim and Structure of Physical Theory*, trans. P.P. Wiener (Princeton: Princeton University Press, 1906/1954).

Dunn, John, *Interpreting Political Responsibility* (Princeton: Princeton University Press, 1986/1990).

Dunn, John, *The Cunning of Unreason* (New York: Basic Books, 2000).

Dworkin, Ronald, *Sovereign Virtue* (Cambridge, MA: Harvard University Press, 2000).

Eliot, T.S., *The Complete Poems and Plays* (New York: Harcourt, 1971).

Falk, W.D. "Morality, Self and Others" in *Morality and the Language of Conduct*, eds. Hector-Neri Castaneda and George Nakhnikian (Detroit: Wayne Street University Press, 1963).

Fischer, John Martin, *The Metaphysics of Free Will* (Oxford: Blackwell, 1994).

Fogelin, Robert, *Walking the Tightrope of Reason* (New York: Oxford University Press, 2003).

Foot, Philippa, *Virtues and Vices* (Berkeley: University of California Press, 1978).

Foot, Philippa, *Natural Goodness* (Oxford: Clarendon Press, 2001).

Frankfurt, Harry G., *The Importance of What We Care About* (New York: Cambridge University Press, 1988).

Freeden, Michael, *Ideologies and Political Theory: A Conceptual Approach* (Oxford: Clarendon Press, 1996).

Freeden, Michael, "Ideology, Political Theory and Political Philosophy" in *Handbook of Political Theory*, eds. Gerald F. Gaus and Chandran Kukathas (London: Sage Publications, 2004).

Gallie, W.B., *Philosophy and the Historical Understanding*, 2nd ed. (New York: Schocken Books, 1968).

Garner, Richard, *Beyond Morality* (Philadelphia: Temple University Press, 1994).

Gaus, Gerald F. and Kukathas, Chandran, eds. *Handbook of Political Theory* (London: Sage Publications, 2004).

Geertz, Clifford, *The Interpretation of Cultures* (New York: Basic Books, 1973).

Geertz, Clifford, *Local Knowledge* (New York: Basic Books, 1983).

Geuss, Raymond, *Morality, Culture and History* (Cambridge: Cambridge University Press, 1999).

Geuss, Raymond, "Genealogy as Critique" *European Journal of Philosophy* 10(2002): 209–15.

Geuss, Raymond, *Philosophy and Real Politics* (Princeton: Princeton University Press, 2008).

Gewirth, Alan, *Reason and Morality* (Chicago: University of Chicago Press, 1978).

Goethe, Johann Wolfgang, *Faust*, trans. Charles E. Passage (Indianapolis: Bobbs-Merrill, 1790/1965).

Goodman, Nelson, *Ways of Worldmaking* (Indianapolis: Hackett, 1978/1985).

Grave, S.A., *The Scottish Philosophy of Common Sense* (Oxford: Clarendon Press, 1960).

Hampshire, Stuart, *Thought and Action* (London: Chatto & Windus, 1960).

Hampshire, Stuart, *Innocence and Experience* (London: Allen Lane, 1989).

Hampshire, Stuart, *Justice is Conflict* (Princeton: Princeton University Press, 2000).

Hare, R.M., *The Language of Morals* (Oxford: Clarendon Press, 1952).

Hare, R.M., *Freedom and Reason* (Oxford: Clarendon Press, 1963).

Hare, R.M., *Moral Thinking* (Oxford: Clarendon Press, 1981).

Hayek, Friedrich, *The Constitution of Liberty* (Chicago: Regnery, 1960/1972).

Hempel, Carl G., *The Philosophy of Carl G. Hempel*, ed. James H. Fetzer (New York: Oxford University Press, 1973/2001).

Hobbes, Thomas, *Leviathan*, ed. Richard Tuck (Cambridge: Cambridge University Press, 1651/1996)

Hoefer, Carl, "Determinism" *Stanford Encyclopedia of Philosophy*, <http:/plato.Stanford.edu/>

Honderich, Ted. *A Theory of Determinism* (Oxford: Clarendon Press, 1988).

Hume, David, *A Treatise of Human Nature*, 2nd ed., rev. P.H. Nidditch (Oxford: Oxford University Press, 1739–40/1978).

Hume, David, *An Enquiry Concerning Human Understanding*, ed. Tom L. Beauchamp, (Oxford: Oxford University Press, 1772/1999).

Hume, David, *Essays Moral, Political, and Literary* (Indianapolis: Liberty Classics, 1777/1985).

Iggers, Georg G., "Historicism" in *Dictionary of the History of Ideas*, ed. Philip P. Wiener (New York: Scribner's, 1973).

James, William, *William James: Writings 1878–1899* (New York: Library of America, 1891/1992).

Joyce, Richard, *The Myth of Morality* (Cambridge: Cambridge University Press, 2001).

Justinian, *Institutes*, trans. Peter Birks and Grant McCleod (Ithaca, NY: Cornell University Press, 533 ad/1987).

Kane, Robert, *The Significance of Free Will* (New York: Oxford University Press, 1998).

Kane, Robert, ed. *The Oxford Handbook of Free Will* (New York: Oxford University Press, 2002).

Kane, Robert, *A Contemporary Introduction to Free Will* (New York: Oxford University Press, 2005).

Kant, Immanuel, *Critique of Pure Reason*, trans. Norman Kemp Smith (London: Macmillan, 1781/1933).

Kant, Immanuel, *Prolegomena To Any Future Metaphysics*, trans. Lewis White Beck (New York: Liberal Arts, 1783/1950)

Kant, Immanuel, *Perpetual Peace and Other Essays*, trans. Ted Humphreys (Indianapolis: Hackett, 1786/1983).

Kant, Immanuel, *Groundwork of the Metaphysics of Morals* in *Practical Philosophy*, trans. and ed. Mary J. Gregor (Cambridge: Cambridge University Press, 1785/1996).

Kant, Immanuel, *Religion within the Bounds of Reason Alone*, trans. Theodore M. Greene and Hoyt H. Hudson (New York: Harper & Row, 1794/1960)

Kant, Immanuel, *The Metaphysics of Morals*, trans. Mary Gregor (Cambridge: Cambridge University Press, 1797/1996).

Kekes, John, *Enjoyment* (Oxford: Clarendon Press, 2008).

Kekes, John, *The Human Condition* (Oxford: Clarendon Press, 2010).

Korsgaard, Christine M., *Creating the Kingdom of Ends* (Cambridge: Cambridge University Press, 1996).

Korsgaard, Christine M., *The Sources of Normativity* (Cambridge: Cambridge University Press, 1996).

Korsgaard, Christine M., *Self-Constitution* (Oxford: Clarendon Press, 2009).

Kuhn, T.S., "Notes on Lakatos" in *Boston Studies in the Philosophy of Science*, 8(1971): 137–46.

Lewis, R.W.B., *The American Adam* (Chicago: University of Chicago Press, 1955).

Lloyd, Genevieve, *Providence Lost* (Cambridge, MA: Harvard University Press, 2008).

Machiavelli, Niccolo, *The Prince*, trans. Harvey C. Mansfield, Jr. (Chicago: University of Chicago Press, 1513/1985).

Machiavelli, Niccolo, *The Discourses*, trans. David Wootton (Indianapolis: Hackett, 1531/1994).

Mackie, J.L., *Ethics: Inventing Right and Wrong* (Harmondsworth: Penguin, 1978).

Malcolm, Norman, *Ludwig Wittgenstein: A Memoir* (London: Oxford University Press, 1958).

Mandelbaum, Maurice, "Historicism" in *The Encyclopedia of Philosophy*, ed. Paul Edwards (New York: Macmillan, 1967).

Mandeville, Bernard, *The Fable of the Bees* (Indianapolis: Liberty Classics, 1714/1988).

Marx, Karl and Engels, Friedrich, *The German Ideology* (Moscow: Foreign Languages Publishing House, 1846/1968).

McKenna, Michael, "Compatibilism" *Stanford Encyclopedia of Philosophy*, <http:/plato. Stanford.edu/>

McCleod, Owen, "Just Plain 'Ought'" *The Journal of Ethics* 5(2001): 269–91.

Mill, John Stuart, *A System of Logic* in *Collected Works of John Stuart Mill*, ed. J.M. Robson (Indianapolis: Liberty Fund, 1843/2006).

Mill, John Stuart, *On Liberty* (Indianapolis: Hackett, 1859/1978).

Mill, John Stuart, *Utilitarianism* (Indianapolis: Hackett, 1861/1979).

Mill, John Stuart, *Collected Works of John Stuart Mill*, ed. J.M. Robson (Indianapolis: Liberty Fund, 1861/2006).

Moeller, Hans-Georg, *The Moral Fool* (New York: Columbia University Press, 2009).

Montaigne, Michel, *The Complete Works of Montaigne*, trans. Donald M. Frame (Stanford: Stanford University Press, 1588/1943).

Moore, G.E., *Philosophical Papers* (London: Allen & Unwin, 1925/1959).

Murdoch, Iris, *Existentialists and Mystics* (London: Allen Lane, 1957/1998).

Nagel, Ernest, *Sovereign Reason* (Glencoe, IL: Free Press, 1954).

Nagel, Thomas, *Mortal Questions* (Cambridge: Cambridge University Press, 1979).

Nagel, Thomas, *The View from Nowhere* (New York: Oxford University Press, 1986).

Nagel, Thomas, *The Last Word* (New York: Oxford University Press, 1997).

Nehamas, Alexander, *Nietzsche: Life as Literature* (Cambridge, MA: Harvard University Press, 1985).

Neiman, Susan, *The Unity of Reason* (New York: Oxford University Press, 1994).

Nietzsche, Friedrich, *Human, All Too Human*, trans. R.J. Hollingdale (Cambridge: Cambridge University Press, 1880/1996).

Nietzsche, Friedrich, *The Genealogy of Morals*, trans. Walter Kaufmann (New York: Random House, 1887/1966).

Nietzsche, Friedrich, *The Gay Science*, trans. Walter Kaufmann (New York: Vintage, 1887/1974).

Nozick, Robert, *Anarchy, State, and Utopia* (New York: Basic Books, 1974).

Oakeshott, Michael, *Experience and Its Modes* (Cambridge: Cambridge University Press, 1933).

Oakeshott, Michael, *Rationalism in Politics and Other Essays*, new and expanded edition, ed. Timothy Fuller (Indianapolis: Liberty Fund, 1962/1991).

O'Connor, Timothy, "Free Will" *Stanford Encyclopedia of Philosophy*, <http:/plato.Stanford.edu/>

O'Hagan, Timothy, *Rousseau* (London: Routledge, 1999).

O'Hear, Anthony, *The Landscape of Humanity* (Exeter: Imprint Academic, 2008).

Popper, Karl R., *Conjectures and Refutations* (New York: Harper & Row, 1963).

Quine, W.V., *From a Logical Point of View* (Cambridge, MA: Harvard University Press, 1953).

Quine, W.V., *World and Object* (Cambridge, MA: MIT Press, 1960).

Quine, W.V., *Theories and Things* (Cambridge, MA: Harvard University Press, 1978/1981).

Rawls, John, *A Theory of Justice* (Cambridge, MA: Harvard University Press, 1971).

Raz, Joseph, *The Morality of Freedom* (Oxford: Clarendon Press, 1986).

Reichenbach, Hans, *Experience and Prediction* (Chicago: University of Chicago Press, 1938).

Reid, Thomas, *Essays on the Active Powers of the Human Mind* (Cambridge, MA: MIT Press, 1788/1969).

Rorty, Amelie, ed. *Explaining Emotions* (Berkeley: University of California Press, 1980).

Rorty, Richard, *Contingency, Irony, and Solidarity* (Cambridge: Cambridge University Press, 1989).

Rorty, Richard, *Objectivity, Relativism, and Truth* (Cambridge: Cambridge University Press, 1991).

Ross, W.D., *The Right and the Good* (Oxford: Clarendon Press, 1930).

Ross, W.D., *Foundations of Ethics* (Oxford: Clarendon Press, 1939).

Rousseau, Jean-Jacques, *Discourse on the Origin of Inequality Among Man*, trans. Donald A. Cress (Indianapolis: Hackett, 1754/1987).

Rousseau, Jean-Jacques, *Letter to Beaumont* in *Oeuvres Completes*, 5 vols. (Paris: Gallimard, 1959–95), trans. Timothy O'Hagan, *Rousseau* (London: Routledge, 1999).

Russell, Bertrand, *Mysticism and Logic* (Harmondsworth: Penguin, 1902/1953).

Russell, Bertrand, *The Problems of Philosophy* (Oxford: Oxford University Press, 1912/1967).

Ryle, Gilbert, *Dilemmas* (Cambridge: Cambridge University Press, 1956).

Scanlon, T.M., *What We Owe to Each Other* (Cambridge, MA: Harvard University Press, 1998).

Scheffler, Samuel, *Human Morality* (New York: Oxford University Press, 1992).

Schneewind, J.M., *Sidgwick's Ethics and Victorian Moral Philosophy* (Oxford: Clarendon Press, 1977).

Schneewind, J.M., *The Invention of Autonomy* (New York: Cambridge University Press, 1998).

Sextus Empiricus, *Outlines of Scepticism*, trans. Julia Annas and Jonathan Barnes (Cambridge: Cambridge University Press, c. 2nd Century AD/1994).

Sidgwick, Henry, *The Methods of Ethics*, 7th ed. (Indianapolis: Hackett, 1907/1981).

Singer, Peter, *Practical Ethics*, 2nd ed. (Cambridge: Cambridge University Press, 1993).

Smith, Adam, *The Theory of Moral Sentiments* (Indianapolis: Liberty Classics, 1759/1969).

Sorell, Tom, *Scientism: Philosophy and the Infatuation with Science* (London: Routledge, 1971).

Strawson, Galen, *Freedom and Belief* (Oxford: Oxford University Press, 1986).

Strawson, Peter F., *Freedom and Resentment* (London: Methuen, 1974).

Taylor, Charles, *Human Agency and Language* (Cambridge: Cambridge University Press, 1985).

Taylor, Charles, *Sources of the Self* (Cambridge, MA: Harvard University Press, 1989).

Taylor, Richard, "Determinism" in *Encyclopedia of Philosophy*, ed. Paul Edwards (New York: Macmillan, 1967).

Thucydides, *The Peloponnesian War*, trans. Rex Warner (Harmondsworth: Penguin, c. 5th Century BC/1954).

Watson, Gary, ed. *Free Will* (Oxford: Oxford University Press, 1982/2003).

Watson, Gary, "Free Action and Free Will" *Mind* 96(1987): 145–72.

Weintraub, Karl Joachim, *The Value of the Individual: Self and Circumstance in Autobiography* (Chicago: University of Chicago Press, 1978).

Whitehead, Alfred North, *Modes of Thought* (Cambridge: Cambridge University Press, 1938).

Wilde, Oscar, *The Picture of Dorian Gray* (Harmondsworth: Penguin, 1891/1949).

Williams, Bernard, *Moral Luck* (Cambridge: Cambridge University Press, 1981).

Williams, Bernard, *Ethics and the Limits of Philosophy* (London: Fontana, 1985).

Williams, Bernard, *Shame and Necessity* (Berkeley: University of California Press, 1993).

Williams, Bernard, *Truth and Truthfulness: An Essay in Genealogy* (Princeton: Princeton University Press, 2002).

Williams, Bernard, *The Sense of the Past* (Princeton: Princeton University Press, 2006).

Wittgenstein, Ludwig, *Tractatus Logico-Philosophicus*, trans. D.F. Pears and B.F. McGuinness (London: Routledge, 1921/1960).

Wittgenstein, Ludwig, *Philosophical Investigations*, trans. G.E.M. Anscombe (Oxford: Blackwell, 1953/1958).

Wittgenstein, Ludwig, *The Blue and Brown Books*, 2nd ed. (Oxford: Blackwell, 1958/1969).

Wittgenstein, Ludwig, *Ludwig Wittgenstein: A Memoir* (London: Oxford University Press, 1958).

Wolf, Susan, "Moral Saints" *Journal of Philosophy* 79(1982): 419–39.

Wolf, Susan, "Morality and the View from Here" *Journal of Ethics* 3(1999): 203–23.

Wollheim, Richard, "On Persons and Their Lives" in *Explaining Emotions*, ed. Amelie Rorty (Berkeley: University of California Press, 1980).

Woodhead, Geoffrey, *Thucydides on the Nature of Power* (Cambridge, MA: Harvard, 1970).

Index